MW00818149

LIFE IN THE KEY OF G

LIFE IN THE KEY OF G

KENNY G

WITH PHILIP LERMAN

BLACK STONE
PUBLISHING

This book is a memoir. The events are portrayed to the best of the author's memory.
It reflects the author's present recollections of experiences over time. Some names,
characteristics, and identifying details have been changed to protect the privacy
of the people involved. Some dialogue has been recreated.

Printed in the United States of America

First edition: 2024
ISBN 979-8-200-75667-4
Biography & Autobiography / Music

Version 1

Blackstone Publishing
31 Mistletoe Rd.
Ashland, OR 97520

www.BlackstonePublishing.com

*To the great jazz masters
who inspired me in the beginning
and who inspire me still*

INTRODUCTION

I like jokes.

I like all kinds of jokes. I like golf jokes. I like relationship jokes. I really love the Jewish jokes I've heard all my life—Mendel says, "Why do Jews always answer a question with a question?" Sam says, "Who wants to know?"

I also love sax jokes, as anyone who's been to my concerts will tell you. When we give away a Kenny G signature-model saxophone at a concert, which we frequently do, I always tell the audience, "I promise you, if you take this home tonight, you're going to have the best sax you've ever had in your life."

But here are a couple of jokes you might be surprised I like:

Kenny G walks out of an elevator and says, "Man, that place really rocks!"

Guy walks into a record store and asks, "Where do you keep the Kenny G records?" Clerk says, "Back there, under 'Difficult Listening.'" Guy says, "Don't you mean 'Easy Listening'?" Clerk says, "Hey, dude, to each his own."

That's right—I even like jokes made at my own expense.

I take my work very, very seriously—and I don't take myself too seriously.

Jokes, to me, are a lot like music, when you think about it. Some people tell jokes just to be the center of attention, to have the spotlight on themselves. That's not why I like telling jokes. I don't need any more spotlight on me. For me, it's the challenge of getting the timing of the punchline just right, with me and the listener in it together. It's a real human connection.

And sharing this moment of humor is very much like sharing music—because when I'm playing before a live audience, I always feel like we are in it together. When it comes to humor, there's a joke teller and a joke listener, and both are equally important (and if you don't think so, try telling a joke in an empty room and see how much of a laugh you get). And at my concerts it's the same dynamic. My band and I are the performers of music, and the audience is the receiver, and when we hit those right notes at just the right time, that's when we make that connection. It's magical. It brings me joy, and I can tell it brings the audience joy, and that's a wonderful feeling. I can't tell you how proud I am to know that my music has brought so much joy to so many people.

I often tell my audiences how lucky we are to be experiencing the giving and receiving of music in this way—to be sharing this together.

To me, as I think about all the things going on around the world, the turmoil, the hardship, the crazy fast-paced chaos that a lot of us experience every day, I believe that what we are doing at my concerts—and in fact the idea that we are all free to come and share this time together, away from the worries of the world outside—just might be the greatest thing happening on earth in that moment. And I don't say that because I'm suggesting that my concerts are better than everyone else's. I'm not here to toot my own horn.

But on the other hand, tooting my own horn is what got me here in the first place!

In this book, I'd like to let you get to know me better. I promise that I'll divulge some stories I've never talked about before. I'll tell you the story of how a skinny Jewish kid named Kenneth Gorelick became the guy named Kenny G with the skinny saxophone. I'll let you in on the little secrets about how I write my songs, as well as the biggest secret of all: how I got that luscious hair!

So let's start. Allow me to explain a bit about who I think I am.

I am a jazz musician. Which means that, at any given moment, I can be struck with a great desire to do something incredibly spontaneous. I'm talking about improvisation. That's the ability that jazz musicians have, and it's a quality that I respect in others. The ability to take the given circumstances and make a quick and confident move based on whatever has just happened. Usually things don't work out the way that you plan them to; a jazz musician goes with the changes (literally and figuratively)—and usually it's better than what you had planned.

I am a meticulous performer, and much of what I've become I owe to my long-standing habit of practicing three hours a day, every day. I always have, and I still do. I do that because I believe practice and repetition are crucial to success in all things, whether it's golf (which I'm pretty good at) or flying a plane (which I'm even better at—I'd better be, since when I'm up there, my life depends on it!) or playing the sax.

When I talk about the success I've had, I say it without ego, I promise. That said, I think ego is the part of me that gives me the drive to be the best at whatever I want to do.

And playing the saxophone, from the minute I picked one up, has been what I wanted to do.

Was it hard? Hell yeah. But I like it hard.

Oops! An unintentional sax joke. But don't worry. I can keep it under control. In fact, self-control is another one of the qualities that I believe are responsible for getting me here.

I don't just accept the hard work that's needed—I thrive on it. I thrive on putting in the long hours it takes, being uncomfortable for long periods of time, knowing that what I'm doing will pay off by allowing me to achieve the skill level I'm looking for.

So this book is about how I tackled the sax life. About how all that hard work and all those long hours get you to the point where you're comfortable enough and proficient enough to play exactly what you want when you want to, and to just wing it when the need arises.

As I mentioned, my favorite parts of a concert are when we're on stage playing a song just the way we rehearsed it, and then suddenly, my keyboard player (and high school friend) will play a note or chord that I wasn't expecting, and I'll look over, and he'll have this big grin on his face, like, What are you gonna do with that, Mister Famous Sax Man?—and I'll get just as big a grin on my face (even though you can't tell because I have the sax in my mouth), and everything we planned will go out the window, and I'll improvise off what he just did, and we'll go in that different direction that makes life so fun and unexpected.

That unexpected fun, combined with the confidence I get from all that practicing and thousands of shows under my belt, and all the joy I've experienced in a life of music, has helped me tune out much of what critics have had to say about me, positive or negative. Those vibes are truly not a big part of my consciousness and never have been.

So as we talk about how Kenneth Gorelick became Kenny G, and as I tell you all about the blessed life I've led and all the great things still to come, I will keep coming back to the basics that I believe are the keys to my success.

That practicing—diligently, intensely, constantly—is the joy that leads to the other joys.

That improvising—being able to adapt to what's around you—leads to the most unexpected pleasure.

That playing from the heart—which is what I do, which is what I have always done—means everything. Whether everyone else loves it or not doesn't change what I do or think is good. That's called trust. And that trust will allow the music to come straight from the heart. And the heart is where we all connect.

And that brings us back to where we started: that laughter—whether you're laughing at the world, at yourself, or at a great joke—is at the heart of it all.

CHAPTER ONE

When you've just played a command performance in the White House, where the elite of the political world have gathered, and you've returned to the Lincoln Bedroom, where you are going to spend the night, and you find Bill Clinton sitting on the foot of your bed with a big sheepish grin on his face, one thought springs to mind:

Shouldn't we go out for a drink first?

Of course, that's not really what I thought. But it is funny, right?

What I actually thought was: Jeez, if only my high school friends could see me now! Especially the tough guys who used to throw me up against my locker and demand my lunch money.

This was in February 2000, and even though I'd been on the national stage for more than a decade, I was still stunned at everything that was happening in my life. (And truth be told, I still am!) As I walked into the Lincoln Bedroom that night, the president stood up. He shook my hand and told me what a terrific evening it had been. And it truly, truly had. It had all started a couple of weeks before, when I got a call to come play for the president at a state dinner. As everyone knows, Bill Clinton is a decent sax player himself. He wanted me to perform at the White House, and I wanted to do it. Not just because he's the president of the United States and because he loves sax (oops, couldn't resist). But because, on top of that, he had been very gracious to say that I was his favorite musician when he had been on MTV a while back. And I have always believed that appearance made a big difference to the success of my album *Breathless*, which had just come out at the time. So there was no way I could say no to that incredible invitation.

I did have one request in exchange, because the invitation also presented me with a chance that not many people ever get: the opportunity to stay in the Lincoln Bedroom. That may sound pushy, but hey, I had nothing to lose by asking, and they said yes! I brought my son Max along, and let me tell you, if you wanna score points with your six-year-old, tell them they're going to sleep in the president's house. Definitely a cool-dad move.

The dinner itself took place before my performance. It was just a humble gathering of more than one hundred incredibly powerful people, including First Lady Hillary Clinton, Secretary of State Madeleine Albright, and about forty governors and other dignitaries, which would have been enormously cool if I'd actually been able to relax and enjoy the moment. Maybe have a drink, eat a little, do the things that people do at parties. And I'm sure the food was incredible, but I never eat before a performance. It's not that I'm nervous; it's just that it makes my whole body feel uncomfortable when I'm taking those big breaths in and blowing those big breaths out. I've learned over the years that I can't deliver my best when I've eaten before a performance, and on this night I really wanted to get it right. And so Max (who did eat) and I sat at a large round table, and I made idle chit-chat with Madeleine Albright. Who was utterly charming, by the way.

I won't pretend that I didn't have butterflies; it was totally natural, given the circumstances. But that feeling is something I've learned to embrace. I don't let that anxious feeling hamper my ability to play my best. And it didn't stop me from having a great time at the dinner, but I was extremely glad when it was time to perform.

After dinner, only about thirty members of the president's inner circle were invited to hear the performance. On stage, it was just me and my old friend Robert Damper up there, me on my soprano sax and Robert on keyboards. We've been playing together since high school, and it's been truly gratifying to share so many years and so many incredible experiences together.

As always, my butterflies floated away the minute I started to play. That's what music and experience—and years and years of practicing three hours a day—do for me. It's a confidence that flows through me and out the sax and into the room. I'm in my element.

Inside my music.

After we played, Robert and I put away our equipment—no road crew on this gig—and then I headed back up to the Lincoln Bedroom, which is where I found Bill Clinton waiting for me. "I thought you guys might like a private backstage tour of the White House," he said. And for the better part of two hours, he showed me and my son the parts of the White House that no one gets to see.

I was pinching myself because I couldn't believe that I was being afforded this rare treat (and pinching my son once or twice to keep him awake). It did go on a little long—Bill Clinton is a very charismatic speaker, but he can take something as simple as a pen that was given to him by the king of Saudi Arabia and talk about it for twenty minutes—and I was starting to worry that the president's second term would end before we got back to the Lincoln Bedroom.

But we finally did. I put Max to bed, but I was too hyped up to sleep. I looked around the room and opened the drawer of a desk, which I was told was the same desk that Abraham Lincoln used. Inside was a bunch of White House stationery, and I couldn't resist taking out a sheet. This was the first chance I had had to reflect on what an unbelievable moment this was. Here I was, this nice Jewish boy from Franklin High School in Seattle, sitting in the White House, sleeping in the Lincoln Bedroom, and hanging out with the president of the United States.

The stationery was thick and embossed with the logo of the White House. It was incredibly impressive, to say the least. I laid it out on Abraham Lincoln's famous desk and did what anyone in that situation would do, because inside we never stop being our parents' kids. I wrote a letter to my dad.

"Hey, Dad," I wrote. "Look where I am! Not bad, huh? Are you proud of me yet?"

I knew he'd know that I was kidding, because my dad has always been proud of me, and he's always told me so. He's always supported me—literally, sometimes—and I know he knows I owe him a lot. And I've told him that often too.

Later I would hand my dad that letter and be overwhelmed by his expression of joy and pride as he processed what that paper meant. But in that moment, that incredibly magical moment, listening to my son snore away on that big bed in the Lincoln Bedroom, I thought of the letter I wished I could write on that beautiful stationery.

Dear assholes,

You know who you are—you used to push me up against my locker every day at Franklin High demanding my lunch money.

Remember me?

I remember you.

Look who wound up in the White House!

Go fuck yourselves.

Sincerely,

Kenny Gorelick, a.k.a. Kenny G

I didn't write that letter. I'm not a vindictive guy, and I don't hold grudges. As crazy as this sounds, I actually would've felt bad for the bullies if I had. But in that moment, I had an overwhelming sense of just how far I had come.

I had started out as a hard-working, straight-A band kid from Seattle named Kenneth Gorelick. Desperate to play music, desperate to do my very best at everything I did. And now, here I was sleeping in the Lincoln Bedroom at the invitation of the president of the United States.

From Kenneth Gorelick to Kenny G.

I still pinch myself sometimes.

Because I gotta tell you, it's been an amazing journey.

I grew up on a quiet street in Seattle in what's called the Seward Park area. Seward Park itself is on Lake Washington. It's a huge park and a great place to go on nature hikes, which I did many times in my childhood. Our house was not on the lake. My dad didn't want to spend the money on one of the lots by the lake, so he built his home a little farther inland, about a mile west of the park.

Years (and millions of albums) later, I was in a position to be able to buy a property right on the lake, which increased in value the second after I bought it, and kept going up. The first time my dad came to see it, I wondered if he would look at how nice it was, acknowledge the smart investment, and think maybe he should have bought a house on the lake himself, back when prices were much cheaper. But my dad wasn't the kind of guy who dwelled on the past. I could tell that he was truly happy for me but still happy for himself and for the choices he made in life.

This was an important lesson for me, because I'm prone to beating myself up if I don't get something completely right (don't worry, folks—I'm working on it). And yet here was my dad, showing me so simply: be happy with what you have.

It wasn't the first lesson my dad taught me, but it was a crucial one.

When I talk about the journey from Kenneth Gorelick to Kenny G, it all begins with family. I firmly believe that family, for better or worse, is at the core of everything that we end up doing and who we end up becoming. My dad and mom made it very clear that family would play a very important part in my life, and that continued throughout my childhood. Growing up, I was surrounded by family. My cousins lived a block away down Mead Street, and my grandparents lived a block away on Raymond Street. While I did have some friends—some of whom I've stayed friends with all my life—my childhood was all about doing things with the family. My parents didn't hang out much with other folks who weren't family members. It was all cousins and brothers and sisters and aunts and uncles, an infrastructure built out of family loyalty, traditions, and love. That was my whole environment.

I was the middle child in our family. My brother, Brian, is five years older, and my sister, Paula, is five years younger. My parents focused a lot of their energy and attention on my brother, because parents often tend to focus on the firstborn, and on my sister, who was the only girl. So I was able mostly to fly under the radar and do my own thing.

The Gorelick siblings got along great. We loved and supported each other but also stayed out of each other's way. Paula went to a private school in Seattle called Lakeside, and Brian and I both went to public school. I didn't have the same closeness with my sister as I did with my older brother back then, because we were on such different paths regarding school and friends. But we always got along really well.

My brother and I had a great relationship growing up. Younger brothers often tend to get left behind, but Brian never treated me like a little brother. He acted like I was more of an equal. More like a friend. That was cool. And that gave me a lot of confidence, because he always included me in the things he did with his friends. I don't remember us ever getting into a fight of any kind, even though we are very different. I would describe my brother as conservative—conservative as in cautious, not the political definition. Come to think of it, I actually don't know if my brother is a liberal or conservative. See? We never argue about anything, including politics.

I was definitely not conservative growing up and always wanted to try things and explore, especially after I learned how to ride a bike. We didn't have cell phones (thank goodness), so once I was "mobile," I was gone. There was something about the fact that your parents couldn't check on you that made freedom feel—well, more free. Every day I would ride my bike down to Lake Washington, around Seward Park, to places like the grocery store, and I wouldn't come back for hours. That was normal for kids then, of course. I loved the freedom, and because I was so curious about things, time would pass, and I wouldn't realize that I had been gone for five or six hours.

My brother wasn't quite that adventuresome. When we were out doing something together, even though I was five years younger, I was the one to take the leap first.

Sometimes literally.

There was a high-dive board at a swimming pool in an area called Lincoln Park in West Seattle, where some of our cousins lived. We'd go out to see them every once in a while, and the first time we spotted that high-dive board, I said, "Brian, let's do that!"

He turned to me and said, "You go first."

So I did. Without hesitation.

One of the things I loved about our relationship growing up was that Brian never made things feel like a competition. Neither of us felt like we had to outdo the other. He supported me and nurtured in me the idea of being the one to forge the path rather than the one to follow it.

Our mom, Evelyn, was not what one would call an overtly sweet lady when it came to her own kids. That said, she could definitely be great. She was a stay-at-home mom, and she made every meal. But her go-to form of communication with us was yelling. Maybe it stemmed in part from not feeling appreciated. None of us, including my dad, ever helped with meals—Dad went to his plumbing-supply business every day and came home to a dinner that was already made—and I don't remember any of us ever actually saying thank you to my mom. We probably just took her for granted.

But the yelling was hard on me. I didn't know how to process that sort of thing, the way I can as an adult. As a kid, I was wired in a way that made me very sensitive to someone raising their voice at me. It upset my equilibrium and balance and made me feel unsafe. So even the occasional yelling was something I would do anything to avoid. As a result, I learned to always be prepared, to not get caught off-guard.

Not that she didn't dish out sweet words too. But those were rare. My mom never once said "I love you" to any of us kids. Years later, when I was mature enough to ask her directly about some sensitive issues, she told me that yelling was her way of keeping us safe—she was a protective mother and that was her way of showing that she didn't want anything bad to happen to us. I can accept that now, but it was harder back then.

But while my mom was not very affectionate with us, my Auntie Diane, who lived a block away down Mead Street, was always loving and sweet to me, and she was my favorite. I went to her house almost every day, especially in the summer.

Sundays in July, in particular, at Uncle Hunsy and Auntie Diane's house were blissful for me. Lots of family around. Lots of fun. They had a swimming pool—which was a big deal—and on those rare summer days that were really hot in Seattle, being at their house was the most fun I could have. My cousins were as close to best friends as I had in those sweet summer days that never seemed to end.

I can still close my eyes and feel the warmth and joy of those moments—the sun on my pale Seattle skin, the love of my aunt and cousins, the heat of the concrete surrounding the pool when you would lie down on it right after coming out of the pool and the stone was almost too hot to touch. Long days when there was nothing to worry about. No future to think about.

Remembering those days helps remind me that that's what life is about.

It's about trying not to spend too much time worrying. Life will work out just the way it is supposed to, with or without the worry, so it's probably smarter to choose the no-worry route. I try hard to remember that it's so important just to be present, to hang out and truly enjoy yourself. That's easy to say but not always very easy to do, and that's why thinking back to those wonderful, carefree summer days is so important. Those days remind me to try my best to put aside the worry and find the joy.

And there was much joy in my childhood. My mother's father, my *zayde* Sam (*zayde* is Yiddish for "grandfather"), had a big farm in Kamsack, Saskatchewan. Every summer my dad would pile us into his Cadillac—always a used one, and every three years or so he would get another "new" Cadillac—and we would drive all the way from Seattle to Kamsack. I loved our road trips up through Canada, through what seemed to me to be exotic places like Moose Jaw, Saskatchewan. I remember we had a little cassette tape recorder that my siblings and I would play with in the back seat, which in those days had no seat belts, and the only "air bags" we were familiar with were the old aunties and uncles who were always full of hot air with advice about this or that. When the tape recorder's batteries were dying, the tape would go slower, and then when you put new batteries in, the tape would speed up and whatever you recorded before would sound like Alvin and the Chipmunks. That was great fun. My first experience with sound engineering.

In those days we never had playdates and never spent the night at a friend's house, so family was everything. My dad's parents lived right nearby, and I literally walked over to my grandparents' house every single day. My Grandpa Harry—a lot of my family called him Hershel—was a very dynamic guy. He taught me to play chess, and he laughed more than anyone I've ever known.

He was also ridiculously buff. Even into his eighties, he had huge and well-defined biceps. And he was tough. Nothing fazed him. It didn't matter how hard the work was or how long it would take to complete a job. He was tireless and loved hard work. He was only about five feet one, but to me, no one was taller than my Grandpa Harry!

Grandma Esther was a typical Jewish grandma, skilled in the two essential talents Jewish grandmothers are famous for: cooking and complaining. Often simultaneously. There was always something to eat and something to kvetch about. Chicken soup with a side of "oy vey" was her specialty. Lots of Jewish kids call their grandmother Bubbe, but I just called her Bub. Sometimes I would irritate her just to get a rise out of her, and she would yell at me and call me a funny Yiddish word followed by, "I'm going to choke you!" If you can imagine the love and laughter with which she delivered that line, then you can understand what it is like to have a true Jewish grandma.

Harry and Esther were from Russia, which is where my dad was born. They came through Ellis Island when my dad was two and a half years old. My dad developed polio on the boat ride over and spent the next five years of his life with braces on his legs. As a result, one of his legs was really skinny, and the other wasn't so great either, but I never once heard him complain. I did hear him fall down a lot, however. You'd hear a crash or a thud from someplace in the house, and you'd run in, and he would've fallen again, and you'd help him up, and he'd be black and blue for days. But not a word of complaint.

I learned a lot from that, and I think I carried a lot of that with me as I grew older. On the one hand, I learned about strength and perseverance by witnessing my loved ones blocking out pain and focusing on the task in front of them. But for better or for worse, the more enduring lesson that seeped in was to suffer in silence.

That might sound noble, and in those days that's how people were—they kept things inside and didn't talk about their pain. Maybe they didn't want to burden anyone. Or who knows—maybe they just didn't want to look weak. But I've come to realize that there's a downside to this. Suffering in silence might seem like you're sparing your friends and family some grief, or like you are taking the high road, but to have healthy, nurturing relationships, I believe we have to share. Share fear, share pain, share feelings. It's taken me a while to come to this place, but I know now that it's more than okay to talk about what's going on inside. It's necessary. And it doesn't have to be hurtful, as long as you do it from a sincere place, do it respectfully, and do it in a gentle, calm, non-threatening tone.

I am also convinced that carrying your pain inside you can be debilitating in its own way. That's what I've learned since those early days anyway. But for a very long time, I fully adopted the idea of suffering in silence myself. When I look back on it, I realize there were good and bad lessons in what was modeled for me. And I'm a good student, so I absorbed both.

I think it would have helped my dad to talk about his pain, but he didn't have that vocabulary. My good old dad just did what he had to do, without letting his disability stop him. That's an enormously important lesson too.

For example, I learned from my aunt that he had been a ballroom dancer in his younger days, and I was flabbergasted. "How were you a ballroom dancer with that leg of yours?" I asked him. He just smiled and shrugged.

My dad wasn't one for bragging. Through him I learned that you don't have to announce your accomplishments to the world. You do your things, work hard at them, and become good at them. That's where real happiness comes from. Appreciating the value inherent in the work itself, taking quiet pride in being good at what you do—those things are the bedrock of the person I would grow up to be.

I should pause here to say that when people ask why I don't strike back at the critics who throw barbs at me, it's because of that lesson. I don't feel the need to say a lot. I just do my thing and work hard at it, and in the end, the music will speak for itself.

My dad started out as a plumber, and when I was young, he and his brother Harold created a business called Thrifty Supply Company. It was a plumbing wholesale business—hardware, heating, pipes, toilets, that kind of thing. I think they assumed that one day I'd take over the business.

On some level, I may have assumed that too. But of course, I eventually followed a different path. I loved being around my dad, though. He was always fun to talk to. He was the kind of guy who didn't do anything quickly—his name was Moe, so we sometimes called him Slow Moe. If you asked him to do something, he'd say, "I'll get around to it," and as often as not he wouldn't. But he was very handy with anything that had to do with the inner workings of a home or with building things. My dad built his desk himself out of some old wood that he found. It was downstairs in our house, and that's where I would go every night to hang out with him. I'd usually find him tinkering with something—a ceiling fan, or part of a dishwasher. He'd take it apart and put it back together, often looking at what he'd fixed with a kind of amused satisfaction, and he'd say, "Hey, look, it works now."

He preferred to fix something instead of getting something new, and that stuck with me. Like him, I love taking things apart and putting them back together. For example, about twenty years ago I noticed that my teeth were gouging an indentation into the mouthpiece of my soprano sax, and that over time I would literally bite right through my mouth-piece. But rather than getting a new mouthpiece or having some music shop attempt a fix, I rigged a solution myself with a Tip Top bicycle-tire patch. I still use that system to this day. I know now they make products like the one I invented, but I'm happy with my own homemade version.

Learning to take things apart and put them back together also ap-peals to my desire not to waste things. I've tried to instill that in my kids, who grew up in a world where everything is disposable. I've tried to teach that rather than toss something out, we should just keep it working. I like that lesson a lot.

All of this adds up to a kid who learned to do his own thing, to take chances, to improvise and improve, to take care of things, and also to have fun.

Music wasn't a huge part of the Gorelick household. My parents had a phonograph, but for the life of me I don't remember them ever playing it. I don't even think they owned any records. The image of Dad coming home after a hard day's work, having a drink and chit-chatting with the family while some songs are playing on the phonograph or radio—that scene didn't happen in my house.

My mom did push piano lessons on us, and we had a piano, so there was some music in our house. My brother took to the piano pretty well, but I hated it. The teacher, Mrs. Rideout, was, as I remember, really mean. (Actually, she could have been great, but I didn't like taking piano lessons and I was only six, so I may have convinced myself that she was a meanie.) We'd all go to her house for lessons, and for me it was pure torture. After two years, my mother finally let me give it up, and an-other two years passed before I even thought about music in any way, shape, or form.

My love of the saxophone started in the mid-1960s, while I was watching *The Ed Sullivan Show*. But not the night you're probably thinking of.

It wasn't the night the Beatles were on. They say seventy-three million people tuned in the night of February 9, 1964—more than a third of the population at the time—but I wasn't one of them. I was a few months shy of my eighth birthday when that show aired and I don't think I even knew who the Beatles were at that time or about any of the pop music on the radio.

But sometime around the start of fourth grade, I was watching TV with my mom and saw a sax player on *The Ed Sullivan Show*. Years later, I tried to figure out who it was—I'm still not quite sure, to be honest. It might have been someone in the Count Basie Orchestra. Woody Herman was on *Ed Sullivan* a lot, and he had a sax player named Sal Nistico for a long time. So I think he might have been the guy.

One way or the other, though, I thought the saxophone looked like the coolest thing I'd ever seen. I turned to my mom and said, "Hey, I'd like to play that instrument."

My mom said, "Well, we're not going to buy you one, that's for sure. We'll rent it, because you might quit like you did piano."

And on that sour note, a lifetime of much sweeter ones was born.

The first sax I got my hands on was a Buffet Crampon alto sax—the shape you're used to seeing when you think of the saxophone, that J shape. The soprano sax—the one I'm best known for, the straight one that looks like a clarinet—came later. The minute I opened the case, I was hooked. It comes with three parts—a body, neck, and mouthpiece—that you have to assemble. I liked puzzles, so that looked like a lot of fun to me. I was hypnotized by the physicality of it, how the sections fit perfectly together. I slid the neck onto the body and then slid the mouthpiece onto the neck—the neck had a cork end, and you had to push the mouthpiece onto it—and attached the reed, that slender little stick of wood, the one that vibrates and makes the sound.

It actually didn't take me very long to get a sound out of the saxophone, but what I did next was something that is to this day one of the most important decisions I've made in my career. I had to figure out where in our small house to practice. Today, when I'm home, I have a specific room that I practice in. When I'm on the road, I choose one of the dressing rooms at the venue to be my practice room for the day. When I'm in a hotel, it gets a lot tougher to find a place to practice, but I manage. At age ten, the first thing I did was find my practice room— the little downstairs bathroom. It was away from everyone in the house, but that wasn't the only reason that I chose it. There were two very important things I loved about that little bathroom. One was the acoustics. The sound. In a bathroom, the sound bounces off the hard surfaces and makes any instrument immediately sound better. Like when you sing in the shower and think you can be the next Luther Vandross. Definitely more fun!

But also, that's where the mirror was.

I was absolutely, 100 percent determined to figure out how to look somewhat like a normal person when I played. A lot of playing the sax, or any reed instrument, is about something called the embouchure— the way you shape your mouth and lips around the mouthpiece. And it affects how your whole face looks. A lot of people make a funny face when they play the sax. Their cheeks go really high, their chin gets tight or juts out, and they look like they're working really hard. Like when you watch someone lifting weights and they're grimacing and grunting and straining.

Not what I wanted.

I wanted to look like I was just walking down the street, sipping a milkshake out of a straw that happened to be big and brassy and shaped like the letter *J*. I wanted it to look effortless, even though there was plenty of effort going into it.

Speaking of how I look when I play the sax, a lot of people have asked me why I play off to one side, and the answer is one of two things.

My two front upper teeth aren't perfectly aligned. One is slightly higher than the other. So when I rest the mouthpiece against my teeth, it fits into that little crevice that my slightly out-of-line teeth make. Now, all these years later, I still don't know if I put the sax that way because my teeth were uneven, or if playing the sax off to the side all those years put my teeth that way.

Hard to say. But I kept with it, because it was the natural way the mouthpiece fit into my mouth, which kept me looking normal, and I loved how it was starting to sound. No need to change that!

I joined the school band, and they made me the first chair right away. I took to the sax pretty easily and learned to read music pretty quickly too. Mr. Bloom, the band teacher, would sit me down in his little practice room and walk me through it step by step: This is a D. This is an E. This is an F.

It was awesome. And I was really having fun with the sax.

I remained first chair all through elementary school. I didn't take it very seriously. At that point, it wasn't something I thought was very important in my life. Just a super fun thing to do. I had no idea that I was taking the first steps on a path that would span a lifetime.

We weren't a very religious family by any means, but being part of a Jewish household played an important role in my life and influenced the lessons I would learn growing up.

I did get bar mitzvahed—another one of those things that came easily to me. It happens when you turn thirteen, and it's a tradition that's meant to take you from boyhood into manhood. On the appointed day, at the Saturday service in the synagogue, you become the leader and have to recite long passages in Hebrew. This was not easy for some of my friends. They truly struggled with it. But I discovered early on that I had the ability to memorize things very easily. This helped me get straight As all through my years of school, something that was very important in my family. And it helped me sail through the recitation when it was my turn.

Even after my bar mitzvah, my mom made me keep going to Hebrew school, twice a week after school and again on Sundays. I hated it, like those piano lessons. But I didn't quit because I had a big crush on one of the girls in the class. I was so shy, though, that I did absolutely nothing about it. (That shyness would start to change later on, after I joined one of Seattle's premier R&B funk bands. In the tale of how Kenneth

Gorelick becomes Kenny G, the ambient coolness of that group may have been a wee bit more transformative than memorizing parts of the Torah. But that was still a ways off.)

The most fun Jewish holiday to me was Passover. That's when the whole family—aunts, uncles, cousins, everybody—all gets together for what's called the seder. It's a big dinner, like Thanksgiving. But in Jewish households, in addition to the big meal, the tradition is to read the story about how our ancestors were slaves to the Egyptians and how Moses beat the pharaoh and freed the Jews.

The seder was always at my Grandma Esther's. In addition to all the usual relatives, various other random old people were there who I'm sure were somehow related, but I never knew how. The seders were great fun. My grandfather would run the seder, and I would sit next to him and help because I knew how to read Hebrew better than my cousins. As my grandpa would be whipping through the Hebrew, I'd be following along and announcing, "He's on page forty-six . . . He's on the bottom of page forty-seven," so that everyone else knew where we were. There is also a part in the service called the four questions, and the tradition is for one of the younger kids to read and sing the Hebrew words in front of the whole family. Since I was the best at Hebrew, that job often fell on my shoulders. I guess that was my first time being "on stage," and I think it helped prepare me for what was to come later.

Those seders are among the fondest memories of that part of my life because they were such a blast. Everyone was laughing and talking, Grandma Esther was always complaining, and my grandpa was in his element, reading Hebrew to his family and being in charge. As he laughed about something, his shoulders would shake, and that would get me laughing. Then the food would come, big heaping platters full of it. And we'd laugh and eat and laugh some more, long into the night.

If you didn't grow up in a Jewish household, it may come as a surprise to learn this, but on Passover the kids were allowed to drink some wine. It's actually part of the service—cheap Manischewitz was a staple of every Jewish family on Passover. It was deliciously sweet and tasted like breaking the rules. (Now I wouldn't touch the stuff. Yuck! I'll take a fine French Bordeaux any day.)

So I learned a lot at those gatherings. But the most important thing I learned at the feet of my grandfather at those seders was this: Eat the gefilte fish. Skip the soup with the egg in it.

I did that by instinct too. My cholesterol still thanks me for it.

So that was my childhood. Enveloped in the love of my family, and learning to suffer in silence in the face of a mom who yelled a lot, albeit with the best of intentions. Relishing the laughter that came from hanging out with my grandpa. And the pleasure that came from playing the sax. I was a good memorizer and a diligent student, and those things were so deeply ingrained in me that they formed the essence of who I would become.

I was a newly minted young man, nurturing a casual crush on music and the saxophone.

And then things started to get interesting.

CHAPTER TWO

I stayed as first-chair saxophone through grade school and into junior high. Sharples Junior High School was about a mile from my house, and I walked there most days. It was kind of an inner-city school, with lots of fights, filled with the racial tension that was gripping the country in the late sixties and early seventies. I was still determined to get perfect grades like I did in elementary school, but I wasn't practicing the sax as diligently as I would later. I was simply having fun with it, and it was coming easily to me.

I remained the lead sax all through junior high. If you are lead alto or tenor, you get the best parts to play. If there's a melodic part to the sax section, you're playing it, and the other horns are doing the harmony. If there were fun little flourishes and nuances, or solos to be played, they usually came my way. Everything sounds so good when the whole sax section plays together, but it's clear that the lead horn player is the most important and has the most responsibility. He also has the most fun.

That's how it always was, ever since I'd picked up the sax, and that's the way I assumed it would always be.

And then I got to high school.

Franklin High was a tougher and more intense version of junior high. I was the classic skinny, white, nerdy guy—glasses and all, and not a hundred pounds soaking wet—and I got picked on a lot, mostly by some of the tougher Black kids. It's just how it was.

They'd see me walking down the hall and push me up against my locker. They'd demand my lunch money, and I'd gladly give it to them. Hey, I was an accommodating guy, even then! It was easier to give them the money than risk losing a tooth. They got the money, I didn't get hurt, and everybody got what they wanted. Win-win, if you ask me.

Honestly, I didn't give this negative situation much thought. And this is something that, today, I think is extremely important. Don't dwell on the bad stuff that is going on in your life. Deal with it, but don't churn it around in your mind and heart. Regurgitating something over and over doesn't help solve it. It's a false sense of doing something constructive. Let it be out there in the periphery and not part of your main thoughts. That was the logic that kept me from getting upset about this whole thing.

I also learned to hide my money in my shoes and tried to smile about it all. I knew that there would be plenty more times that I would walk down the hallway after the bell rang and imagined the situation might go something like this:

"Hey, white boy, what are you doing walking by yourself?"

"Oh, I'm trying to get to class. That's what I'm doing."

"Well, why don't you come over here?"

"Okay, here's my money, anything else?"

"No, keep going."

"Okay, nice hanging with you. See you tomorrow. We'll do this again."

There were a lot of fights at the school—usually involving fists, although sometimes there were knives and guns as well. The police were at the school often enough, breaking things up or taking kids down to the precinct to give them a good scare, which it absolutely did not do. The next day we'd be right back at the same dance. And I was a lousy dancer.

But for all the tension in that school, the band room was the place where everybody seemed to get along. It was like, for this hour of class, we're not Black kids and white kids. We're altos and tenors and sopranos. We're piano and string and horn.

That's where I wanted to be, and given all my success to this point, that's where I knew I would be. After all, I had been the best in elementary and junior high school.

There was only one problem.

All the kids in the band or trying out for the band were also the best sax players at their respective junior high schools. And they were all better than me. I knew it the minute I heard them.

Spoiler alert: I didn't make the band.

You'd think I would be upset, but I swear, in my memory, I wasn't upset at all. Even though it had come so easily to me, after hearing all those other guys who played so much better than I could, I had only one thought about the saxophone: I need to get better.

I knew I could learn to do it, and that led to another decision that would have a monumental impact on my life and career. I started practicing—a lot. At the time, I was focused on getting better and making the band the following year. Those kids had been markedly better than me, and I was determined to improve. Also, I had a natural curiosity about the sax. I was almost addicted to finding out what else it could do.

So I started an intense practice regimen that I maintain a version of to this day. Even after more than fifty years, I still practice three hours a day. Every day. Maybe perfectionism and the desire to please my not-so-easy-to-please mother jump-started the engine at the time. But once it was going and the jumper cables were removed, the car began running by itself.

I started practicing. And practicing. And practicing. I didn't practice any songs, mind you—not once. Although that might seem strange, at that time I was all about the mechanics, not the music. I wasn't listening to records of other sax players. In fact, I didn't even know anything about other sax players. I liked Earth, Wind & Fire and Tower of Power because of their horn sections, but I was years away from knowing about guys like Stan Getz or John Coltrane. Practice was about perfecting the technique. If you learn to play a song, then you know how to play that song. If you get your mechanics right and learn to read music well, then you can play any song ever written. I wanted to get better and better. I wanted to really nail it. But I also knew that the first thing I needed to do was to get better than those other guys in high school.

Day in and day out, for an entire year, I practiced nothing but the mechanics of the sax.

I made a major breakthrough during this period. It was during the summer, just before I went back to school. One morning I woke up and could play twice as fast. And twice as clean. I'm not sure how that happened—maybe all the scales I was doing led me down a path I didn't realize I was walking until I got there—but once that happened, I said to myself, I'm not going back.

Because being that good was way more fun.

And I wanted more of it.

All of that practice also led me to something else, something that further powered the engine: It led me to the magic and beauty of sound and melody. To the joy of music.

The more I played and the better I got, the more motivated I was to keep reaching for that joy, to delight in the music, to simply enjoy the sound of something beautiful, to revel in the pleasure of figuring things out and getting them right. It became like a drug. I wanted more and more of it. That's still true today.

It's possible that being motivated by an unconscious fear—the fear of disappointing my mother—drove me, at first, to work hard at things. But now I am motivated by joy. The joy of trying your hardest, and the joy of doing something really well. The joy of making music.

Joy works better.

That fall, I went back to audition for the school band again. I was way better than everybody else.

And everybody knew it.

The band director made me first chair.

Lest you think I went from nerd to insufferable egomaniac in a single bound, my friends were there to keep me in check. In fact, after my dear friend since junior high Tom Ikeda heard me play a solo, he told me, "Maybe you should stick to math." (We've remained friends to this day, and when I play in Seattle, where he still lives, I like to introduce him and announce this fact at my shows, because it draws a big boo from the crowd. He's a great guy and he knows it's all in good fun.)

By now you might be picking up on something about me. I have an overwhelming desire to try to be the best I can possibly be at whatever I do. As a kid, it wasn't just about being *a* top student; it was about being *the* top. If there was a situation where I could possibly be number one, I was gunning for it. Somebody else was gonna have to settle for number two, because I was gonna be number one.

Here's something I'll admit: I don't like dancing. Why? Well, first of all, I'm a terrible dancer. You might think I'd have enough rhythm to get by on the dance floor, but sadly, nope.

But the main reason is this: I don't like dancing because it doesn't have a right way or a wrong way. There's no objective means of measuring your success. That's why I'm drawn to golf—maybe even obsessed with it—because if you do it right, you know it. The score tells you how well you did. Now with music, of course, there's no "right way" or "wrong way" to make it—but that never mattered to me, because in my heart, I've always known whether I'm doing it right.

But still, there was that part of me that wanted to be as close to perfect as possible. I was searching for that clear if unattainable "perfect score," something I could see in the far distance and always be reaching for.

But striving for perfection also gave rise to a voice in my head that grew more and more powerful as I got older. Along with my perfectionist tendencies as well as my innate competitiveness, a relentless taskmaster took hold in my head, one that made no room for "good enough." For a long time, I thought that voice was me, and I thought it was a motivating voice, and I thought it was correct. Why not be perfect, right?

Eventually, after years of listening to this inner taskmaster, who relentlessly encouraged me to continue my quest to be perfect, I've come to the realization that one can never actually attain that. And pursuing this goal will lead to a much lower quality of life. So I've changed the narrative. Now I push for "best efforts." I hope for great results, but I focus on giving something my best effort. You can't guarantee the result, but you can control the work you put in. It's a huge and crucial distinction. Whether it's the sax or golf or something else, I know I'll keep improving if I keep practicing. And that's where the fun is. The results usually follow eventually, so it seems to work out, but I know that focusing on the effort instead of the result keeps me from being overly disappointed or unhappy if things don't turn out the way I had hoped.

Which is one of the reasons I'm a very happy person.

But it's not the only reason. I also love what I do. I love my instrument. I love performing and the challenges of putting on a great show. I love the amazing people in my life that I'm fortunate enough to spend time with. It's a wonderful life, and I'm so grateful for it—and it is from that gratitude that the drive to be my absolute best continues to grow stronger every day, if that's possible.

Knowing I'm giving my best efforts allows me to feel peaceful, because I'm aware that I'm doing everything I can. I feel I owe it to those who have brought me here—the people who love and support my music—to try to be the best possible musician and person I can be.

And so I continue to practice three hours a day. And as time goes on and the hours continue to add up, I find that the distance between where you are and what your idea of excellence is seems to get smaller and smaller and smaller. You're never quite there, but if you practice some more, you can keep getting a little closer every time. And that keeps me coming back to the practice room!

Once I made first chair, I never looked back. I've never been one to dwell on the past. Life is about the front windshield, not the rearview mirror.

I did start listening to more sax music. I actually bought my first record, Tower of Power's *Soul Vaccination*. However, that is not the record that changed my life. But I was about to discover the one that would.

Our high school band director was a guy named Charles Chinn—a nice guy, but pretty conservative, and he did everything by the book. As kids under his guidance, we didn't know the difference, of course, so we played what we were told. But one day, this very interesting Black dude showed up to our practice room. His name was Jim Gardiner, and Mr. Chinn told us he was a musician and was going to be the composer in residence.

Like we knew what that meant.

We soon found out. Jim started writing charts for us—the notated musical parts that told each of us what to play—based not only on the kind of musicians we were but also on the music he was doing at the time, which happened to be what we were listening to at Franklin High: R&B and Motown. There was a lot of that flavor in what he was giving us.

One day, I walked into his office, my sax in tow, and there was a record on the record player—yes, listening to music on vinyl LPs wasn't a hip, retro option then; it was the *only* option—and I was amazed by what I was hearing.

"What *is* that?" I asked him.

"Come in. Sit down. Listen," Jim said.

I listened for a minute to this mystical, magical, flowing sound, smooth and rough at the same time. It was perfect technically—that part I knew—but it was something more than that, something I hadn't experienced before. I knew it was some kind of horn, but I'd never heard anything like it. It was a beautiful tone. The notes were soulful and jazzy, uplifting and heartfelt at the same time. It filled me with inspiration and motivation and joy and wonder. It was amazing.

"What instrument is that?" I asked.

He looked at me and smiled. "That's Grover Washington. He's playing the same instrument you play."

I think my jaw actually dropped open. I was dumbstruck. "Are you kidding me?" I asked and looked down at my sax. "Wait a minute. This can do *that*? Jim, can I borrow that record?"

He got up, carefully lifted the needle off the record, and slid it into the white paper sleeve and then into the album cover. He handed it to me, and I stared at the photo on the cover, a warm sepia-toned portrait of a man filled with a calm confidence. My eyes met Grover's, and I thought, I'm going to learn how to play my horn like this guy.

And then I'm going to get even better.

Hey, if you're not gonna be full of cockeyed optimism in high school, when else?

That night, before I went to bed, I put the album on. There's so much magic in that album. If you want to hear one of the funkiest cuts ever made, listen to the first cut, Grover's take on Marvin Gaye's "Inner City Blues." If you want to hear one of the sweetest cuts ever recorded, listen to the second cut, Grover's version of "Georgia on My Mind." In fact, every cut on that album was another lesson in what the sax can do.

So I set about learning how to do it.

I recorded the album using that little tape recorder we played with on car rides with my parents, so I could stop and rewind again and again, back and forth, figure out what notes he was playing, and write them down. To this day, I have those stacks of paper, all those licks I wrote down on those afternoons alone in my room, just me and my sax and Grover.

Years later, when my album *Duotones* had come out and had sold about five million records, I was doing an interview in Chicago at the jazz station WNUA, and they said they needed to wrap it up because Grover Washington was coming on after me. He was playing at Chicago's famed Park West jazz club that night.

I convinced them to let me do the interview, arguing that no one knew his music like I did. Secretly, I was hoping he might invite me to jam with him.

During the interview I kept trying to steer the conversation. "So, Grover, you're playing at Park West tonight? Gee, that sounds great. Boy, I'd love to play there sometime. I hear it's a terrific venue."

Subtle.

He finally took the bait, and that night, I jammed with my hero face to face, horn to horn, trading solos. I'll never forget how he treated me as an equal on that stage. If the audience thought they might have seen a tear in my eye when the night ended, I could say that it was just the lights.

But you know better. And Grover did too. (Thanks, my friend, and rest in peace.)

Things are different for today's sax students. Kids have access to everything on the internet. The young sax players I see on Instagram today are absolutely amazing. But the problem is, everyone in the world is listening to the same stuff. A sax player in Finland is watching the same videos as a sax player in Kazakhstan or Boston, and they're getting the same licks down and playing the same style. Which is amazing, but it's not unique. I guess you could argue that they have access to tons more stuff than I did, so their chances of doing something different are that much greater, and there's some validity to that. But the reality seems to be that certain licks go viral, and a lot of kids learn to do exactly the same thing. At least, that's what I see.

But alone in my room as a teenager, with no chance of seeing what anyone else was trying to do, I started figuring things out on my own. My brother was off at college, so I had my own bedroom by then. And every night when I went to bed, I'd put that Grover Washington record on the phonograph and lay my head down and close my eyes, letting the record take me off to dreamland. I probably listened to it every night for two or three years.

That was the sound that launched me forward. Most of the music I heard through other kids at school was R&B. I liked it, but I don't think I ever bought a single record. There was an R&B radio station, KYAC, and I listened to whatever they were playing. Most of the other popular music of the time totally escaped me. I didn't pay one bit of attention to Bob Dylan or the Rolling Stones or the Beach Boys. The East Coast folk scene and the West Coast music explosion went right past me.

For me, it was mostly Grover, and Tower of Power, and at some point, I bought a Blood, Sweat & Tears album, as well as one by Chicago, and I listened to the horns on those too. Jim also turned me on to a phenomenal tenor sax player named Michael Brecker. He had a group with his brother but went on to forge his own career. He became what many young sax players today think of as the greatest tenor sax player who ever lived. Although Michael was absolutely phenomenal, I would give that title to John Coltrane and Stan Getz. I think Michael would probably agree—at least with the Coltrane part—because to me it's clear that he got a lot of his inspiration from Coltrane.

At this point in my music career, in addition to the alto sax, I was also playing clarinet and flute a little bit. I didn't get my soprano sax until I was seventeen, but I fell in love with it right off the bat.

Here's how that momentous event came to be.

I had always wanted to try soprano, so I decided to put an ad in the paper. (Yes, you youngsters out there, we did not have eBay.) A guy answered it, and I went to his house and gave him $300 for a used Selmer Mark VI soprano sax made in 1959. Today, I look at the soprano Mark VI as the most famous saxophone the world has produced and consider myself the lucky keeper of this sacred horn. It's literally a treasure to me. But when I first put it in my mouth and made my initial sounds, it didn't sound like the soprano saxophone I had heard on the record, and I was bummed. And no matter what I did, it only sounded like . . . me.

The more I tried to sound like someone else, the more I sounded like . . . me.

Little by little, I learned the incredibly important lesson that shaped everything that came afterward: that it is a blessing to have your own sound. Little by little, I came to appreciate it. And little by little, I came to understand that I would carve my own path when it came to how a soprano sax would sound and be played.

I learned that invaluable lesson one note at a time.

I developed a couple of other loves during my high school years. Ping-Pong was one. I got pretty damned good at it and still play pretty well. Another was golf, and I became captain of the golf team. Years later, that skill would lead me to playing more high-level golf—I'll tell you more about that later—but more importantly, golf allowed me to become friends with Tiger Woods, Jack Nicklaus, Arnold Palmer, Clint Eastwood, and Ray Romano, to name-drop a few. (While we're at it, can I brag a little and tell you that I won my club championship twice?) As I said, golf scratches the same itch that music does. It's something that if you practice, over and over and over again, you can become very good at.

The goal is very defined. To this day, I'm actually more proud of my golf trophies than my music ones. Music is subjective. A music award means some group of people decided they liked what I did. But golf is objective. Either you got the ball on the green or you didn't. Either you sank the putt or you didn't. You have to beat everyone else to win.

I will admit I like that.

I also fell in love with my first car, a 1968 Oldsmobile 88. It was rusted out when I got it, and I sanded the whole thing down, put the primer on by myself, and then took it to Earl Scheib, the place you'd go for a cheap paint job, and I got it painted blue for $99.95. I put a swan hood ornament and Godfather whitewalls on it and drove it to school every morning. But I promise you that I wasn't trying to be hip. I actually just liked the way it looked with the Godfather tires and the hood ornament. Unfortunately, I didn't have any money at the time, so I faked the whitewalls. Yep, I put fake whitewalls on a fresh set of retread tires—old tires with new treads on them. It was way cheaper than new tires.

But more than anything, that tricked-out Oldsmobile represented long, wonderful afternoons with my Grandpa Harry. By that point, Harry was close to one hundred years old, and my father didn't let him drive anymore because it wasn't safe. And he was clearly right. The last time Grandpa drove, as he told it later, he was crossing some train tracks while a train was coming. He said he "saw red lights and heard vissles," so he stopped—with the car's wheels still on the tracks! By the grace of God, the train only hit the back of the car and spun it around a bunch of times. Grandpa was just a little banged up, but it could have been a lot worse. So that was the day my father took his keys away.

Since I was the one with the cool car, I started driving him around every day in the summer. We would drive to the junkyards, and he'd find stuff—copper wire or old tires or whatever—and buy it up, only to sell it to another junkyard for a few pennies more.

The stories he would tell during those drives! He told me once about trying to get out of being conscripted into the Russian army, because he didn't want to fight. In Grandpa's words, "I vent to this guy, and he gave me an eye." Which meant—I kid you not—that he paid a man to stick a needle in his eye so he couldn't be drafted. To his dying day, Grandpa had one cloudy eye—but the irony is, they drafted him anyway.

Grandma Esther died of stomach cancer in her mid-eighties, but Harry lived to be a hundred and three, so he survived her by almost two decades. At one point, my dad decided Grandpa should go into an old-age home. When my grandfather turned one hundred years old, my dad and I went to visit him at the home. I was already friends with President Clinton at this point, and I'd asked him to write a letter to my grandpa congratulating him on his one hundredth birthday. I gave the letter to Grandpa, and he turned to my dad, who he called Moey, and said, with perfect comic timing, "Moey, your son is friends with the president from the United States. You have to start dressing better."

Anyway, that's Grandpa. He was always laughing—enjoying his life and telling great stories or giving his unique brand of advice. Those were very special summers, and when I think back on those days in the Olds 88 with the fake Godfather whitewalls, it makes me think of Grandpa Harry. And it makes me smile.

During the school year, I'd get in that car each morning and make one stop before school. To pick up my friend Lee Turner, the drummer in the jazz band. Lee was the best musician in our high school band, by far. He was an amazing musician, although he didn't pursue it as a career. I saw him recently when he came to one of my club dates in Seattle at Jazz Alley, and I swear, he looked as young as he did when we were in school together.

Can't say the same for myself. But at least I still have all my hair and it hasn't turned gray yet. And we all know that when my hair goes, my career is gonna go right down the toilet with it.

I'm joking! (I hope!)

When I talk about my loves in high school—music, of course, and golf, and my old car, and Ping-Pong—one question inevitably arises:

Weren't there any girls involved? And the answer arises pretty quickly. Not really.

Not for lack of desire, I should mention. I had plenty of that. And not for a lack of thinking about it, either, which was pretty much confined to the time between waking up and falling asleep, and also dreaming. No more than that, though.

But as I said, I was incredibly shy around girls. Even my hair lacked game. I was in the process of growing it longer—in accordance with the seventies hairstyles—but it wasn't there yet. And neither was I.

Then there was sex. Or I should say, then there *wasn't* sex. I knew nothing about it. My brother never told me anything. Because that wasn't the type of relationship we had. So I had to learn about it from my friends at school, which didn't ensure that I was getting the right information. I looked forward to going to school every day because I could look at the girls. But I never actually imagined doing anything about it. Like so many other shy boys, I was waiting for the girl to make the first move.

My first real kiss happened at a New Year's Eve party during my junior year. It was midnight, and I was drunk for the first time in my life—I didn't drink at all in high school, or smoke pot, but I was good and smashed that night, drinking whiskey. At midnight, I was sitting with a girl named Lynda, and she leaned over and kissed me happy New Year, and we made out for quite a while. I remember thinking, Hey, this is fun. I should do more of this.

I didn't do more of it with Lynda. We stayed friendly, but nothing ever came of it. That girl, by the way, was Lynda Barry, who went on to become a fabulous and very famous cartoonist. I love her cartoons, and I always smile when I see her name. Hey, that artist gave me my first kiss. That's pretty cool.

During high school, I started taking sax lessons with a couple of teachers, including a man named Johnnie Jessen, who was pretty famous around the area. He also taught flute, so I started to learn that too. I can't say the lessons helped me develop my sound, but I do think it was good to practice under the watchful eye of a pro. I've never made a conscious effort to get a certain sound, but I kept practicing and my tone kept developing.

Whatever people call "the Kenny G sound" came from practicing and evolving. After twelve years, twenty-five years, and now fifty years of playing sax, the truth is that I can't tell you exactly what I'm doing that's different from year to year. There's a finessing, a different way I'm tightening the muscles of my throat, or adjusting the pressure of the mouthpiece on my lips, or pressing the keys in a certain way. Over the years, things have kept evolving and getting better and better, but I never consciously tried to make my saxophone sound a certain way. It was all instinctual. I'd listen to records, try to emulate what I was hearing, and never really thought about exactly how I was doing it. As I said before, whatever I did, it still kept sounding like me. And that, I came to understand, was a good thing.

I was also taking clarinet lessons at a music school called the Cornish College of the Arts from Larry McDaniels, who at the time was the lead clarinet player in the Seattle Symphony. I didn't enjoy the lessons, but not because of the teacher. Larry was a great guy and a great teacher. I just didn't love playing the clarinet. But it was a skill I wanted to learn. And I loved the time right after the lessons, because my mom would take me to Dick's hamburger joint. They had the best fries and really good burgers, and sitting with my mom in the car and having fries and a burger was one of the sweeter moments we shared together as I was growing up. We didn't have all that many, so that was pretty special.

In addition to the jazz band, I played in the school marching band too. The music there was a lot less interesting to me, but the band was a ton of fun, because I'd go on the school bus with all these guys and girls on the way to football games at night. Since I was so shy, this was a great chance to talk to some of the girls without it being too awkward. Most days, I didn't do much after I got home from school—just hung around the house night after night—so these trips were pretty exciting.

Other than that, nothing too thrilling was happening to me.

But it was about to.

In a huge way.

CHAPTER THREE

When I was a senior in high school, Barry White was the biggest Black music star in the world. He was like Michael Jackson, Luther Vandross, and the Weeknd all rolled into one. One weekend, Barry and his Love Unlimited Orchestra were headed to the West Coast to play a series of gigs. The "Love Unlimited Orchestra" often consisted of a number of musicians Barry would pick up along the way—in this case, players from the Seattle Symphony. Barry always traveled with the same core musicians: his rhythm section and his sax soloist. But that weekend his sax player was sick, and Barry needed someone to fill in. The guy who was putting the band together turned to a local jazz expert to find a replacement.

As fate would have it, the guy he turned to was his friend Jim Gardiner, the composer in residence at my school who'd taken me under his wing. "I need someone who plays sax with a soulful feel, but he also needs to be able to read music," he told Jim. "Know anyone?"

Well, there were a lot of sax players in Seattle with soul—the town was teeming with them—but they couldn't read music. And lots of guys could read music but couldn't play with soul.

"I only know one guy," Jim told him.

And that guy was me.

The band was going to play Portland, Seattle, and Vancouver that weekend. Our first gig was in Portland. The plan was for me and all the members of the Seattle Symphony to take a bus down there, and on that Friday I showed up, ready to board the bus.

They'd told me to wear a suit. I know now that they meant a black suit, but the only suit I owned was my bar mitzvah suit, which consisted of a plaid jacket, maroon pants, and a white shirt with a maroon tie. Those were the only dress-up clothes I owned, and when I showed up at the bus, they took one look at me and said, "Hey, kid, who the hell are you?"

"I'm the sax player," I told them. "I'm supposed to be on the bus."

Keep in mind I'm also about ten years younger than everyone else and all of maybe 105 pounds. They took one look at this skinny kid in a bar mitzvah suit and said, "We think you're on the wrong bus."

Fortunately, at the last minute the guy who hired me—Jim Gardiner's friend—showed up and vouched for me, and I sat on the bus, uncomfortable around all these older, professional musicians, wondering if I really was supposed to be there. Those words, "you're on the wrong bus," kept ringing in my ears, like a mantra of self-doubt, as I headed off to Portland for my first professional gig.

That night was our first time playing the music, so thank goodness I was a good sight reader. There I was, playing along on my soprano sax, when all of a sudden, the whole orchestra—those Seattle Symphony players who were on the bus with me—dropped out, leaving this nerdy white teenager with just Barry's rhythm section, just me and all these thirty- and forty-year-old Black guys on drums, guitar, keyboard, and bass. And suddenly, even they stopped. Everything stopped. And it was time for me to take a solo. I hadn't known I was going to solo.

You may be thinking I was as nervous as hell. But here's the truth: I wasn't scared in the least.

Everything I'd done for the last couple of years, all those hours and hours of practice in the bathroom, everything I learned from the various lessons I'd had and the records I listened to, all the R&B I'd heard on KYAC, kicked in. And I started wailing, playing these really fast licks, running through the changes like I'd been doing it all my life—which I had, but in my room or in the bathroom, not on a stage with three thousand people in the audience—and when I was done, I looked out at the audience.

And they were on their feet, giving me a standing ovation.

It was the coolest moment of my life.

By the way, just to bring me back down to earth, years later, in 1994, I was given an award at the Soul Train Music Awards—I have two of them, by the way, one of the few white guys who've received that honor twice—and a little later that night, I'm in the restroom, when who walks in but Barry White. A few minutes later he's at the sink washing his hands, and I can't help myself. "Hey, Barry," I say. "You're never going to believe me, but my very first gig was with you in Portland."

He raises an eyebrow. "Really?"

I can't stop talking. "Yeah, I played all the solos. I have *got* to tell you, if it wasn't for that weekend, I don't know if I would be a professional musician. Getting up on stage with you made me feel like, 'Hey, I can do this! I can do this! I'm playing with *the* Barry White! Doing those gigs showed me that I was good enough to play with the pros!"

Barry turns off the water and says, "Hey, that's great, baby. Hand me a paper towel."

So if you want to bring a jazz icon back down to earth, remind him that in the temple of great artists, sometimes you're the headliner, and sometimes you're the bathroom attendant handing out the towels.

Kidding really. I wasn't offended in the least. It was a funny moment. Barry was getting the Soul Train Heritage Award that year, for a lifetime of achievement, and that whole night, being at the Soul Train awards and being honored alongside the greats like Barry, Whitney Houston, Toni Braxton, and Janet Jackson, I was thrilled to be acknowledged as one of their peers.

Remember how, on that bus with Barry White, that mantra kept ringing in my ears—"you're on the wrong bus"? Well, it's moments like this that told me:

Yes, Kenny Gorelick. It's okay. Breathe. You belong on this bus.

The night after my first solo with Barry White, we got on the bus and headed back to Seattle to play at what was then called the Paramount Northwest Theatre, a three-thousand-seat hall that was the city's premier venue. Playing the Paramount in Seattle was like playing Carnegie Hall in New York. Only the top acts played there, and it was stunningly ornate, like a Broadway theater. Pink Floyd, the Guess Who, and the Grateful Dead had all been there in the last year. So there I was, playing the Paramount with Barry White, and I swear to God, every Black kid from my high school was there, including the guys who pushed me up against the locker on a daily basis demanding my lunch money.

I stood up to play my solos and got another ovation, and when I got back to school on Monday, everything had changed.

On Monday morning, in the halls of Franklin High School, right next to the famous locker that had a close and personal relationship with my backside, the same kids who used to beat me up were coming up to me and telling me how cool it was that I was playing with Barry White. Barry White! Suddenly, the nerdiest kid in the school had become the coolest.

I mean, not really. I was still the nerdiest kid in school.

But a lot of things did change.

For one thing, what I said to Barry White all those years later in the bathroom was absolutely true. I was infused with the idea that I had become a professional musician. Not only had I gotten paid for playing the saxophone, but I had played along with seasoned lifelong musicians, and not only had I held my own, but I had stood out. And people recognized it. I thought, for the first time, that I could really do this. I could become a professional saxophone player. The thought blew my mind.

For another, in a school filled with racial tension, in a town where just about all the local bands were segregated—there were Black bands and white bands and nothing in between—I was the kid who crossed over.

It wouldn't be the last time I stood out.

Seattle has a rich, deep music history. In the forties and fifties, there was an incredible after-hours jazz scene that gave rise to legends like Ray Charles, who recorded his first single in Seattle, and Bumps Blackwell, a bandleader who gave guys like Quincy Jones their start. Jimi Hendrix also started his career in Seattle.

Everyone knows Seattle, of course, as the birthplace of grunge music years later.

But between the Rays and Jimis of the fifties and sixties, and the Kurt Cobains of the nineties, there arose an incredibly rich funk scene, which was in full swing by the time I was a high school senior in the fall of '73. To much of the world, the bands of that era were largely unknown.

But I sure knew about them. Robert Nesbitt, a very well-known DJ at the R&B station KYAC, really championed the Seattle funk bands. Bobby is a truly wonderful guy. He was someone I really looked up to and was one of my first big supporters. He told me when I was just starting out that he thought I was a really good player. His kind words gave me a ton of confidence when I needed it the most, and I'll always be grateful to him for that. It truly made a difference. Bobby became a great long-term friend, and years later, he wrote this great description of the Seattle scene:

> There was a minimum of twenty live-music clubs specializing in funk and soul, and all those joints jammed. There must have been twenty-five hard-giggin', Superfly-like, wide-leg-polyester-pant-and-platform-shoes-wearing, wide-brim-hat-and-maxi-coat-sportin', big-ass, highly-"sheened"-afro-stylin',

Kool & the Gang song-covering live bands playing four sets a night from 8 p.m. 'til 0-dark-thirty in the morning . . . Each night, some band, somewhere, was kickin' it. You could find Manuel Stanton of Black and White Affair doing flips while playing bass on a Monday at the Gallery. Meanwhile, you might catch Robbie Hill, flashing like a Christmas tree in a red rhinestone-studded jumpsuit, matching red Big Apple cap and the huge hair, keeping the beat for his band Family Affair at the District Tavern. The Dave Lewis Trio, the highly stylized Overton Berry and the ultra-funky Johnny Lewis Quartet regularly played the Trojan Horse, while Cold, Bold & Together was house band at the legendary Golden Crown Up. Cookin' Bag, with their heavy horn vibe was a major draw from Perls' Ballroom in Bremerton to Soul Street.

So how does the skinny little white guy get in with the coolest of the cool kids? Chalk it up to a little bit of fate, a little bit of luck, and a little theft of property.

At one point, a few of us from the high school jazz ensemble decided to start a band of our own. We called it Energy and somehow booked a gig. The problem was we didn't have a sound system.

This was our solution. One night, I suggested we break into the school and "borrow" the high school's sound system. And somehow, no one in the band had the wherewithal to say, There's no way we're going to get away with that—because, like, teenagers. You think you can get away with anything. And when you're the one who goes off the diving board first, "fear" is not in your vocabulary.

Unfortunately, "smart" isn't either. At least not in this case. This was one of the more fearless things I'd done. We played the gig and returned the equipment, but the next day the band director, Mr. Chinn, found out about it and made us pay the school all the money we made from the gig, which was maybe twenty-five bucks apiece. Not a fortune, but we were all pretty bummed. Philip Woo, the keyboard player, was so mad that he quit and never played in the high school band again.

Which turned out great for him.

And even better for me.

Because of that, two things happened. For one, Philip's leaving created an opening in our jazz band for a piano player. One of the trumpet players, Robert Damper, was also a killer piano man and played piano in his church. We'd always told him he was better at piano than he was on trumpet, but he was stubborn and refused to switch. Now, however, he had to step in and fill the void on piano. (Flash forward about ten years and he becomes the piano player in my band, which, as I mentioned earlier, he still is.)

The other thing that happened when Philip left the band was that he became the keyboardist in a great Seattle funk band called Cold, Bold & Together. They had formed in 1971 when they were in college in Bellingham, Washington. When they moved to Seattle, they found themselves short a keyboard player right around the time Philip quit the school band. So he quickly became their keyboardist, and one day they were holding rehearsals for a sax player. The rehearsals were at the home of that DJ who I mentioned earlier, Robert Nesbitt. His house was the band's house. Philip told me to come by and sit in on sax.

The leader of the band was Tony Gable, a big, six-foot-four, 245-pound guy, and he loved me right away. But the other guys didn't want to bring a white kid into the band. Philip was okay, they'd decided, because he was Asian. But in the end, Tony convinced them that a good player is a good player. And everyone agreed that I was more than good. So I was in.

Only one more problem: we had to convince my mom. Seattle, like most cities at the time, remained pretty segregated when it came to nightlife, and while I never once witnessed my parents being in any way overtly racist, I knew they wouldn't like the idea. My staying out late at those inner-city nightclubs was not something my mom was going to go for, because she would be worried for my safety.

"Tony," I told him, "my mom's not gonna let me be in the band and spend all my nights in the Black clubs. You're gonna have to talk to her."

So a few days later, Tony showed up at my door. Fortunately, my mom tended to treat strangers very well. There was a certain softness and tenderness that came out in my mom when she was around strangers, a quality that, for whatever reason, she kept inside when it was just family. Luckily for me it was there when Tony came over. So while this might have been the first Black person she'd invited into her home, other than my friends like Lee Turner, she invited Tony in like a long-lost cousin. Of course, it didn't hurt that Tony was a very kind and articulate guy and also quite charming and was doing his best that day to charm my mom.

She didn't ask him about the clubs we'd be playing in or what the clientele was or anything like that. She just offered him some cookies and made some idle chit-chat, and the deal was done.

In later years, I came to understand my mom better. She wanted only the best for us kids. And of course, she worried for our safety. She might have had a loud bark, but behind it was the sweet love that a mother has for her children. And she could tell that day that it was important for me to be part of this professional band. So being kind to Tony was her way of showing me love. And even though she couldn't know it at the time, her decision led to so many wonderful things in my life.

Because as of that moment, I was officially in the band.

The band's first gig had been opening for the Chambers Brothers in front of two thousand people. Later they'd go on to open for bands such as the Ohio Players, KC and the Sunshine Band, and Earth, Wind & Fire. But during my time with them, it was all about those clubs in Seattle's Central District, a.k.a. the CD. Tony and I became fast friends. I'd go to his apartment a lot, or we'd go out for burgers.

I liked all the guys in that band. There were the twins—one played bass, and one played guitar. The lead singer, Harrison Allen, was this good-looking guy with an absolutely beautiful voice and an even more beautiful attitude—he decided it was his job to teach this nerdy kid how to get it on with the ladies. You gotta smell good, and you gotta know how to say the right things, he would tell me. Be respectful.

When we were out at the clubs, and I was often the only white guy in the room, he would tell me that race didn't matter, but attitude did. If you see a beautiful lady with a guy, make sure you look that guy in the eye. Don't just look at her. Make sure you show him respect. I was still just a senior in high school, so I was soaking all this up like a sponge. Remember, I definitely hadn't had sex yet—that kiss with Lynda Barry was not only the highlight of my love life but pretty much the extent of it—so I was all ears. Well, maybe not *all* ears. I'll let you insert your own sax joke here while I get back to the story.

My white friends would rarely come to see me because they were afraid to venture into an all-Black crowd. I understood that and never pressured them. They knew that I was aware of their support, even if they didn't come to the gigs.

But I was with the band. I was with Tony, me and this big, intimidating Black guy walking shoulder to shoulder into these clubs, and people would look over, size up the situation, and turn back to whatever they were doing. In retrospect, I can see that I was being given entry to a milieu and a culture that very few other white kids were privileged to take part in. At the time, though, I didn't think much of it. I thought, Hey, I'm playing with the coolest band in town. And we are blowing the roof off these joints, night after night.

I'll talk more about this later, but because there have been critics who've brought up the idea that there's a problem with a white sax player becoming successful playing jazz music that came from an African American milieu, I do want to say a little more about my introduction to that world. Because from my perspective, I was being given a great gift. It's a gift I feel I earned with my sax playing, but I never want to talk about those days without acknowledging what a gift I was given.

There was a cultural difference that I saw in those rooms, a sense of togetherness that I didn't feel had the same vibe in the white places. A sense of commonality, of shared experience, of "we're all in this together."

Recently, at one of my shows, I talked with the percussionist in my band, Ron Powell, about this. Ron happens to be Black, and he and I have been good friends for forty years, so I'm very comfortable talking with him about things that, unfortunately, white and Black people don't always feel comfortable talking about together.

During my shows, I often invite a couple on stage, and I play a song for them. One night, an older Black man and his wife won the drawing to join me for one song, and after the song was done and as the man stepped off the stage, he spotted Ron and gave him a kind of knowing nod. Later I asked Ron about that, and he said, "It's all about being a Black man in America. We know each other's struggles and ac-knowledge them."

That's what I sensed and what I loved about being in those Black clubs. It was that feeling of connection. And when people in those clubs heard me play and because of my playing said, Okay, we accept you here even though you don't share our experience; you can share this part of it—that just filled me with a sense of great pride. And a sense of awe, too, at the fact that my sax was going to take me places I could never go on my own. I didn't go to hear the other bands in town much. On my own, I was just a skinny white kid who didn't belong. But with Cold, Bold & Together, I had a place where I belonged.

So I will always be grateful to Tony, to the CBT crew, and to the folks in those clubs for allowing me into that world, to witness and absorb and participate in a culture and a music that very few white guys were privileged to be a part of. I know it shaped my music forever. And for the better.

There was a lot more money in playing the white clubs in the 1970s, but they wouldn't take a Black band. I remember a couple of places, like Pier 70, that wouldn't let us in the door. I played there occasionally when I sat in with a white band called Big Joe and Push. Big Joe was like 380 pounds, could really sing, and was a great entertainer. He used to say to me, "Bro, you're in the wrong band. You got to come join my band. We're making like ten times the money you are."

But I liked where I was, because the vibe was so cool and the music was way more heartfelt for me. So I told him no.

That might have been the first time I began to understand the ad-vantages I had as a white musician in the predominantly Black mediums of funk and jazz. Because the white bands were still almost entirely seg-regated, the opportunity to play with them—and make ten times as much money—wasn't going to be presented to any of the very, very worthy Black musicians who could have stepped in. I'm also quite aware of how lucky I was to be in a position where I was given that choice. As well as the opportunity to play with the predominantly Black bands who weren't as segregated, and to have a choice between the two. And of course, how fortunate I was to be in a position where I wasn't desper-ate for the money. I had grown up in a nice middle-class home, where my needs were taken care of.

I try never to forget all of that.

I'm so glad I turned Big Joe's offers down. The music I was playing was so much more of the sound that I felt was in my own soul.

I may have thought I had soul in my sound before I joined Cold, Bold & Together, but the time I spent with them really got my groove going. At first we played mostly the soul standards, like Earth, Wind & Fire and Con Funk Shun and such. We did play the Wild Cherry song that goes "Play that funky music, white boy," and of course they had me sing it—the one and only time I've sung on stage. It always got a good, warm laugh. Eventually we started adding in more jazzy sounds, like a Grover Washington song or two, and the audiences loved it when we played those. And of course, on those songs, I got to really shine.

We became kind of the house band at a cool club called the Golden Crown Up, so named because it was above a Chinese restaurant called the Golden Crown, and you had to schlep all your equipment up this steep and narrow staircase. We'd hook up a U-Haul trailer to my Olds 88 and then haul all the equipment up there—a whole Hammond B3 organ, the full drum kit, and all the rest.

Those gigs were a lot of work. We'd start our first set at 11:30 p.m. and finish around 4:00 a.m., and then Tony and I would go out to break-fast at a Denny's kind of joint called the 13 Coins, which never closed. It was a wild scene, the Golden Crown Up, with a lot of cocaine flying around. I never did any, but it was pretty much everywhere. And it was a pretty tough crowd too.

I remember one time coming up the stairs for the third set and hearing someone playing a saxophone. When I got to the top of the steps and walked into the club, I saw that somebody had just taken my saxophone off my stand and started playing it. Just as I started to say, "What the fuck are you doing . . . ?" I looked up and realized it was this six-foot-four tough guy with a big brim on, staring down at me and daring me to do something about it. He stopped playing and stepped toward me, clearly ready to kick my ass. Just then, I heard a voice behind me saying, "Hey, brother, that's his saxophone." It was Tony. The big guy said, "Oh, okay, that's cool, that's cool," and handed the sax to me. Like I said, Tony always had my back.

I loved being in that band, and I loved our music. And when I graduated from high school and went to college, I stayed with them. Because . . . who wouldn't?

But even while I was grooving with CBT, my musical horizons were about to get a lot broader.

And, some might say, in the strangest ways.

CHAPTER FOUR

I went to college at the University of Washington and immediately joined the jazz band. The band director, Roy Cummings, singled me out as someone who could really play. Luckily, when visiting artists came to town and needed a few local artists to fill out their bands, Roy was the one they turned to. And Roy would turn to me.

One day Liberace, the famously flamboyant piano player, was coming to town, and he needed a saxophone player who could also play the flute, clarinet, and oboe. I could play the flute and clarinet at this point—I'd picked those up along the way pretty easily. But I didn't play the oboe.

When Roy asked me if I could do it, of course I said yes.

I had a week to learn, so I tracked down the oboe player in the Seattle Symphony and convinced him to help me. It's a woodwind instrument, so the finger positions are similar to the sax, which is half the battle. My fingers basically knew what to do. But the oboe is a double-reed instrument, and learning to play it was more about my mouth figuring out how to make the right sound. Then I practiced a ton. All that week leading up to the show, I'd practice a few hours, stop long enough to eat, then get right back to practicing. The thing is, if you practice something for two or three hours, at the end of that session you're probably going to be pretty good. The key, though, is where you are with it when you come back to it later. Did you learn it, or was it crammed into your head temporarily? That's become a big test of whether I've really learned something. When I come back to it, where am I with it? It can't just be a cram session.

That's why one session doesn't do it. You have to come back to it over and over and over. Which is another reason that I still practice three hours every day.

At the end of that week, I had the oboe down well enough not to embarrass myself. I wasn't great at that show, but I was good enough. Normally, especially back then, being anything short of perfect would make my teeth ache, but in this case, given the circumstances, I gave myself a pass. Fortunately, so did Liberace.

Now, a lot of people have asked me: Here you are, the only white guy in one of the hippest soul-and-funk bands in one of the hottest soul-and-funk scenes in the country. Wasn't it strange for you to be on stage with, arguably, the whitest guy in America at the time?

And my answer is no, because in the end, music is music.

My job was to play his charts. It was a fascinating and fun challenge. You don't have the charts to practice with for weeks. You don't know his music. You just open up the book and there's "You Don't Bring Me Flowers," and you have to nail it, right from the start. You're in a big orchestra, and you're holding your own, and I was very proud to be there, sight-reading along with the band. To me, it was still the magic of realizing, Holy shit, I *am* a professional musician. And what could be cooler than that?

There was something else I picked up from Liberace. I would watch him from a vantage point few people have ever had, and I could see how polished and impeccable his playing was. Night after night, he played meticulously, perfectly, the same notes in the same way, never missing a note, with a precision that was incredible. I remember thinking, That's how to do it, to put on a show and nail it every night. That's how I wanted to be. That's what musicians do. We want to master our instruments. Even though they can never truly be mastered, we want to keep trying anyway. To this day, I still think about Liberace playing each note perfectly. I still try to emulate that example in my shows. I don't always succeed, but I try.

So I didn't care that a lot of people—my friends, especially—thought his music was corny or schmaltzy. I was happy to be there. And I kept getting more gigs through Roy. They ran the gamut. When the Ringling Brothers circus came to town, that was me playing the silly circus music. When Sammy Davis Jr. came to town, I was up there with the Candy Man.

In fact, during Sammy Davis's show I had a little solo, and he pointed to me and said to the audience, "That kid will have his own band in a week." It was just part of the show, but my mom happened to be in the audience, and she was really proud. I think it finally hit her that her son was actually an accomplished professional musician who got to play with some of the greatest stars in the country.

Thanks for that, Sammy.

From all of them—Sammy and Liberace and Barry White and Diahann Carroll and so many others—I learned about being a professional musician and the discipline it takes. But I learned something else too. How to put on a show. How to be an entertainer. How to read a crowd, know when you have them, and know how to keep them. I was a sponge, soaking it all in, knowing—knowing for certain—that one day, I would have that chance in the spotlight as well.

In between those gigs, I was still playing the clubs with my soul mates in Cold, Bold & Together. After a while, we got a chance to go into the studio and record a couple of singles. My favorite—everybody's favorite—was "Somebody's Gonna Burn Ya," the song the band was best known for at the time. It's worth your time to go check it out on Spotify or YouTube. It's a great period piece, and I think it stands up as a great piece of music on its own. And yes, that's me in there.

If you listen to those records now, you'll hear that, as with most funk bands, it was all about the bass and the drums and the vocals. The horn section, such as it was, was featured, but not prominently. When we were live, there was room for some sax solos, but mostly I was keeping our little section together—just me and a trumpet player—and I was fine with that. After the gigs, we sold the 45s out of the trunk of one of the guys' gold four-door Buick Electra 225.

So between that and having breakfast with Tony, it'd usually be getting light outside by the time I was back on campus. Still, I managed to get enough sleep and keep up the straight As I felt compelled to earn. It was pretty easy actually. I'd read and memorize the material and write it on the test and go about my business.

I didn't make the golf team, but I did make the ski team, and I spent a lot of time working out at the gym.

And then—cue the drumroll—I finally, finally managed to have actual sex.

I met the young woman at a party. We wound up going to my dorm room, and I swear, I didn't have any idea what I was supposed to do. But somehow, we managed to find our way through it, and soon we started dating. She wouldn't come see me at the clubs, but a few months later, Cold, Bold & Together was playing some gig near the Sea-Tac Airport, and she walked in on the arm of another guy. On one of our slow numbers, they started slow-dancing right in front of me.

I guess that was her cold and bold way of telling me we were no longer together.

I didn't take it that hard. I was the cool guy in the cool band, and I was finally learning how to talk to girls. I was never a big Casanova, but I did okay. Between the girls and the music, I was having the time of my life.

A lot of the fun I was having with music was thanks, as I said, to Roy Cummings, the band director at the University of Washington, who kept getting me great gigs with acts that were coming to town. He was a terrific guy, and I'm very grateful to him.

It may surprise you to learn that I was not a music major. I started to take music classes, and my intent was to major in music, but after the first day in music theory class, I knew it wasn't for me. The professor was talking about the standard jazz progression being the "two five one," which for some reason he wrote as "ii V I," and was explaining why those chords sound so good together. Then he started talking about the difference between the Mixolydian scale and the Dorian, and all I could think was, Did I accidentally wind up in Greek 101? Because it sure sounded like that to me.

After about an hour of this, of which I understood less than none, the class mercifully ended, and I ran screaming from the room and directly to a practice room. There, I spent six delightful hours, playing the sounds and scales that sounded good to me, not what a professor said sounded good on paper.

And that's what I've done ever since.

Thus ended my career as a music major—but certainly not my career in music.

I really enjoyed being in the school band, and I could play anything that director Roy Cummings threw at me. He was a great guy, except for when he wasn't, and for the most part, we got along great. There was only one time I remember butting heads with him. At the time, I was furious about it; it was only later that I realized how important this moment would be.

Here's what happened. One day, I was doing a solo in a jazz rehearsal, and Roy got annoyed, walked up to me, and swatted my sheet music off the stand. "This isn't a Grover Washington solo," he snapped. "Everything isn't Grover Washington."

My cheeks burned, and I heard some snickers behind me. Not cool, I thought. That's not the way he should have handled this. I was churning inside.

And as much as I had learned from my father to suffer in silence, I was also learning that there were times when I would do anything but. In later years, this would become very natural for me—especially when it comes to my music, nothing stops me from saying or doing what I think is correct. (Wait'll I tell you about my first visit to *The Tonight Show*.)

But back then, for a kid who'd learned not to fight back against authority, it was a new experience to stand up for myself. Nevertheless, after class, I went up to Roy and looked him right in the eye. "I think you were out of line," I said. He looked a little taken aback, but I was on fire. "There are a lot of ways you could have handled that. You didn't have to grab my sheet music from me. I'm just a student, but I'm still worthy of your respect. You embarrassed me, and quite frankly I'd say you embarrassed yourself too." I stopped and thought, Oh shit, did I go too far?

But his reaction was the opposite of what I expected. A little smile bloomed on his face, and he nodded his head a little bit, then told me to sit down. "You're right," he said. His voice was quiet, almost fatherly. "But the reason I got pissed is, you're too talented to be stuck where you are. You know I believe in you. And I believe you can do so much more." He walked over to a little shelf on the opposite side of the room and grabbed a handful of records. "John Coltrane," he said to me, showing me the cover of *Blue Train*, and then flipped through a few others. "Charlie Parker. Stanley Turrentine. Listen to some of these guys. Then come back and show me what you got. Because I know you got it. It's time for you to go beyond."

It was, in a lot of ways, one of the most important conversations I've ever had. For one, it taught me that there are times when you have to stand up for yourself—not an easy lesson for a kid from my house. But also, and more importantly, it opened me up to a world of music that I'd never heard. Frankly, I didn't even know they existed. As I said earlier, playing sax in isolation has its benefits, because you can develop your own sound, but obviously it can also be enormously limiting. So getting turned on to the greats of jazz for the first time was like pouring water onto a sponge.

I mean, Miles Davis, where have you been all my life?

I started listening to all the jazz greats: Sonny Rollins, Stanley Turrentine, Dexter Gordon, Cannonball Adderley, Miles and Coltrane, and Stan Getz. I particularly loved Stan Getz. There was something about his sound that was exhilarating and quiet and playful and serious and moody and romantic, all at the same time. And years later, when

I recorded my *New Standards* album in 2021, I actually managed to create a posthumous duet with Stan Getz. Even though he'd been gone by then for thirty years.

Wait till I tell you *that* story.

Just like when I first heard Grover, I was listening to these amazing, amazing players, and I realized there was power and possibility in my instrument that I hadn't even imagined.

All I wanted to do was to be able to play like that. Sort of.

To be more precise, I wanted to be able to play like that and then add my own vibe to it. I never wanted to sound exactly like any of the masters. I wanted to understand how to play what they were playing and add that to the mix to make my own style and sound.

When critics say that I borrow from the greats, I plead guilty as charged. But when they say I don't acknowledge my roots, nothing could be further from the truth. Those guys were the milk that nourished my sound, the soil that my sound grew from. And not a day goes by that I don't say thanks.

I listened so much to these guys that I can tell who it is after a few seconds. I can tell that it's John Coltrane playing "Naima" or Stanley Turrentine playing "Sugar" after one note. I do have trouble sometimes catching the difference between Dexter Gordon and Sonny Rollins—they remind me of each other a lot—but that usually clears up after I hear a bit of the song. Everybody has his own sound. That's what jazz is about.

One day, I heard that Stanley Turrentine was going to play the local jazz club, and I was determined to see him. The problem was, the drinking age was twenty-one, but I wasn't; so when I went to the club where Turrentine was playing, they wouldn't let me in.

I went around to the side and put my ear to the door. I could hear Turrentine's unmistakable sound. It was incredible to be so close to greatness. But I hated that I was missing a chance to hear him in person. I kept an eye on the front door, and when the guy checking IDs turned his back for a second, I snuck in. There was Stanley Turrentine himself, wearing a suit and skinny tie, wailing away on that tenor sax. I felt like

I had stepped through a portal into another dimension. A dimension of unparalleled musicianship. Next thing I knew, a heavy hand grabbed my shoulder, and a bouncer was ushering me out the door.

Now that I was bitten by the bug, I couldn't stay away. A few weeks later, Cannonball Adderley came to a club called the Heritage House. Once again, I sat outside, with my ear to the door, absolutely enthralled by the muffled sounds of one of the greats playing only a few steps away. As before, I felt like I had entered some alternate realm of existence. And all I knew was that someday I wanted to be somewhere in that universe. And stay there as long as I could.

In college, I wasn't sure what I was going to focus on at first. I took a calculus class early on because it seemed like fun at the time (yes, I'm one of those people who think calculus could be fun). In retrospect, it feels kind of meaningless to me—I mean, when are you ever gonna use calculus in real life?—but a friend of mine reminded me that I go to the gym every day and lift weights, and it's not like anyone in real life is ever gonna ask me to lift fifty pounds of something straight up ten times in a row, over and over again. You do it to build those muscles for other things—which is exactly what calculus did, in my opinion. It built brain muscles. I liked that exercise for that reason. I like anything that gets the brain going and is challenging.

Sixty percent of the final grade in this particular calculus class was the final exam. In preparing for it, somehow I had gotten ahold of the previous year's test, which included one particularly complicated problem. It took me three hours to solve it, and I had a feeling it would be on the final again. It was. The exam was open book and open notes, so you could bring in anything, and since I had that exact problem already solved, I wrote out the solution in four minutes. I can still see the look of surprise on the proctor's face when I handed in my test and said, "Okay, I'm done." I got an A-plus on that one.

Even so, calculus was still feeling pretty meaningless, and I wasn't interested in studying music, just playing it. I started taking economics and accounting classes and graduated as an accounting major. Those courses were easy for me. I've always been great at memorizing things, and for better or for worse—definitely not for better, I think—so much of school is about memorization. If you ask me right now to name all the presidents in order, I'll get stuck somewhere after Washington, Adams, Jefferson . . . well, somewhere around there. But give me the list and come back tomorrow, and I'll nail it, 100 percent. I can picture the page in my brain, and mostly I just read off it.

I'm not saying this is a great way of educating our youth. Quite the opposite. I was just good at it, and it served me well. I mean, here I was, getting straight As not for really having to know the material, just for memorizing it for a short time. If I had my way, we would focus more on whether our young people actually learn the material we want them to know, rather than memorizing it to get a good grade on the test.

But that's how school was for me. Test after test, 100 percent after 100 percent.

Today, the ability to visualize information comes in incredibly handy. It's good for remembering the notes I play every night, of course, and it's also handy when I perform concerts in other countries, which I do a lot. When I first played Japan, for example, I wanted to say a few things in Japanese, so I wrote down, phonetically, "*Sumimasen, watashi no nihongo wo amari uma koo arimasen*," which means, "I'm sorry, my Japanese is not very good." When I got up on the stage, I pictured those words on the page. The audience loved that I was making that effort to connect.

After that, I started doing it in as many countries as I could. I've found that if I recite the words and look at the page I've written them on the night before my concert, it sticks. It's important to do it the night before because when I wake up in the morning, the page is imprinted on my mind. These days, in countries I visit frequently, I can do the entire show in that country's language. I can tell jokes in Japanese. Spanish and French are pretty easy. Chinese was tricky until I figured out the tones. I could see the words and say them correctly, but the meaning was lost without the correct tones. As a Westerner, that takes a while, but I've gotten pretty good at "concert Mandarin."

So that's the process that let me slide through college. I have a Phi Beta Kappa key and a 3.96 GPA (and it galls me no end, to this day, that that's not a 4.0).

Even so, I should count my blessings. I almost didn't graduate at all.

Back in those days, you could take a pass-fail class. I needed a few final credits to graduate, so I took a meaningless one in my senior year, and I knew I had enough points to pass, so I didn't bother to show up for the final. And I failed. Which meant I couldn't graduate.

I went to the teacher to argue my case. "Look," I said, "I had enough points to pass."

"Yes, but you have to take the final," he said. "If you don't, it's an automatic failure."

I stared him down. "Where is that written? When was that put out there?"

He stared right back. "That's just the way it is," he said.

I marched right into the dean's office and stood up for myself. "Look at my record," I said to him. "Do you think I'm going to actually fail this dumbass class? Seriously. This can't stand. I have enough points to pass this class easily. You can't go with this. It isn't fair."

He waited a long time to answer. Finally, he leaned forward and said, "Kenny. Look. Will you just take the final? Even if you get a zero on it, you'll pass. Just take the test."

So I did. The next day, I sat down with the teacher, and he gave me the test. I answered one question. Boom. Done. I handed it back to him. I failed the test, passed the class, and graduated.

Look, I don't want to paint myself as someone who doesn't take shit from anyone. In my personal life, for many years, I was still ruled by the commandment to suffer in silence. I'd go along with things because I didn't want to upset the applecart.

But don't let this wimpy Jewish exterior fool you. I can be a tough guy when I need to be. I've learned to overcome the deeply ingrained lesson I was taught about keeping your mouth shut. That is no longer part of my DNA. It took years of hard work with a great therapist to flush that out of my system. Now I'm okay with voicing my own opinions on things and not staying silent. Especially on what I think are objective matters. If I know A plus B equals C and you try to tell me otherwise, I'll *really* fight you tooth and nail. That's what I did with that pass-fail course.

And that's what I would eventually learn to do in my music career. It's been central to my happiness as a musician—and a person. Learning what's right for you, trusting that it's okay, and sticking with that conviction are vital to achieving personal happiness. Once I figured out what I thought was the best way to play—the best way for *me*—then it didn't matter what anyone else said about it (which was good, because as I became more and more successful, plenty of people had plenty of opinions about how I play and how I should play). That's not to say that I don't listen to advice from others, especially those close to me, but I'm not going to take that advice unless I'm convinced that the new information is better. Especially when it comes to my music. No album of mine comes out until it gets my stamp of approval—and sometimes it can take years to get it where I want it to be. Once I put my stamp on it, it goes out and I don't doubt myself. If someone else loves it too, that makes me happy, and if someone else doesn't, I can live with that, because I've chosen to trust myself first and foremost. And that trust is everything. It has brought a lot of happiness and peace to my life.

When I graduated from college, I was at a fork in the road. Down one road were toilets and hot-water tanks—i.e., Thrifty Supply Company. I knew my dad was hoping that I would go into the family business with him, and with my accounting major and business emphasis, it seemed like a perfect fit. I could see a long way down that road; I'd probably wind up managing and owning that company someday.

But down the other road lay music. I couldn't see very far down that other road—I had no idea where it led—but I knew I wanted to take a chance on that path and see where it took me.

A few days after graduation I did an afternoon gig out at the Seattle Center, a big complex that was built for the 1962 World's Fair, and afterward my dad picked me up. As we were driving away, I told him I needed to talk to him about something. So he pulled over in a parking lot near the big Space Needle, and I laid it on the line. "Dad, I really want to give music a try," I said. "I think I'm good at it. I'm making some money now when I play these gigs, and I can afford to have my own apartment and do my thing. I want to take a couple of years and see what happens. Just a couple of years before I say, 'Hey, I'm going to come work at Thrifty.'"

He wasn't the least bit disappointed. Or if he was, he never showed it to me—not that night, and not any time after that. "No problem," he said.

That was the first step. Then I had to gear myself up for step two. The sun was going down, and I squinted over at the Space Needle—a great monument to people building something great based on a crazy idea, if you think about it, which is not that far from what I was thinking about myself in that moment—and then I turned back to my dad. "But I'm gonna need some help," I said. "I can pay my rent, like I said, but if I'm gonna do this, write songs and make my way in the business, I'm gonna need some stuff."

Technology was changing rapidly at that point, and if I was going to create music, I was going to need a new thing called a synthesizer, with a device inside called a sequencing computer that seems insanely simple now but was pretty radical at the time. With it, I could play a certain sequence of notes, and it would play them back as often as I needed. That and other equipment, like a drum machine, as well as a multi-track recording deck, which had been pretty esoteric a few years earlier but was now becoming the industry standard. And all of this wasn't cheap.

"I need you to loan me some money," I told him. "But I swear, I'll pay you back."

Slow Moe took almost no time to answer. "No problem," he finally said, with a big grin on his face.

That was my dad. The equipment was going to cost tens of thousands of dollars, but he didn't even ask me the price tag. I am eternally grateful to him for that sunset conversation by the Space Needle.

And it has never been lost on me that there are not a lot of musicians in this country who had that kind of support at that crucial moment. That so many others had to give up their dreams because they had to go to work, or support a family, or struggle to make ends meet, because they didn't come from the secure, safe, supportive background that I did. I can, and I do, point to the enormous amount of hard work I have put in to reach the place I am today. I am not shy about talking about my talent, and I think I owe a lot of my success, in those early days, to the fact that I worked harder than everyone else. No bones about it. But I am just as quick to acknowledge the enormous privilege I had. Even today, when I do my charity work to help underprivileged youth find their way to music, I always remember that when people thank me, they're also saying thanks to my dad for a conversation by the Space Needle some forty-odd years ago. When he said the two words that let a hopeful young musician pursue his dream: "No problem."

I stayed in the little $125-a-month off-campus apartment I'd been living in and started laying in the equipment—the synthesizer with the sequencer, a drum machine, and a big Otari eight-track recording machine (for those old enough to remember, this has nothing to do with those big eight-track tapes that competed with cassettes for a hot minute in the seventies). The Otari let me record eight different tracks at different times, then play them back together. So I could lay down a drum pattern, then a bass line, then play one sax line over that, and put another sax solo on top, and so on. And then I needed a mixing console, one of those things you see in control rooms with the sliders that change the volume of each track.

This is the very equipment I would write "Songbird" on a couple of years later. The song that changed everything.

But before that I had a huge musical adventure to go on.

CHAPTER FIVE

The 1970s was a time in which my life would change in many unimaginable ways. A real turning point in my unplanned transition from Kenny Gorelick to Kenny G. Because this was, after all, the decade when my hair would finally achieve the greatness that I always believed was possible.

If we were to map my career trajectory by the growth of my hair, this would be a time of great tonsorial promise. It was growing out but still defied gravity, the kind of frizzy curls that had a force of their own.

I, too, was guided by my own unique gravitational pull. Because during this time, I glimpsed my future, and as a result, I knew where I wanted to go.

For those too young to remember—those who have come of age with Stephen Colbert, Jimmy Fallon, Jimmy Kimmel, Seth Meyers, Trevor Noah, and James Corden—it can be hard to conceive of a time when there was only one place for an up-and-coming musician to perform. One platform that stood higher and shone brighter than any other. In the sixties, that was *The Ed Sullivan Show.* In the seventies, it was *The Tonight Show Starring Johnny Carson.*

Appearing on *The Tonight Show* wasn't even a remote possibility in my mind back then. Years later, when I actually did appear on that show, it would change my life. But my first brush with *The Tonight Show* came not long after I graduated from college, when I learned that the *Tonight Show* band's sax player would be playing in Malibu.

Johnny Carson had a great house band, fronted by a bandleader with a big smile and a bigger personality, a trumpet player named Doc Severinsen (who later became a friend of mine, which shows you how crazy and amazing life can be). Same as on the late-night programs today, the band was kind of a sideshow, and you didn't usually get to focus on the individual members. But every once in a while, they featured their sax player, Pete Christlieb. He would take a solo, and I remember thinking, Hey, this guy is good! Pete was kind of well-known in jazz circles around the time I graduated from college. Fans of Steely Dan know he's the guy who played the great sax solo on their big hit "Deacon Blues," and he backed up a lot of other well-known musicians.

I was eager to see him on his own. I'd never seen a sax player do a whole set, fronting a trio instead of backing up someone else, so I got in my trusty Olds 88 and took my first honest-to-God road trip, driving all the way from Seattle down to Malibu to a place called Pasquale's to hear him play.

It was like taking a master class in the future.

My future.

I watched him intently, looking at his fingers, listening to his tone, absorbing not only his music but his presence, both the notes he was playing and the way he was presenting himself as an entertainer.

And a feeling welled up in my chest. My face flushed, and I took in a deep breath and realized:

I can do this.

I know that might sound terribly egotistical—a young kid, watching the ultimate professional on stage, thinking he could do just as well, if not better—but I swear, in that instant, I believed with all my heart and soul that one day I would be up on that stage, fronting my own band, making my own music.

That was when I knew, without a doubt, that what I wanted more than anything else was, if I worked hard enough, something I could achieve.

Thanks for that, Pete.

The other thing that changed my life, after college, was a phone call.

In the seventies, a new kind of music had become popular. It was called jazz fusion. It was a mix of straight jazz melodies and improv, with a good dollop of funk and R&B thrown in. The instruments were a mix of the electric guitars and keyboards that rock bands were using, and more traditional jazz instruments like the sax. It kind of exploded on the scene when Miles Davis released *Bitches Brew* in the late sixties, and had gained a small but fervent following that had been growing year by year.

Jeff Lorber was a pretty well-known name in fusion in the late seventies. Not that I'd ever heard of him. Again, I was still living in the lo-fi Gorelick family world of my three-record collection and the occasional show I could get into in Seattle. So when Jeff called me on the telephone at my parents' house and said, "Hey, this is Jeff Lorber," I responded with a very unenthusiastic "Okay . . . and?"

If he was put out by that, I couldn't tell. He said he had heard about this Seattle sax player, and he wanted me to audition for his band. I guess he expected that I knew who they were, but I was still only half paying attention. "So, tell me about the band," I said.

"Well, we've got a record deal with Clive Davis at Arista Records and one record out already, and we're touring the country playing gigs. Things are going pretty well."

Clive Davis. Now *that* was a name I knew. He was the head of Arista Records, and Columbia before that, and he was famous for signing everyone from Springsteen to Sly and the Family Stone. Barry Manilow, Janis Joplin, and Tony Orlando were some of his other discoveries.

Now I was interested.

I did my research on Jeff after our phone call, heading down to the local record store to find a Jeff Lorber record. I took it home and put it on, and I loved what I heard. And now I was super excited, because I really wanted the gig. I got even more excited when I drove down to Portland to audition. I liked the band a lot. What they were doing was exciting and different, and they were really, really tight. Lorber liked me too—he couldn't have been more complimentary—and before the day was out, I had the gig.

Within a couple of weeks, we were out on the road, all of us taking turns driving a van from city to city. I was making $150 a week and having the time of my life.

Nothing says adventure like your first time.

Not *that* first time, which we've already discussed (and which, in my case, as you know, skewed much more toward awkwardness than adventure, but I know I'm not alone here!).

But it was because of Jeff and the band that I had the next life-changing experience—that I did something for the first time that I'd continue to do the rest of my life.

We were playing gigs all over the country, and Jeff always gave me lots of room to shine. He was very generous when it came to stepping back and letting me have solos. And audiences loved it; their reactions gave me the confidence that I had what it takes. I took more chances with my solos, and the wilder they got, the more the audiences seemed to go crazy.

Jeff's sound man, Rick McMillen, liked to experiment with the most cutting-edge technology, and he'd gotten his hands on some wireless microphones, which were still pretty new at the time. For one show, he had me attach one of the wireless mics to the end of my saxophone, and it was like the first time your dad takes the training wheels off your bike. Suddenly I could move so much more freely now that I didn't have to aim my sax right at the microphone.

Rick got me a little monitor so that on stage I could adjust how much sax I was hearing. For the first time, I was in control of the sound, which made it a lot easier to play my best. It was liberating.

But what he said next was even more liberating. "G-man," he said. That's what he called me. I was still billed as Kenny Gorelick, but I was starting to be known as Kenny G or G-man to the guys in the band. "G, you gotta walk off the stage. Come on. You gotta walk out there. In the crowd. Just do it, bro. Just go."

I was nervous about it. Not because of the audience—but because of Jeff. Though he was generous, he could also be difficult to read, and very often it was hard to tell if he was upset or not. I didn't want to take a chance of upsetting him and spoiling the good vibe we all had.

I was hesitant to step out, but Rick was persistent. He kept bugging me about it. One night in 1979, at the Bass Club in San Diego, I started one of my solos—a high-flying, fast-moving riff, interspersed with a bunch of the intricate patterns and long, long notes I would become well-known for later—and I looked over. There was Rick, going bananas off stage, waving his arms like a third-base coach trying to send me home.

My new home.

Out in the audience.

Like the fearless kid who used to jump off the high-dive, I did it. I stepped off the stage.

The stage was pretty low, so I could step off without missing a beat, and the minute I did, the crowd went crazy. I loved it. It wasn't that it was *more* fun than playing on stage. All my life, ever since I was in my high school band, playing on stage was what I was used to. I had not known any other way. Occasionally, they would move the microphone into the middle of the basketball court for me to play the national anthem, but I could never just . . . wander. It was absolutely incredible to do that and be so close to everyone. I had to learn very quickly how to move around without putting my horn at risk. For a long time, being on stage had been the most exciting part of life, but this was a different kind of excitement. I was so close to the people, looking at them eye to eye. We were sharing the music in a close and personal way that I had never experienced before. I'm 100 percent sure the audience had never experienced this before either; as I said, this technology was new and cutting edge at the time. And although they couldn't tell, I was smiling ear to ear behind my sax.

I'll be honest—it was so close and so intense that it forced me to immediately let go of the control that I usually play with. I don't like to use the term "control freak," but I do like to be in charge of everything that happens around me. And that's especially true when it comes to making music and performing my shows. Only during my improvised solos would I let that all go out the window. So to be performing those solos in the middle of the audience—that was the perfect place to abandon control, because I was totally caught up in the flow of the moment.

And what a moment that first time was.

People were dancing and slapping me on the back, shouting my name. And I was playing my heart out right at them—picking someone in the crowd and playing just for them. It was exhilarating.

It was my first time, but I knew for certain it wouldn't be my last.

Over the years some crazy things have happened out there in the audience. Once I was playing at Wolf Trap, a beautiful amphitheater nestled in the woods outside Washington, DC. I have to say that it gives me a special feeling when I get to play in venues like that, and that day, as I walked out into the audience and was just starting to feel the majesty and grace of that unique space, this big guy jumped on my back while I was playing. And he would not let go.

By this point I'm like a bucking bronco—pointing my tenor sax up at the sky, down at the ground, spinning in circles—and he's acting like he's about to win the rodeo. He wants his golden lasso, and I'm trying to get him the hell off my back, all while not missing a note! Eventually my tour manager whacked him with a big Maglite, at which point the guy made the quality decision to dismount and fall to the ground. I have to say, it took everything in me not to just stop and totally crack up. On the outside, I remained cool, hitting all the right notes, but on the inside, I was laughing my butt off. The sheer spontaneity of it, the absolute not-knowing-what's-gonna-happen-next of it, filled me with a real sense of excitement for what was yet to come.

All of that was still in front of me that first night at the Bass Club in San Diego. After my inaugural solo out on the floor among the people, I got back up on the stage, and the crowd gave me a huge ovation. At one point I peeked over at Jeff Lorber to see how he was reacting. He looked over at me, and I swear to God, to this day I have no idea what he was thinking. He was the kind of guy who was probably great at poker because so often you couldn't tell a single thing by looking at his face.

I hadn't known I was going to do it until Rick egged me on from off stage, so there'd have been no way to prepare Jeff or make sure he was okay with it beforehand. He didn't say much about it afterward, but Rick was completely jazzed about it. "Way to go, bro!" he yelled when I came off stage. "You've got to do that every night!" I looked over at Jeff at his keyboard, to see if I could get any reaction, but it was like looking at the Lincoln Memorial and trying to figure out if Mister Lincoln was having a good day. There was just no sign.

Those sax solos were the culmination of everything I had learned. Jeff never told me to stop, and the crowd was eating it up, so I kept at it. Performing in the audience is still a huge part of my shows. In fact, it's how I start all my concerts these days. The lights go down, there's a polite wave of applause and some excited whoops and hollers, and then the room goes quiet. I slip into the audience from the back and walk slowly but deliberately down the aisle to a place we've worked out ahead of time, so the guy running the follow spot—the movable spotlight—can find me. And yes, we call it the "G-spot." There have been countless times along my walk when I've been pinched in places very similar to that exact spot!

That first time performing in the crowd is a big part of how I went from Kenneth Gorelick to Kenny G.

CHAPTER SIX

My sax playing was evolving. And I was getting better and better. As I've said before, that's what happens when you work on something consistently for years. I was practicing a lot, as usual, and working on all the things that I felt would make me a better sax player—my technique, speed, articulation, and so on. But I also wanted to improve on something I was doing during my live performances that was getting a lot of very positive feedback.

There would be a point when I held a very long note or sustained a pattern for a long time. This became a kind of signature of mine, and it got a tremendous response, and so naturally I wanted to keep doing it.

It centered on a technique known as circular breathing. It's where you breathe in through your nose and out through your mouth at the same time. From what I know, Rahsaan Roland Kirk was the sax guy who started what we know as modern circular breathing. (He was also the guy who was known for playing multiple horns at once.) Unless you were a real jazz aficionado, you'd probably never heard Rahsaan, and so when I started doing it, most people had never seen it before and thought I invented it. And when I did it, they went absolutely wild.

But once again, it was never about trying to imitate what came before me but about learning from it and mixing in my own magic.

What I had heard from those who had done circular breathing before me was either holding one note for a long time or doing the circular breathing with a simple pattern. I decided, Hey, what if I tried to do the circular breathing but also play my sax normally at the same time? All the patterns, scales, riffs, syncopation, melodies, intervals—the whole shebang? How hard could that be? Turns out, pretty hard.

It took me about ten or fifteen more years of hard work to get that down. But now it's second nature to me, and I'm super proud of that skill, because it's something that very few people can do; because it's something that required a long time to master, which always matters to me; and because it makes playing the sax a whole lot more fun and interesting, which matters even more.

I was adding all these elements to my solos—the arpeggios, the circular breathing, the long notes, all those things that were getting an amazing reaction from the audience. But even while I was becoming extremely comfortable on stage, I still didn't forget that this was Jeff's band and his vision, and I only wanted to add to that, not detract from it in any way. I was simply trying my best to play the best solos possible. Sometimes we'd be driving the van late at night—sometimes I'd be behind the wheel with Jeff next to me—and he'd put in a cassette tape of the night's performance. We all hated when he did that, and we all braced for whatever criticism was coming. When my solo would come up, he'd say, "Don't do that."

I'd think, What? Don't do the thing that the audience is loving? Don't do the fast notes, the cool solos? What exactly do you not want me to do? Usually I said nothing. I'd just nod and then do whatever I wanted the next show. Maybe his gruffness came from the late hours, or maybe we were all tired. I figured if it was an important issue, it would come up again.

And as you know by now, I usually do what I think is best without too much regard for what others think. Even the boss! Although since it was his band, he ultimately had the final say. And rightfully so.

But I want to be really clear that at this point I was feeling very grateful for my time with Jeff and the band. Jeff guided me, taught me so much, and gave me incredible opportunities. It was because of Jeff and the band that I learned how to take my solos to another level. It was because of the Jeff Lorber Fusion that I first stepped off the stage and learned the joys of connecting to the crowd. It was because of the guys in the band calling me G or G-man that Jeff's manager, a thoroughly nice guy named Jeffrey Ross, suggested I make that my name. I can't overstate the importance of Jeff and the band. Because of them, I literally and creatively went from being Kenneth Gorelick to being Kenny G.

The first album I ever played on was Jeff's album *Wizard's Island*, and I got to co-write one of the songs. It was called "Fusion Juice," my first writing credit. Making that album and writing that song was a profound experience. Jeff was a great musician and a great songwriter, and when he asked me to co-write with him, I didn't know if I was even qualified to try. But after I heard his piano intro, it only took a couple of seconds for me to come up with the melody of the song.

And just like that, I became a songwriter.

Over the next couple of years, as he released one more album as the Jeff Lorber Fusion and then a solo album, *It's A Fact*, I started writing more and more. If you want to hear the moment that I think I started actually finding my own sound, it's a song called "Tierra Verde" on that solo album. There's about a twenty-second intro, and when my sax comes in, I hear, in a very early form, the vibe that I felt was my own and the beginnings of everything I was going to do going forward. If I look for the early ancestor of "Songbird," the song that put me on the top of the charts, this is the source of its DNA.

I loved the musicians I got to play with in those Jeff Lorber years, but one guy on those albums I was sorry I didn't get to jam with was Stanley Clarke. Stanley was absolutely the greatest bass player around—hell, one of the greatest of all time. He played bass in Return to Forever, Chick Corea's band, which was the most famous of the jazz fusion bands, and with good reason. But I was never in the studio with Stanley. He recorded his parts separately.

Three or four years ago, I saw Stanley at Nobu in Malibu, and he called out my name and called me over and I was so thrilled. I was thinking, Hey, I'm on Stanley Clarke's radar enough that he recognizes me! To this day, those moments make me feel wonderful. I tried to keep my cool as best I could, but when he said I should come and sit in with him sometime, I could barely contain myself. Every time this happens, I have to pinch myself (unless I'm in the audience starting a concert, when that job is often claimed by an audience member). Later on, when I got to play with Earth, Wind & Fire, I had the same feeling—I mean, Stanley Clarke! Earth, Wind & Fire! These are musicians I absolutely idolized when I was a kid, and now they're asking me to come play with them? It still feels unreal.

The Jeff Lorber Fusion played New York City a lot, usually at a cool little Greenwich Village club called the Bottom Line, a small venue for huge names. Everybody who was anybody passed through the Bottom Line. We played there twice in 1980, and it was during the second of those gigs, a cool Monday evening in October, that I finally got the break that every musician dreams of.

Clive Davis, Jeff's legendary record producer and the founder and president of Arista Records, would come to our gigs whenever we were in the city. Clive was—and still is—such an important person in my life. He was such a gentlemanly presence—respectful, smart, and not like so many fifty-year-olds at the time who were desperately trying to be hip. Clive was Clive, and he was cool with that.

I was lucky enough to be invited to Clive's ninetieth birthday party in 2022, and I finally learned what those years meant to him. He invited Gayle King to interview him in front of his adoring music family—hundreds of us—and I learned things about Clive that I hadn't known. I learned that his parents died when he was a teenager, and he was raised by a sister, so family became enormously important to him. To this day, he said, going on vacations with his four sons, and having Sunday-night dinners whenever they can, remain the most important things in his life.

As one of his artists, I've always felt like he treated me like family too. Not just me but all his artists. Understanding how important family is to him makes me understand why he cares so much and worries so much about us and our careers. How lucky for the few of us who were in that special Arista family.

That very, very special man, the man who would mean so much to me throughout my life, was the man who walked up to me after our set that cool night in October in Greenwich Village. We were standing next to the stage, and Clive said, "Kenny, you were fantastic. It was good to see you tonight."

I thanked him and thought that was all he was going to say. But there was more.

"You know," he said, "I think there's an audience for your particular saxophone sound. Would you like to do a solo album?"

How I felt: Holy shit! I can't believe it! After all these years, the thing that I've been working so hard for is finally happening!

What I said: "Yes, Clive. I think that would be a good idea. Let's do that."

I do have to clear up one thing before I go on. If you look at the Wikipedia page on Kenny G, it will tell you that Clive signed me after hearing me do ABBA's "Dancing Queen." There's absolutely no truth to that. I'm not at all sure how that rumor started, but it's been everywhere, all my life. But it didn't happen that way.

Clive did sign me, and a few months later we were in a studio in Malibu, recording the album. That's when the importance of what I was doing truly hit me. There weren't that many sax players putting out records at that time. There was Grover Washington Jr., of course, and David Sanborn, and a few others. Michael Brecker and his brother had done some stuff, but his first solo album was still a few years away. So I felt an enormous amount of pressure but also a great sense of good fortune to be given this opportunity.

Things started moving quickly. Jeff Lorber's manager, Jeffrey Ross, the guy who dubbed me "Kenny G," became my manager, and he was the one who decided it was the name I should record under. Then Jeff Lorber was signed on to produce the album. Jeffrey and Jeff each took

25 percent of my whole record contract, which was absolutely fine by me, because frankly, without them I wouldn't be here, so that seemed fair enough at that time. I was all of twenty-five years old, not very confident in my songwriting skills, and not at all sure what direction the album should go in, so I was glad to have a couple of more experienced guys on my side and as part of my career at that time.

We decided on the songs first. Jeff and I wrote a few of them together, and we added a cover version of the Eagles' hit "I Can't Tell You Why," because Clive and the guys at the record company thought we needed something like that for people to latch on to. As a result of this, it was more of a Lorber album than a Kenny G album. When you listen to that first album, *Kenny G*, you hear that same Lorber sound—very professional and catchy, with lots of hooks and fun little riffs, but it doesn't have my sound and my groove as much as it has Jeff's. The truth is that I wasn't sure what my sound was yet. I was still experimenting with the idea that I could actually write songs, so it was natural for this first record to basically be a Jeff Lorber Fusion album with me playing all the lead lines instead of Jeff. It was a good place to start but also left me feeling very not-special and slightly lost as far as direction.

We were working at Indigo Ranch Studios, up on Barrymore Drive in Malibu, California, one of the most beautiful places in the country. It's a big sixty-acre ranch surrounded by craggy rock formations and overlooking the endless blue of the Pacific Ocean. A lovely place to try to make music. And the equipment was astounding. Some of the microphones, I learned later, had come from Abbey Road, including Paul McCartney's favorite mike.

Not bad for a kid who didn't make his freshman year high school band.

Oddly enough, years later, Indigo Ranch Studios became the home of some of the angriest music ever—the post-metal music of Korn, Limp Bizkit, Slipknot, and others—but what we were doing could not have been more the polar opposite. This was happy music. Maybe even a little too happy sometimes. The first song was "Mercy Mercy Mercy," the classic Cannonball Adderley number. His version is soulful and hopeful, a little mournful but uplifting as well. Jeff did his own arrangement of that song, which was more light and upbeat. I liked it, but I didn't love it. But at that point I wasn't going to argue; I just wanted to hit all the right notes and make it sound as good as I could. We were doing multi-track recording on a big twenty-four-track machine, but we didn't have the digital editing capacity that we have today to go in and fix mistakes. So I couldn't tweak my sax parts and make the melodies and solos exactly the way I wanted to, like I can today. Back then, I did the best I could and pretty much focused on not messing up.

And since I was pretty new at this, I was happy to record songs that everyone else was happy with. That's a sentiment I've left behind long ago. Some things you carry forward as you get older, and some you leave by the curb when you move on. Making musical choices based on what other people wanted was one of the latter.

The second track, "Here We Are," features Greg Walker doing the vocal. Again, I wasn't crazy about the idea of having a vocal track on an instrumental album. This was supposed to be a Kenny G album, not an album of Kenny G doing backup for vocalists. But I acquiesced to the idea that this is the way you do records, slapping in some vocals so maybe you'll get air play on a different kind of radio station. This philosophy of having me do sax solos on vocal songs on my records, in order to get air play on stations that wouldn't play instrumentals, would follow me from album to album. It's something that I'll talk about in more detail later, but I think you're getting the idea that I don't like it.

One of the songs I did like on the first side of that album was that Eagles song we did. It was the first time on this album that I felt like I was getting to play the melody with my own take on it. Was this the beginnings of what would later become my sound? I'm still not 100 percent sure, but it was definitely headed in the right direction.

Up until now I'd pretty much been playing syncopation with Jeff, but here I was carrying the melody all by myself, singing the lead line with my saxophone for the first time. And on this song, finally, I can hear myself relaxing into the melody, expressing it just the way I felt it.

On this first album, with that song, I started to get a taste of what it felt like to actually play a melody the way I wanted to. I wasn't in total control yet, so I couldn't truly do this, but I got enough of a taste of it that I knew that there was no going back. That I had to be in control of how I played and how I recorded. And that was my goal. To get to the position where I could just play music from my heart and soul the way I hear it. It was never about selling records. I felt that record sales would come naturally if I was sincere about the music and if I created great music. And I planned to do both.

My philosophy was: Do it from the heart. Do it with skills honed by hard work and practice. Do it from your soul. Do it from inspiration, and do it with sincerity.

That, pure and simple, is what the Kenny G sound is about. Nothing more, and nothing less. Everything else comes from there. You can tell me you think it's too simple, you can tell me you think it's not real jazz—whatever that means—but you can never say it doesn't come from the heart.

Well, you can say that, of course. You can also say that goldfish have antlers. Neither would be close to the truth.

Because even way back then, it was all I ever wanted to do. To find my own sound and to play it from the heart.

As the sessions went on, I became more and more comfortable, and more and more assertive. Jeff and I wrote a song together called "The Shuffle," which I think is the best song on the album by far. It's a call-and-response between me and Jeff, and still a bit Lorber-esque, but I'm playing mostly what I want to play and having fun. There's a lot of room for improv in this one, and I'm trying to keep my head out of the way and let the music flow. It's pretty easy, and I'm pretty happy with how it came out. This one is the closest to where I wanted to be at that time.

And frankly, I was thinking—but not saying—that I was getting to the point where I didn't need Jeff to make music. I felt I was ready to do this on my own now, and I knew that I needed to be in total control so I could truly play the music the way I wanted to. It was the first time I started seeing the full potential of what my music could be, how I could write *more* songs like "The Shuffle" and beyond that and do it differently than anyone else. And there was only one way to do this.

All by myself.

I also started getting comfortable with the equipment and noticing how I could change my position in relation to the microphone to get the sound I wanted.

Much to the chagrin of the lead engineer.

What happened was, when we started recording me playing the soprano sax—the straight one that looks like a clarinet—he placed the microphones the way he always had, the way soprano saxophones had always been miked: one above my sax and one below it, with him blending the two. When you play any saxophone, some of the sound comes out of the tone holes, the little holes that your fingers are pressing the keys down onto, and he was trying to capture all that sound. But I didn't like the way it sounded. So I started experimenting, and at one point I discovered that if I put the mike right in front of the bell of the sax and got so close I was almost touching it, I got exactly the sound I wanted.

He said, "You can't mike a soprano sax like that."

And I said, "But that's the sound I like."

And he said, "I don't like it."

And I thought, Here's the top engineer at one of the best recording studios in the country, hired by a major record label headed by the genius Clive Davis, and here's a twenty-five-year-old kid from Seattle who has never recorded his own album before. So what could I say?

Well, here's what I said:

"You don't like this sound. But I do. And this is my album. And this is the way we're going to do it."

It wasn't until years later that I learned that Miles Davis, perhaps the most innovative jazzman ever, had done the same in the 1950s, using a mute with his trumpet and putting it right up to the microphone to capture the subtleties of his sound. It would have been reassuring to know I was following in the footsteps of greatness, but at the time I was just following what my ears were telling me.

And as much as learning to pull away from the Lorber riffs was the beginning of me finding the "Kenny G sound," learning to mike the sax the way I wanted to was a big part of it too. So while I wasn't able to play as freely and as true to my own heart as I would later in my recording career, I can hear in this album the seeds of what I was hoping would flower in the years to come.

When it comes to my music, I have always stood up for what I know in my heart is the right way to be. And my advice to any kids or adults who find themselves in a similar situation—which everyone does, at some point—is this: It's a two-step process. First, make absolutely certain that you are examining the issue at hand intelligently, and then base your decision on that. That's how you know in your heart whether you are right or not.

And if you're certain, then stand up for yourself.

I actually felt sorry for that engineer, because he was not going to enjoy himself. He was doing something he didn't want to do, and the part of me that wants to please people and do what I can to help them enjoy themselves—which is still an enormously strong part—felt awful for him.

But not bad enough to change what I wanted.

Because I knew what was right.

I do want to say one more thing about that first album. In the genre that's now known as "smooth jazz" (a term that hadn't been invented yet), there are a lot of songs that I label as "snappy tunes." That's how I describe it when artists record a song because they think it will have a good chance of getting some radio air play or sell well, or just do a song to fill a space on the album, instead of doing music that is true to their own heart. And that's why all those songs come and go and are not memorable. I don't like them. They are not truly heartfelt. And unfortunately, I will admit, a couple of those kinds of songs existed on my first record. I just wasn't in a position to do anything about it at that time.

As I've mentioned, I became extremely precise later, when I was recording my own albums, and it took years sometimes to get an album right, from the writing to the production. But I didn't have the elbow room at this point to do that. At the end of the recording sessions, as I said earlier, I realized that was precisely what I needed next: elbow room.

That album, simply titled *Kenny G*, didn't do well at all, frankly. But once again, I consider myself very lucky to have been making music at the time I was making it. I was one of Clive Davis's family, and it wasn't like he was going to throw away a family member because it didn't work out on the first record.

The business is very different today, and the analytics are much more precise. It's true that thanks to the internet, some folks are able to work independently and go viral in a way they couldn't have on their own in my day. But it's also true that it's still vastly important to have a label that believes in you and helps to promote you, and those labels today are so much more likely to drop an act and go on to the next one than they were in my day. You wouldn't believe how many flops big names like the Supremes and the Temptations had before they became famous, but Berry Gordy stayed with them at Motown until they had time to develop. That's exactly how I felt with Clive. He had my back. He saw the first album get a tepid reception and said, "Okay, let's move on to the next one." He was totally willing to give me a shot at another record.

Even when I told him that I thought it was time for a different producer.

Let me say again that I learned so much from my time with the Jeff Lorber Fusion. But it was clear that my sound and the Jeff Lorber Fusion sound had hit a fork in the road, and I knew which road I had to take.

I can't look back at that time now, though, without an enormous sense of gratitude to Jeff—for helping me get my first record, for showing me the ropes, for being open enough to let me start to find my own sound. But the time had come—graduation day. Maybe I wasn't his student anymore, but as I threw off my cap and gown and struck out on my own, it wasn't without a fond wave to the teacher who helped get me there.

CHAPTER SEVEN

It wasn't until years later, when I became a pilot, that I noticed the co-incidence in the names of my first albums and my first big hit. I had been given the freedom to come up with the titles of my own albums, and maybe there was some subconscious theme running inside me.

Or *flying* inside me.

Because after the *Kenny G* album, the one that cemented the name that everyone now knew me by, came *G Force*, which is the experience a pilot has as the plane accelerates, followed by *Gravity*, the force he conquers when he lifts off. And then, of course, by chance—I guess—the first mega-hit was "Songbird," an image of a creature in effortless flight. But as I said, none of that occurred to me back then.

Nor did it occur to me that my career was about to take flight as well.

After the first album, while Arista was more than willing to let me split from Jeff Lorber as a producer, there was no way they were going to give me the money and let me produce on my own. And I had no problem with that. At that time in my career, I didn't have the confidence yet to produce an entire album on my own. I knew that day would come, but at this point I was fine with Arista assigning me a producer—and then much more than fine with it when they assigned one of the hottest producers in the business.

Kashif Saleem, who was known simply as Kashif, had made a huge name for himself when he wrote and produced "Love Come Down" for Evelyn "Champagne" King. She was best known for her huge disco hit "Shame," but disco was long gone when Kashif teamed up with her, and "Love Come Down" soared to number one on the R&B charts. So Arista was hoping Kashif would work some of that magic on their new sax player. I was too.

Kashif was based in New York, so that's where I went to work. One of the first nights we were together, we had dinner in Tribeca, and he decided he wanted to show me where he grew up in Brooklyn. We started to walk the streets of the city together. It was one of those steamy New York nights, and he bought a melon at a fruit stand before we got to the Brooklyn Bridge. We were tossing it back and forth like a football as we crossed the bridge, and I remember thinking, This is so cool. I'm with one of the hippest, hottest producers in New York, just laughing and having a good time like old friends. He walked me through his old neighborhood in Brooklyn, and I thought, I am gonna love working with this guy.

It wasn't all peaches and cream, though. I absolutely loved the R&B chops he was bringing into the mix. I was right back in my old Cold, Bold & Together groove. But what I didn't love so much was how incredibly flaky he could be. I mean, I had flown in from Seattle to work with him, and I figured we'd get down to business and work every day. But each day, there was another reason we had to push the start of recording back another day. And another, and another. Two weeks went by, and I never saw the guy. He'd say, "Hey, show up at my apartment on Thursday," and then he wouldn't be there, and I wouldn't see him until Saturday. All that said, I knew he was in high demand and that working with me was definitely not super high on his priority list, so I had patience and hoped it would all be worth it in the end. Besides, I didn't have anything else to do at the time.

It wasn't like you could text the guy and say "LMK when you're ready" and then go do something else. In those days, when you waited around for someone, you literally just waited and did absolutely nothing. For hours. That was hard for someone like me who likes to be productive with his time.

Kashif had assigned a young bass player named Wayne Brathwaite to work with me, and we were having a lot of fun in the studio noodling around. But Kashif was still not showing up, and I was getting nervous. When I did see him, he was brilliant and warm and fantastic. He actually let me move into his apartment in Tribeca for a couple of weeks—a huge place. Finally, we did get into the studio together. And what we started doing together was terrific.

All my natural melody ideas for the *G Force* album were very well received by both Kashif and Wayne. My favorite tune, which the three of us wrote together, was called "Tribeca," and it was a song that I ended up performing at every one of my gigs for about twenty years. It came easily and bonded us all. It was another step closer to believing that I could actually write songs. The album as a whole was soulful and funky and genuine, and I knew we had something special.

The album took off like a rocket. Within a short time, sales had topped two hundred thousand records, which was enormous at the time for a jazz instrumental record. Enormous. I was happy because I had justified Clive Davis's faith in me.

And I had justified my dad's faith in me too.

When the album was done, I came back to Seattle and moved back in with my parents to reassess and figure out my next moves.

But the man who moved back into that house was not the same person as the boy who'd moved out years before. My mom was about to find that out.

One day I was in the kitchen cooking some rice, and she came downstairs and started screaming at me that the smell of rice was stinking up her house.

For some reason, her yelling at me at that moment hit me like a brick. Everything I had held inside me for all those years, all those unconscious feelings of trying to please her and so often feeling like it was never quite enough—it all came pouring out of me, like I had left the top on the pressure cooker too long and the rice finally exploded out. "Mom, I'm almost thirty years old," I said, calmly and firmly, though on the inside I was pretty angry. "The days of you yelling at me are over."

"You don't tell me what to do in my own house," she said, in the most threatening voice she could muster.

I remained calm but firm, and somewhere between a growl and a yell came my response. "I'm a grown man now, and you are not going to yell at me. Do you hear me? And do you understand me?" I got right up in her face and said, "You need to start talking to me with respect. Have I made myself clear?"

She immediately backed down. And I was glad. Not just because I had "won," but also because I really didn't want to talk to my mother like that. I mean, she was my mom! I felt bad for her in that moment. I didn't take pleasure in winning at her expense; I just didn't want to be yelled at anymore, and I needed to make that clear. After that we never talked about it again, which isn't necessarily the healthiest thing. But the end result was that she never yelled at me again. Not once, ever again.

We all have things we carry with us. Everyone has burdens they've had to bear. Some of us learn to let them go when we're young. Sometimes it takes into your twenties or thirties. Some I'm still carrying and just learning to let go of now.

But to anyone who feels they've carried their burden long enough, and that it's time to lay that burden down, I don't care if you're sixteen or sixty. I am here to tell you that I'm living proof of this simple fact: You're right. It's time to let it go, and just know that it's okay to let it go. Do it calmly and respectfully, the way you would like to be treated. But do it.

I did.

And it made all the difference.

I had done a number of gigs to support the first album, but after the success of *G Force*, I started touring more in earnest. I'd never been the frontman in all my years on stage, but it came pretty naturally to me.

I think I learned, from backing the greats like Liberace, Barry White, and Sammy Davis Jr., that there are a lot of ways to get it right. They all had their own shtick. But one thing they shared was a comfortable ease on stage. They'd crack a joke here and there, and if something went wrong, they'd never sweat it. From them, I realized both that I could be myself—there was no one formula I had to follow—and that I could lean on my instincts, the natural connection I'd developed with audiences ever since that first time I stepped on stage (and the first time I stepped off it!). That innate perfectionism that drives me, in the studio and in my daily life, never got in the way once I started fronting my own band. I would work as hard as I could to get every note precisely right, and when something went wrong, I'd accept it as part of the moment—sometimes even calling attention to it and joking about it with the audience—which would make me feel all the more comfortable and connected to the people I was playing for. And, I like to think, it made them all the more comfortable with me too.

I was also having so much more fun touring on my own. I'd put together a small ensemble of guys I knew back in Seattle, and we were playing fifty- or one-hundred-seat venues, and we were perfectly happy with that.

But that was about to change in a huge way.

I was starting to get air play on a new radio format called "quiet storm." It had started at a radio station in Washington, DC, back in 1976, and little by little it was working its way across the country. Some stations would do straight R&B all week, and maybe on a Saturday night at midnight they'd have a "quiet storm" show that was more mellow and had a smooth and soulful groove. It was "sensual and pensive," as one journalist wrote at the time. They played Grover Washington Jr., and they played David Sanborn, and they'd play me.

When I say *G Force* was successful—and it was—I need to put this in perspective. I started thinking, Well, who is the most successful instrumentalist in the world? The answer was easy: George Benson. At the time his big hit was *Breezin'*, an album mostly of instrumentals. But George is known for his beautiful voice as much as his instrumentals, and that album included him singing on one track, "This Masquerade," which became a gigantic hit and won the Grammy for record of the year.

Still, I thought of it as similar to what I was doing—an album that was 90 percent instrumentals. So when I looked it up and saw that *Breezin'* had sold three million records—three *million*—I had only one question: Who the hell is his manager?

I bought the record and looked on the back to find that his management team was Fritz/Turner, on North Robertson Boulevard in Los Angeles. Then I did what any self-respecting obsessive-compulsive musician would do. I got in my car, drove to LA, and showed up at their door.

I walked in, said hello to the receptionist, Pam, politely introduced myself, and said, "I'd like to talk to George Benson's manager."

"Oh, that would be Dennis Turner," she said. One of the guys whose names were on the door. Somehow, I wangled my way into his office. When I need to be, I can be a good wangler.

"Hey, you don't know me," I said to the heavy-set, good-looking guy with a scruffy goatee, "but I'm a sax player. I already have a record deal with Clive Davis, and I would like you to manage me."

He said, with a very warm smile on his face, "Well, I have to say that I'm not familiar with you, so tell me more." My first impression of him was that he was a good-natured, intelligent guy, and I got the feeling that he was also a very competent businessman.

I said, "Well, I actually happen to be playing a gig in a club in Redondo Beach called Concerts by the Sea."

Probably not my best move if I was trying to show I was a rising star—the club sat maybe all of fifty people, and I had to do three shows a night to make any money—but it was the only card I had to play.

I knew if I could get him to see the connection I'd developed with my audience, I at least had a shot. Somehow, I convinced him to come. And sure enough, he saw what a great time we were all having. I gave it everything I had, and the audience was right there with me, reacting to everything I was doing, from jazz licks and R&B grooves to the fast-paced arpeggios and the crazy long notes. It was an amazing night, and I was really happy—and maybe just a little relieved—about how great everything went, because I really wanted Dennis to be impressed.

I guess it must have clicked, because afterward, Dennis came up to me and said, "You've got yourself a manager."

I caught my breath and dropped the other shoe. "Well, here's the part I didn't tell you, Dennis. I don't have any money to pay you." It was true—even with a hit record, I was just eking out a living, because record company expenses had to be paid back first before any money would go to the artist, and there were a hell of a lot of expenses accrued so far for my first two records. I sure as hell wasn't going to go to my dad and ask for any more help either. I was into him for about $125,000 by this point, and I still had no idea how I was ever gonna pay him back.

"Don't worry about it," Dennis said with a little grin. "We'll work that out later."

The first thing he did was get me to open for George Benson at what was then called the Universal Amphitheatre in Los Angeles, a beautiful and famous venue that seats six thousand people. I mean, I'd never played for six *hundred* people as a frontman, let alone six thousand. When he told me he was going to pay me $5,000 for the gig, it blew my mind.

Here I was, George Benson's opening act, making grown-up money, with a big-time manager. I truly felt like I was beginning to soar.

Unfortunately, it was right around this time that I hit some real turbulence.

After our smash success together with *G Force*, everyone was excited for me and Kashif to get back into the studio for the next album. Unfortunately, lightning didn't strike twice. I went back to New York, and it just wasn't the same.

Part of the problem was that Kashif had gotten way too big and way too famous. And way, way too busy.

One night, back when we were still working on our first album in New York, Clive had asked me to go with him to a club in Harlem called

Sweetwater's to watch the young cousin of Dionne Warwick. He was thinking of signing her. We went, and I thought she was the most amazing performer I'd ever seen. Incredible voice, incredible stage presence.

"Clive," I said, leaning over to him, "you should sign her."

I don't take credit for it, but he did sign that young woman. And by the time I'd gotten back to New York to do the second album with Kashif, he had started working with her and produced her first single, "You Give Good Love." It became a massive, massive hit. It's the song that cemented Whitney Houston's much-deserved mega-stardom and the song that cemented Kashif's much-deserved reputation as the best producer around.

So I absolutely understood why he didn't have much time or attention to give to this little sax player back in town from Seattle.

By now I had absorbed the vibe that he had brought to the first session, so even though he wasn't around much, I was able to reproduce it, pretty much, for the second. But without Kashif in the room, the record wasn't coming together the way I knew it could.

I was spending weeks and weeks waiting around for Kashif to give me some time, some direction, some anything. And eventually he gave a little. Just a little. I had to somehow finish the record and do the best I could with it. I was not in the position to be the final say on the music and mixes, so I couldn't just power through it, but I didn't have Kashif around much either, so it was all very frustrating. I knew that if I got a chance to make another record, I would make sure to have much more decision-making power.

As the recording sessions went on, my frustration with Kashif got worse and worse. One afternoon, I was waiting outside his Tribeca apartment for him to show. I waited. And waited. And waited. Finally, after four hours of cooling my heels, I gave up and went back to my hotel. The next day, I went down to the record company.

Clive wasn't around, but I did get in to see his second-in-command, Roy Lott. My manager, Dennis Turner, was on the speaker phone. I laid out the problem for Roy, and then said, "Look, I harbor no ill feelings, but—"

And that's all I got to say. Roy got right up in my face, nose to nose, and started screaming at me. Making the point that I should be counting my lucky stars to be working with Kashif no matter how long I had to wait. Because Kashif was in high demand, and very, very important, and was producing Whitney Houston, and who was I to challenge him.

I can certainly understand it from his point of view. But from my point of view, I had already had enough yelling in my life, so I stood up and told Roy that he needed to lower the volume and show some respect to one of his artists. I wanted to have an adult conversation about how we were going to get the record finished.

Eventually everything did calm down.

But the damage was done. I knew the record was not going to be a success, and it wasn't—*Gravity* sold only about twenty-five thousand copies.

Somehow, we managed to move on from all that. I bear no ill will to Roy Lott. We were friends then, and we remain friends. I look at it as a memorable, if heated, business conversation. And I bear no ill will to Kashif either. The album wasn't very good, and the responsibility for that rests solely with me. I'm enormously grateful to him for the brilliance he brought to *G Force*, and if it weren't for the success of that album— much of the credit for which goes directly to Kashif—I don't know if I'd have been given the chance to keep going and trying new things.

But the fact is, our relationship was broken, the album was lousy, and when it came time to move on and try again, there wasn't a single thought of pairing Kenny G and Kashif Saleem one more time.

Which turned out to be the best thing that could have happened.

I don't know that in this day and age the Clive Davises of the business would have given an instrumentalist with one successful album and two mediocre ones another chance.

All I know is that Clive did give me one more chance. And I knew that this time, right or wrong, sink or swim, I was gonna do it my way.

CHAPTER EIGHT

I want to share a very intimate part of my life with you right now.

I want to invite you into my studio while I'm composing a song.

Not just any song, mind you. I want to invite you in while I'm composing the song that changed everything—a little tune I called "Songbird." We have to go back in time to the mid-eighties. To a little room in a little house in Seattle called Studio G.

Come on in and have a seat. Sorry if it's a little cramped in here. I had moved into my own little place by then, and you've probably noticed Studio G is merely a small room in that house. But it's filled with all this cool equipment, which I once again have to thank my dad for, for loaning me the many thousands of dollars that made it possible for me to buy all this stuff. Over there, you'll see a synthesizer, which is kind of an electronic keyboard that can do all sorts of things that a piano can't do. That machine over there makes drum sounds, and that one over there is an eight-track recorder. In this room, there is everything I need to do what I really want to do.

Which is to make some beautiful music all by myself.

By this point, when it came to songwriting, I had some confidence. Hey, why not? Some of the things I wrote with Jeff Lorber got to be pretty popular. I got good feedback from Kashif, too, and when a legend like that says you've got talent, it gives you the feeling, Hey, maybe I actually have the talent to do this all on my own.

Which is what I set out to do.

I have to say I probably had more instinct than talent at that point. I had a good sense of what a melody should be, even if I didn't have a lot of practice at turning that melody into a song without the help of someone else. And as you have no doubt figured out about me by now, I'm all about the practice. If I wasn't good at something right away, I would just stick with it and stick with it and stick with it. I knew this process intimately and knew that eventually I would get better at whatever I was trying to get better at.

And when it came to creating music all by myself in my own little studio, there was no way to do that except to just get started. So I started to mess around.

It was such a joy to play around in that room, with no downside in trying this or that, with no one looking over my shoulder, no one saying, Hey, that part sounds wrong, or, just as bad, Hey, that part's good. Stay with that. I got to listen to what sounded good to me alone, and I went with it.

When you're with other musicians or producers, they'll often tell you things like "You can't do this or that on a keyboard" or "You can't make a drum loop like that." Or "That drum loop doesn't sound like something a real drummer would do." Or "That isn't really a song." But just like when I was a teenager, alone in my room, trying to figure out how to make my own sounds come out of my saxophone, I was in uncharted waters, following my own instincts on what sounded good to me.

And loving it. Loving the freedom to create things that haven't been created before, not knowing if anything is going to be good but also confident that something great is going to come out of all this at some point. There isn't a set time frame of when something amazing will happen. But I knew in my heart that, just like when you go to the gym, getting stronger is all about the reps; in the studio, I was hoping that all those reps would ultimately lead to something special.

So let's go. Ready? Here's what happened.

A lot of folks probably think "Songbird" started with the sax melody. That certainly makes sense since I'm a sax player. And the melody I play on that song is what the song is known for. But the truth is, this humble sax player started this special song on his fancy new synthesizer keyboard.

As I mentioned earlier, the synthesizer had a sequencer, which allows a musician to play things on the keyboard and then, as if it recorded those parts, the synthesizer will play it back for you. If you play the wrong note, you can go back and correct it. This was a huge innovation in technology in the eighties. It's very similar to correcting a typo in a sentence you typed on your computer. This was great for me because I was not a virtuoso piano player, but now I could make up the keyboard part myself and it would end up being perfect. And I didn't have to figure out how to tell a keyboard player what to play, which very often takes away from the creative flow. I could mess around with the notes as long as I wanted. Until I found what I was looking for.

So in the privacy of that room, I started playing different little arpeggios on the electric keyboard. As you would imagine, some didn't come out so great. Okay, some were pretty lousy. But some sounded pretty good. I started to tweak the things that sounded good to my ears, and after a while, I created a keyboard part that I really liked. If you listen to the beginning of "Songbird," that's what it was. It's not that complicated. Just sixteen notes. The second time I played them, I shifted them a bit so the song would grow a little. Here's the beauty of being alone in that room. Once I found that little arpeggio, I put it on a loop and listened to it over and over and over again. At the time, this was a revelation. This wasn't something that a normal human being could do. It was repeating this pattern that I liked, over and over again, without embellishing or adding chords or changing the time or changing the feel. Or if I felt like the part actually did need a little change here or there, I could insert that change easily. So I put the pattern on repeat and used yet another brand-new technology called "quantizing," which did a couple of incredible things. One thing was that it meant I could tell the keyboard how many beats per minute I wanted it to play, meaning how fast or slow the music would be. I could speed it up or slow it down as I chose without changing the pitch, which is something I didn't want to change, and it would be perfect every time (as opposed to when you speed up or slow down something on tape and make someone sound like a chipmunk, or like they're talking in slo-mo). And the other thing was if a note I played was a little ahead of or behind the beat, it would fix that to my liking as well. Meaning that the timing would be perfect.

Am I getting too technical for you? This might sound like some unemotional exercise in technology without any beauty or heart. But it was the opposite for me, and I want to get that across. Picture writing a long essay with an old typewriter. Okay. You can do it, and that seems sort of romantic, right? But now write the same essay on a computer, and you get to rewrite awkward phrases, cut and paste and move things around, run a spell-check, fact-check on the internet, and so on. See what I mean? I think you can get *way* more creative if you have a real handle on the latest technology. Then you can use these innovations to let your creativity flow, instead of being held back by old-school technology. With this new technology, I was feeling more creative than ever before.

I was listening to this sequence that had a special sound and flow to me, adjusting the tempo to where it felt right, and I thought, Hey, that sounds pretty good! Let me put a little drum on it. I added a drumbeat, which again was groundbreaking because before this, I would have had to get a drummer to play, and that would be another person to deal with when all I wanted was to create and keep the creative flow going since I hadn't done anything like this musically before.

Now I added a little bass part, and ta-*da*! I had this bed of music, and the sequencer was repeating it and repeating it. I loved what I was hearing.

That's when I took out my sax.

It's not like I heard a melody in my head and started playing it. What happened was, I listened to that musical bed and started playing notes that I thought went with it.

Quickly—like, maybe on the second or third try, at most—the melody that became the first riff of "Songbird" revealed itself. Now we're getting somewhere!

Okay, see that machine against the far wall? That's an eight-track recording machine. If you're a real music geek, you'll know how the Beatles and others dealt with that back in the days when they only had four tracks to play with. They'd mix the music down, so all the drums would be on one track, for example, or the bass and drum on the same track. But the downside is that the sound quality degrades as you mix it down—and you also lose control of the various parts if they are combined on a single track. With the eight-track recording machine, I could record each instrument—the real ones and the ones coming out of the synthesizer—on a different track. By the way, there were twenty-four-track machines by then, but my humble budget could only afford an eight-track machine for my home studio. That was enough for me at this point.

So I had two tracks for the keyboard, because it was stereo. One track was for a kick drum, one for a snare, and one for a high hat—that's the double-cymbal part of the drum set—so that's five tracks. I put the bass on track six, so I still had two tracks to play with for the saxophone.

So I put that little sax part I'd been playing around with on its own track and listened back. And I listened back without anyone commenting. I can't stress to you enough how important that is to me. I and I alone decided what sounded good and what needed to change. And I thought, That's really good so far. Where can I go with it now? What's the B section?

A song would get pretty monotonous if it stayed on the same section over and over, so it usually has to go somewhere after the first melody is established. That next section is often referred to as the "B section" (see, you're getting an "inside the ropes" look at songwriting and recording). The B section on some songs can be a complete departure from the beginning melody; on this particular song the B section is similar to where I started, but then it takes things to a different place. Changing the melody so the song grows and goes . . . somewhere.

After that, I thought it would be a good place for a little more complicated sax solo to take the melody and basically run with it. Don't forget I still had two tracks for the sax, so I put the melody on one track and started messing around with the solo section on another track. Again, I have to say, it came pretty fast. This is where my years of improvising on stage came in handy. I knew how far to go with the solo so it stood out but didn't overpower the rest of the song.

And then I went back and finished off the melody. It all happened very quickly. I think the whole thing maybe took me an hour or so.

What was revolutionary was that I could hear what I had done, and change what I wanted, and keep what I wanted. There was no producer saying, "That's good, Kenny. Let's move on," or "Try something different at this part, Kenny." I got to be the guy who played it, recorded it, listened to it, evaluated it, and all the rest.

But I wasn't done yet. The sound of my sax wasn't quite right to me. The notes were there, and the tone was my tone, but it didn't have a certain ambience that I was imagining. I knew that there was one more step I needed to take. I was going to have to add this quality, this ambience, to the sound of my saxophone in order to make it right. And as it turned out, this ended up becoming one of the important signatures of my sound.

It's called the reverb.

When you listen to "Songbird" and just about everything I've recorded that came after, you'll notice that the sax doesn't sound like I'm standing right next to you when I play. It sounds like I might be in a big concert hall, or a church, or even a cavern. It has a kind of ethereal quality, like it's being played in a bigger, almost infinite space.

And the reverb machine allowed me to get that sound in my little very-not-infinite room.

Creating echo and reverb effects in music goes way back to Elvis and his producer, Sam Phillips, at Sun Records in the 1950s. But reverb as we know it is a special kind of effect that was used on recordings starting in the early sixties. A sax player named John Klemmer started using a machine called an Echoplex and got pretty well-known for his sound.

Reverb is like the sound you'd get if you played your sax standing in the middle of Saint Mark's Cathedral—a huge sound in that giant, acoustically amazing room, a sound that seems to linger long after you've finished playing the note. Now you get the idea.

Now we have to work on the parameters. Those are the things that one can adjust to create the right reverb. Maybe Saint Mark's is too big of a room for the sound you want on a particular song. But your living room is sounding too small. Get it? Again, this great technology allowed me to dial it in. What did I want? Was it a small room, a large hall, a big cathedral?

I am usually drawn to what one might call the Carnegie Hall sound—the sound of a big hall. It's less than the cathedral sound and more contained than the sound of a big cave or the Taj Mahal—which would sound great on some things, but for my "Songbird," the sound would get lost in the vastness of the space. And in a small room, the sound would be too harsh. I wanted that middle ground, that big-hall sound.

So I had control over a variety of these parameters to make a reverb sound I liked. I could adjust the reverb time, which is how long the note lasts for. I could adjust another thing called pre-delay. Now, I hope I'm not getting too technical, but again, all these things allowed me to get very, very creative, and so I fooled around with all this stuff until I heard the sound I was looking for. I didn't have any set idea, so I just turned the dials up and back and fooled around and fooled around some more, until I finally found the sound I liked. Ahhhhh.

And that, my friend, was the birth of the Kenny G sound.

Hey! Thanks for your patience in letting me tell you how my

"Songbird" was born. And now for your reward: I give you all permission to take five and take a listen. You know what? I think it's pretty good, if I do say so myself!

When "Songbird" was finished, I didn't call anyone up and say, Hey, listen to this song I just wrote and recorded! I didn't need to call anyone. I liked what I did, and I didn't feel like I needed anyone else's approval.

That was a trait that came in pretty handy later on.

I mean, for the first time, here was a piece of music that truly represented me, that expressed what was going on in my heart and my brain. Like going into a room with a piece of wood and a chisel and some sandpaper and coming out with a little sculpture that you can look at and say, Hey, I made this!

It made me enormously happy. I thought it was so cool to be able to do this.

And by the way, when you listen to the finished recording, it's almost exactly what I did that day in that room. Later, in a bigger studio, we may have added a little more keyboard or another layer of bass, but basically, what I did in that room was the final song.

How cool is that? For me, it was really, really cool.

So then I wrote a few more instrumentals, in the same way, with the similar reverb effect. One of them, "Esther," I wrote for my grandmother, and a lot of people have told me that when they hear it, they can almost hear their old Jewish grandmother's voice in my melody, which means a whole lot to me. That's especially satisfying, because it tells me I captured the feeling I was trying to capture.

I sent the songs to Arista Records and told them that these were the songs I wanted to build the new album around. I figured I'd finally found my road forward.

But the next day, I hit a speed bump the size of a small elephant.

Here's what happened. Remember, my previous album, *Gravity*, didn't do so well, which was okay with me (even though normally I'd be unhappy with lousy album sales). It was okay because I didn't love the way the record came out anyway; and since it didn't sell so well, it meant the record label wasn't going to go, Well, this is working. Let's keep on this path. It meant there was a new path ahead for Kenny G.

I didn't know that I was about to take a hard left, while Arista wanted me to take a crazy detour.

While I was finishing up those songs in Studio G, I got a call from a man named Ed Eckstine at Arista Records' offices in New York. Ed was the son of the legendary Billy Eckstine, a bandleader from the time when big band music was giving way to bebop. All the greats of that era played in Billy Eckstine's band—Charlie Parker, Dizzy Gillespie, Dexter Gordon, Miles Davis, everybody—so Ed kind of came from music royalty.

But he wasn't riding his dad's coattails. Ed had been in the business since he was eighteen, when he worked for Quincy Jones, and would later go on to become the president of Mercury Records, the first Black person appointed the head of a major label. So he was no slouch.

I was excited to tell Ed about all the cool new songs I'd come up with. But before I could, here's what Ed had to say to me on the phone: "For your next record, we want you to record songs that the fifteen-year-old kids in the ghetto can groove to."

Now please understand, Ed is a good guy, and I like him a lot, but I was flabbergasted. I didn't know what to say. Here's what I did say: "Ed, stay right there. I'm coming to see you. Don't move." I literally hung up the phone, drove to the airport, and got on a plane from Seattle to New York.

I was in his office first thing the next morning. Ed was sitting behind his desk, and in his big, deep voice, he repeated what he'd told me on the phone. The people in charge at Arista thought my next record should be something that fifteen-year-old kids in the ghetto could groove to.

"Ed," I said, "with all due respect, I'm a twenty-nine-year-old Jewish sax player from Seattle. What do I know about what fifteen-year-old kids in the ghetto can groove to?"

And here's what I said after that, as dramatically as I could: "I quit. I'm done."

Now before I tell you what happened next, let me tell you a little behind-the-scenes stuff about how the record business works. I owed Arista probably a couple hundred thousand dollars by then—the cost of making those first couple of records, minus sales from those records. Jeff Lorber didn't come cheap. Kashif didn't come cheap. Recording studios don't come cheap. But thankfully, it's not like I had to reach into my pocket and pay that money back; it's a debt that's put against future sales. If I kept recording for Arista, they'd take that couple hundred thousand out of the sales of my next albums before I would see one dime from any of those sales. At this time in my career, this felt like an insurmountable debt to overcome. And on top of that, there was the fact that I wasn't being allowed to make the music I truly wanted to, and in fact I was being told to make music that I couldn't relate to.

So I thought, Maybe the best thing would be to walk away, find a small jazz-oriented label that would put out my new stuff, and start fresh. And more importantly, I'd get to do the kind of music that was starting to flow from my heart, and not have to keep trying to fit into whatever concept the big shots wanted me to do.

I wasn't sure what Arista was going to say. Maybe they would be happy to get rid of me since I wasn't making them any money at this point. Fortunately, that wasn't the case. Clive Davis saw something in me and wanted to see things through.

So they came up with a compromise.

Ed got up from behind his desk, walked around, and sat on the front of it, next to where I was sitting. "Look, Kenny," he said, "we don't want to do that." He was probably about my age, but he was talking to me like a kind uncle. "Here's what we think you should do. We want you to go up to San Francisco and work with a guy named Narada Michael Walden. We think you guys can work together." He told me about a song by Junior Walker called "What Does It Take." He said, "It has vocals, but everyone knows it's really a sax song. Why don't you give it a try?"

I had never heard of Junior Walker, because as I've said I kind of live in my own musical vacuum in a lot of ways, but I told him I'd think about it. And I also told him, "By the way, I've got all these instrumentals I've done—do you want to listen to them?"

And as politely as you can say no to that question—which, frankly, is not all that politely—he said, "No."

Ouch! That stung. But I didn't let him see my disappointment. I knew I had something special in these new songs.

I went off and listened to the Junior Walker song, and I liked it a lot. It was a vocal song, but just as Ed had said, it was really a saxophone song. I realized that what Ed was offering kind of made sense—and besides, I realized that I did know who Narada Michael Walden was, and he wasn't just a good producer but a good musician—so I decided to give it a shot.

Narada Michael Walden was riding pretty high at this point. He had just co-written and produced a big hit for Aretha Franklin called "Freeway of Love," which, by the way, featured a cool sax solo by Clarence Clemons, the big man from Bruce Springsteen's band. I loved that sax players were getting great exposure in rock and soul music, just as they had in the fifties. But I still wanted to find a way to get there on my own without the vocals. Narada was also a huge drummer in the jazz fusion world—he'd played with John McLaughlin and the Mahavishnu Orchestra, Chick Corea, and a bunch of others.

So by the time I got to Marin County, which is one of the rich parts of the San Francisco Bay Area, I was super excited. First off, the place is absolutely beautiful. Tarpan Studios was in Sausalito; I walked in, carrying my sax of course, and it seemed great. And I'd been listening to the Junior Walker song, and I was liking it more and more. So I couldn't wait to get started.

I found Narada Michael Walden and introduced myself, and he told me, "Good to meet you. You're going to be working with baby love."

I didn't have the slightest idea what that meant. Was that a nickname for some kind of new music technology I hadn't heard of? Was that a person or a way of softening your sound? Did my sound need to get any softer? Baby love?

"Baby love is upstairs. Head on up there. I've got some things I have to do. I'll catch you later."

So he walked away, and I walked to the stairs, and I thought, Well, this is some kind of adventure I'm on.

I had no idea what was waiting for me at the top of those stairs.

CHAPTER NINE

I got to the top of the stairs, and there was a guy sitting at a piano. Before I could say anything, he looked up, gave me a big warm smile, and said, "Hi, I'm Walter. They call me Baby Love."

Oh! It was a person after all! Working with Baby Love! Now I got it.

We chatted for a bit, and I told him I was working on some new material, to which he said, "Yeah, I've been thinking about you and your sound. What do you think of this?"

Walter "Baby Love" Afanasieff, I came to discover, was the keyboard/synthesizer guy who was making a lot of the sounds that came out of this studio. He wasn't getting credit at that time as a producer, but he was basically doing the work of a producer. I didn't know any of this at the time. All I knew was that when Walter put his fingers on the keys, I liked what I was hearing. A lot. He noodled around, and what he was noodling was one of the most beautiful things I'd ever heard. I immediately connected with what he was playing. It had these beautiful chord changes, and I said, "Walter, what's that you just played?"

He said, "I don't know, just some little idea."

Then I said four very important words: "Walter, play it again."

I know that sounds like a line out of *Casablanca*, but I promise, I remember this moment very clearly, and I'm not trying to be overly dramatic. He started playing it again, and I whipped out my sax and started playing along. If you want to hear what this sounded like, listen to my song "Pastel," because what we came up with right there was almost exactly what wound up on the record. I love listening to that song because it represents the very rare sound of two people truly connecting. Of course, in our case, musically.

Have you ever met someone you immediately clicked with, and the communication was easy and the feeling was comfortable and effortless? Because that's what happened between me and Walter. We were two people who were meant to make music together.

To borrow another line from *Casablanca*, it's like when Humphrey Bogart says to Claude Rains, "Louie, I think this is the beginning of a beautiful friendship." That's precisely how I felt.

Except in *Casablanca*, that line comes at the end of the movie. For Walter and me, we were just getting started. And we would make some very beautiful music together over the next twenty-five years.

Narada Michael Walden would stop in from time to time, but for the most part he was executive-producing—approving finished songs or making a tweak here or there. Mainly the work was being done by me and Walter, with some help on a few songs by another producer, Preston Glass. I was in heaven! Given the freedom to do what I wanted to do, with two guys who really knew what they were doing. Except for occasional suggestions from Narada—some good and some we ignored—I was doing it all my way.

Doing things the way I wanted was a habit I was starting to develop. And being vocal about what I wanted and what I was willing to do was starting to become my MO. A few years later, when I recorded a song called "Silhouette," I was asked to fly all the way to London to do my first TV show appearance in England. One of the producers told me, "Okay, we want you to play your song 'Silhouette,' and we're going to have two ballet dancers dancing around you."

That idea sounded horrible to me. It was like saying that my music wasn't good enough to stand up by itself, that it needed some dancers to make it worth watching and listening to. I was actually angry.

I said, "I don't want to do that."

And they said, "We know our audience, bloke, and this is how it's going to go."

I said, "Well, I know how I want my music to be portrayed, and no, I'm not comfortable with that."

Things got quiet for a second. Then the producer leaned back and said, "Well, it looks like you're going to be taking an early flight back to the States."

I stayed calm and said, "Well, okay, I'll go back to my hotel. If you change your mind, let me know in the next hour, because then I'll be heading to the airport."

About thirty minutes later, they called and said, "It's fine, we don't need the ballet dancers."

By then, I'd become much more comfortable with pushing for what was right for me creatively. But of course, it's even easier not to have to fight at all. Which is how I felt back in the studio with Walter and Preston. They'd suggest lots of things, and most of them were wonderful, and we'd go with them—but if they didn't feel right to me, there was no struggle, no hard feelings, not even a grimace. We moved on until we found the right notes, the right chords, the right sounds.

And man, I think we found a lot of them.

I brought in the songs I had recorded on my own at home, including "Songbird," and those basically all sailed through with very little additional work. The other songs came pretty easily too. We did that Junior Walker song, "What Does It Take." Ellis Hall, from Tower of Power, came in to do the vocals, and he did an amazing job with them, and I did my tenor sax riffs on it, and it came out terrific. I didn't truly love that one, though, because I wasn't as into the vocal songs as I was the instrumentals. But the album had a lot of really good songs on it, and I was satisfied that I had gotten my way with almost every one of them. I was very happy with the end product.

When the photographer was showing me the pictures he'd taken for the cover of the album, he printed them in a couple of different ways. One of them looked especially interesting—not quite black and white, not quite color—and I asked him what it was. "That's a duotone," he said.

"Oh, cool," I said because I didn't feel like saying, "I have no idea what you're talking about."

But the image—and the word—stuck in my head. So when it came time to choose the album cover, I went with that picture, and when it came time to pick a name for the cover, I used that word too.

And *Duotones* was born.

"What Does It Take" was the first single that Arista released (with "Songbird" on the B-side), and it started climbing the charts. Then the album followed suit. Whereas *Gravity* had sold all of twenty-five thousand copies, *Duotones* started going nuts—one hundred thousand, then two hundred thousand, then three hundred thousand. And that's when things really started taking off.

I put a band together with some great musicians I knew from Portland and Seattle, and we took the show on the road. (One of those guys—John Raymond, who is a fabulous guitarist—still plays with me to this day. How cool is that?) And remember my new manager, Dennis Turner, who was George Benson's manager? Well, guess who he decided to have me open for on tour? That's right. He teamed me up with the one, the only George Benson. So once again, this little sax combo was playing in front of thousands of people!

It was scary. For about two minutes.

The minute I played my first note and the crowd reacted, I knew I was in my element. It was no different from the small clubs, really—I just did my thing. And instead of connecting to a hundred people, we started connecting with thousands. That's what hours and hours and hours of practice will do. It gives you the confidence that you know what you're doing, and you know it's good. The only difference was the size of the venue and the number of people in the audience. The size of the venue did in fact change the sound of what we were doing, so I had to learn to adapt to hearing my sound in those bigger venues—that took about ten seconds. I also had to learn to adapt to the sound of the cheers of an audience that big. That took one second! I gotta admit, though, the first time I heard it, it gave me a chill. And then I got right back to the business at hand: playing that horn.

Let's be honest: They didn't come to hear me. They came to hear George Benson. But I was confident. For one, I knew they would like some of the songs, like "Songbird" and "Midnight Motion," because I'd already played them for smaller audiences, and I knew people liked them. But I also knew we put on a great live show, and I did a lot of things this crowd probably had never seen before: the circular breathing, the wild arpeggios, the walking out into the crowd. I knew the way we fashioned the set and played with great energy and enthusiasm would win over the crowd, just as it had in the past.

And it did, for sure.

A performer can tell when he's getting polite applause. Polite applause is like getting a handshake after sex.

Nice job. There's the door.

What you want from the audience is, Wow! You rocked my world! I felt the earth move! Can we do that again? I wasn't expecting that!

That's the kind of reaction we were getting. And I loved it!

Because I knew I was giving them great sax. No handshake here!

But one night, there were two particular audience members I had to win over. Dennis had called the people at *The Tonight Show* and told them he had this sax player he wanted them to hear. By this time, some other late-night shows had started up, but Johnny Carson was still the king, so it was a huge deal.

He got the producers to come to see us at the Universal Amphitheatre in Los Angeles, and they liked what they saw. *Boom!* I was booked on *The Tonight Show*.

I thought, Man, I guess I impressed them. It wasn't until later that I found out I had had a little help. Dennis had told the producers, "Would you like to have George Benson on the show? Well, if you have Kenny first, you can have George." Leverage, baby, leverage.

Thanks to Dennis, a couple of weeks later, I was off to Burbank to do *The Tonight Show*. When I got there, the producer told us that we would come on and do the single "What Does It Take," which was the main reason they booked me, and then they'd go to commercial. After Johnny said good night, we could play whatever we wanted as the show ended, which was when I was going to play "Songbird."

But after the taping started, just before we were about to go on, the producer came on and said, "Look, Johnny's running late, so you're only going to be able to do one song, and so you're just doing your single." He left the room, and I made what was probably the biggest decision of my career.

I told my band, "No, we're not. We're not doing the vocal. We're doing the instrumental. We're doing 'Songbird.'"

Now, to understand what a high-wire trick we were about to pull, you have to know how they did *The Tonight Show*. It hadn't been shown live for years, but it was done as what they call "live to tape"—they taped it earlier in the day, but they did it like it was a live show. Lots of people do that now and go back in and fix things and edit things, but Johnny Carson was a fanatic about keeping it feeling like a live show. So he had all the clocks in the studio set to the time the show would air—even though they taped at 5:30 p.m., the clocks said 11:30 p.m.—and with extremely rare exceptions, they never stopped and fixed anything or went back and redid anything. If someone flubbed, they flubbed. The show ran for exactly sixty minutes, and they taped it in exactly sixty minutes. So for all intents and purposes, it was like doing a live show.

That was the key to what we were about to do. Because until I went out on stage, we weren't gonna tell anyone that we were pulling a switcheroo.

My old friend Tony Gable was playing percussion for me that night, and his brother Andre was going to be the singer on "What Does It Take." I apologized to Andre—after all, I was taking away a potential big break for him, I knew that, and I felt bad about it—but I had to do what I had to do.

I looked around the room at the rest of the band, and they looked pretty scared. Then I looked over at Dennis, my manager, and I couldn't tell what he was thinking. So I said, "Look, Dennis, this is my one chance. I've watched Johnny Carson since I was a kid. I'm on the show tonight. I have to play the song I want to play. What do you think?"

And to his eternal credit—and my eternal gratitude—he nodded his head, smiled, and said, "This is your career. These have to be your decisions. If that's what you've decided to do, then I'm behind you one hundred percent."

Wow! Did I pick the right manager or what? I mean, I thought that was awesome. Having his support at that pivotal moment was crucial, because the record company wanted me to play the single, the *Carson* folks wanted me to play the single, everybody wanted me to play the single. That's the only reason I was booked—not to play "Songbird," obviously. Not a chance. So for him to say he had my back was the ultimate act of coolness.

Look, I had learned a thing or two about my audiences. They liked "What Does It Take," sure. But when I did "Songbird" and went into my cadenza—the big solo part at the end where I show off the crazy scales and the circular breathing—they went wild. So I wasn't afraid that people watching weren't going to like what I did. I knew it would translate even if everyone at *The Tonight Show* thought otherwise. So I went into it with a lot of confidence.

So now it's time. We're walking out onto the stage. I say to the guys, "Don't worry! It's gonna be all right. You're starting this, so please make sure you start the right song."

And we go out there—and I'm in total sensory deprivation.

Remember, this is my first time on TV. I don't know what to expect. I'm used to looking out and seeing the audience, but with those bright lights in my eyes, I can only see darkness out there behind the huge cameras. I can barely even see Johnny while he is introducing me.

Fortunately, he just mentions the album and not which song we are gonna play.

So we begin, and the keyboards start in on the first notes of "Songbird." Whew! I had been worried that the guys were going to be too scared to play it.

I still can't see the audience, but I can see the guy who hired us standing right behind the cameras.

And he looks like he wants to kill me.

He starts flipping me off, but I just focus on my playing. My heart is into it, and I'm feeling great. I go into the melody, then the solo, then the cadenza, and it comes out really well. I look over at Johnny, and he gives me the okay sign, which is a big deal, but honestly, I don't know if he is paying much attention. Then we finish up and go backstage.

And there is the producer who hired me. He is not, to put it mildly, in a very congratulatory mood. Instead, he is looking like I just peed on his blue suede shoes.

"I can't believe it!" he shouts. "I can *not* believe it! I can't believe that you would fuck me the way you did!"

I am kind of taken aback. I didn't expect him to kiss me on the lips or anything, but I sure didn't expect this. "Look, bro, I'm super sorry," I say. "I've wanted to be on *Carson* all my life. I used to watch it with my dad when I was a kid. So to have this chance, well, I just had to do my song. I'm so sorry you're upset, but I really want you to know how much I appreciate being on this show."

"Oh yeah?" he says. "Well, I'm gonna make sure you never play this show or anyone else's show in this town again."

I don't like it when people yell at me, but what he said was such a cliché, I had to stop myself from laughing. I just apologized again and walked away.

I ended up watching the show that night while I was working out at a gym in town—hey, I gotta get my workout in, even on a big night like this!—and I thought, You know, I did a pretty good job. But what was life-changing about that broadcast was that there was somebody else watching who thought the same thing.

All the Arista executives were watching, of course, and expecting me to promote their single. I'm sure they were perplexed when the wrong song came out of their TV sets. But the head of promotion, Donnie Ienner, was watching with his wife, Michelle. He told me later that after I finished "Songbird," before he could say whatever he was thinking (which was probably the same thing as that guy behind the camera who gave me the finger!), his wife turned to him and said, "Honey, now that's the kind of music you guys should be doing. That's beautiful."

And if I were making a movie of this, this would be the scene when the heavens open and the light pours down and the celestial music starts playing. (Of course, in my movie, the celestial music would be "Songbird"!) Because right then a light went off in Donnie Ienner's head.

And it was the light that would lead me on the path to stardom.

Monday morning came, and Donnie Ienner walked into Clive Davis's office and said something like, "Hey, Clive, we got it all wrong. We gotta push this instrumental." He explained that his wife, who he felt was representative of young women all around the country, loved the song. And Clive, with no ego attached to the fact that he was the one who was basically spearheading the movement for me to go in the other direction, said, "Let's do it."

Let that sink in, folks. Clive had a lot invested—literally—in that other direction, and in a split second, he changed everything.

Because he just knew.

He knew that there was something very special about that moment on *Carson*. He knew there was something special about the song I played. And, God bless him, he believed there was something special about me.

And boy, did he go all in on it. Clive did something I don't think any record company executive had ever done before—certainly something *he* had never done before. He started writing letters to radio programmers all over the country, telling them they should play "Songbird." Then he sent me and Donnie around the country to tell them the same thing.

And one of them listened.

KMEL, a top-forty station in San Francisco, had just hired a guy named Hosh Gurelli as their new music director. He got Clive's letter and figured, Why the hell not. Let's give it a shot. It was four in the afternoon. They played the song, and their phones started lighting up. All women, all twenty-five to thirty-five years old—the very demographic they were looking for—and they were saying, "That's beautiful! Who is that? Why don't you play more songs like that?"

From there, it snowballed. San Francisco called their colleagues at the station in Miami, who called the station in Chicago, who called Detroit, who called Atlanta, and suddenly the song was a big hit. My little instrumental went to number six—not on the jazz charts, not on the R&B charts, but on the pop charts!

And here's the kicker. A few months later, we got a call from the *Carson* people. The ones who said I'd never work in this town again. They said, "Would you please come back on the show and play 'Songbird'?"

And I said, "No chance. Now it's my turn to give you the finger!" Only kidding. What do you think I am, crazy? Of course I said yes.

That night, after I played, Johnny motioned me over to come sit down on the couch. If you're too young to remember, Johnny asking you to come sit on the couch was like the pope inviting you to join him in the Jacuzzi at the Vatican. I mean, I don't know if they actually have a Jacuzzi at the Vatican, but if they do, it's like that.

I was sitting there with my sax, and when we went to commercial, the band started playing a song called "Killer Joe," which I happened to know, and Doc Severinsen, the bandleader, who was sitting next to me on the couch, said, "Hey, Kenny, play along!" so I did. I thought, This is amazing! I'm playing with Doc Severinsen and the band! He and I became friends because of that. A few years later, at another performance at the Universal Amphitheatre, Doc came to my gig and hung out with me backstage. He was a real mentor to me, and playing with his band is one of my sweet memories of that time.

But the best moment came a little while later while I was driving down Sunset Boulevard, one of the most famous streets in Los Angeles. I was listening to one of the big pop stations on the radio, and "Songbird" came on. Right there and then I looked up and saw a huge poster with my face on it.

How I didn't crash the car is a testament to my good driving instincts. Because I have to tell you, that feeling was just overwhelming. I mean, they had just played an Elton John song, and Celine Dion, and then Sade, and then Kenny G! That's pretty cool.

It wasn't so much like, Oh, you're a big star now, Mister Gorelick. Why don't you get a swelled head as big as that billboard? The feeling, if I can put it into words, was, Wow. I did it. I stuck with my integrity and did the music my way, and because of that, I'm really part of the mainstream music scene. I'm one of the members of an elite club.

It's like trying to figure out how to solve a puzzle that's important to you, and people are telling you how to go about it, but you know that you have to do it your way to solve it, and then, *boom!* There it is, right in front of you. You got it right, and here's the proof that you got it right. Go to the head of the class.

I mean, I always knew what I was doing was right, for me. But here was the universe saying, It's right for a whole lot of other people too.

Here's why this was so important to me. It told me, clearly and conclusively, that I could do the thing I loved the most and do it at a level equal to the top artists in the world, and because of the success, I would get to keep doing it. To keep making my own kind of music, my way. And that meant more to me than anything.

Two other things happened around that time that were great in terms of synchronicity for me. One was the creation of a TV format. The other was the creation of a radio format.

Let's talk radio, something that almost doesn't exist anymore with all of our streaming platforms. I have a guy named Allen Kepler to thank for this one. Allen was the jazz music director of WNUA radio in Chicago in the late eighties, and their motto—"Music for a New Age"—wasn't working for them anymore. They had made some programming shifts, away from New Age music into a new format of mostly instrumentals that featured contemporary jazz and R&B—right up a certain sax man's alley—and were looking for a name for the new format. Allen became the head of in-house research for the company. He started bringing people in and playing different kinds of music for them to see what they liked best. And guess which sax man made the needles light up!

But they still needed a name for the format. They'd brainstormed a number of terms—"contemporary jazz," "light jazz," and the like—but nothing was working.

Then suddenly, one of the women they'd brought in looked up and said, "You know what that is? It's *smooooooooth* jazz."

And voilà, a format was born.

What happened next was, WNUA became the first station to call itself Smooth Jazz. It started the format on August 3, 1987. What's funny is that when they started, they decided to not have announcers, so listeners couldn't find out whose music they were listening to. It took a few months of complaints before they figured out they needed DJs.

They weren't alone in playing my music. Other stations—like KTWV in Los Angeles, which billed itself as a "new adult contemporary" station—were playing my stuff as well. They may have been the first to adopt the concept of no DJs and music that fit a certain groove that I was a part of. But once the smooth jazz format had a name, it started to spread like wildfire.

They were playing me, George Benson, Sade, Anita Baker, and Luther Vandross—so some instrumentals and some vocals (just like my albums!).

What I learned from Allen was that at first KTWV was resistant to playing my music—because they thought I was too mainstream. I thought, Too mainstream? The irony was almost funny. I was finally breaking big on the pop charts, which is only a plus for instrumentals in general, and now they were going to hold it against me.

And they did hold it against me—for about a second. They did their research and realized that of all the stuff they were playing, seven of the top ten songs people were reacting to were my songs. So that resistance dropped away pretty fast.

That's how I became the poster boy for smooth jazz. My sound defined the genre, and as more of those stations started popping up and as the format started to get more and more popular, a lot of other musicians started to follow my lead. I suppose you could say that I opened the door to a lot of competition. Now that those stations needed more of the kind of music I was making, all sorts of people started trying to emulate my sound. If I were a territorial guy, I guess I would have been upset, but a lot of musicians have told me they wouldn't have had a career if it weren't for me, and that makes me proud.

But as proud as I was about helping other artists, I was just as upset about a certain situation that emerged as a result of this. I'll try to say this without sounding conceited or harsh.

Here goes.

It was obvious to me that many artists were being signed to basically do the "Kenny G sound." In my humble opinion, these artists had no business making records. They simply weren't that good. And I say this from a very kind and respectful place in my heart. Listen, I'd like to think that I know a thing or two about what it takes to really play an instrument well. And if I had to break it down, I'd list great tone, great technique, and great timing as three of the essential qualities one would find in a great musician. And to my ears, a lot of these newly signed players were mediocre at best in these qualities. But most importantly, when you're trying to imitate someone else, you're playing from your head, not your heart, and so the music ends up being a more calculated product, instead of a reflection of your heart and soul. As a result, the music isn't really expressing your feelings. As I've said, that is the true essence of what I aspire to do. And that, to my ears, was what was also missing from those musicians who were trying to do the "Kenny G sound." It was missing the heart.

Maybe they had the "look" that the record company was searching for, or maybe the folks signing these artists couldn't tell the difference between a really good musician and an average one. But record companies wanted to cash in on this sound and the new popular format, so they were very eager to sign these new artists and put out records. We all know that money makes a lot of things happen that aren't always in the best interest of the art form. Again, I'm not trying to throw shade on anyone, but in my opinion, too many artists were signed when their musicianship didn't warrant them becoming recording artists, and eventually the whole format got diluted and lost strength. But at this moment in time, it was still going strong.

WNUA out of Chicago was becoming popular, and they decided to make a television commercial to further promote the station. I got called in to be the featured artist of the commercial, and that's how yours truly literally became the face of the station. I have to tip my cap to Richie Balsbaugh, the head of the company that owned the Chicago station. Richie was a very charismatic guy, and he had a lot of say-so about how things worked in the radio world. And the radio world was the only world we had at the time, since social media was decades away from being born. Richie was super supportive of me, my career, and my music, and his support made a big difference back then. And that commercial I was featured in became their main promo! Just me and my tenor saxophone walking the streets of Chicago, playing my song "Midnight Motion." That, my friends, is pretty darn cool. So thank you very much, Richie B.!

Now, here's a surprise for you. I didn't really like the name "smooth jazz." That's right. The guy who became synonymous with the genre wishes they called it something else. Or actually I wish we didn't need to label music at all. I get why we have to. It would be like going out to eat and not having any idea what kind of food a restaurant serves because it's just called "Restaurant" instead of having a name that would give someone a little insight as to what kind of food is being served. Something like "Le Canard Chanceux" for a French restaurant, or maybe "El Pollo Estúpido" for a Mexican restaurant. I think you get my point. We kind of need labels so we know basically what we are getting before we get it. I simply didn't like the label "smooth." For me, it evokes a feeling of something that's too light, too fluffy, and not strong enough. Like the music doesn't require real musicianship, and you know how I pride myself on that. I would have come up with a different name, like "today's modern contemporary jazz" or maybe just "instrumentals for today."

But I didn't program those radio stations. (If I did, they would have played even more Kenny G!)

Truth be told, I didn't care that much one way or the other. I just loved that there were stations that wanted to play my music, and that I would be able to keep doing what I loved. Still, "Songbird" and the other singles from *Duotones* did dovetail nicely with this serendipitous innovation. It helped the surge that followed. *Duotones* reached number one on *Billboard*'s Contemporary Jazz Albums chart and number five on the Jazz Albums chart.

"Songbird" went as high as number three on the Adult Contemporary chart and number twenty-three on the R&B chart.

That's a lot of charts! But the chart that really indicated if a song had connected with millions of people was the *Billboard* Hot 100 chart, the industry standard for success. And on that one, "Songbird" soared up to number four. That's pretty darn good for an instrumental! Since then—in the past thirty-eight years—only three more instrumentals have reached the top ten, and, ahem, another one of those was mine too. My version of "Auld Lang Syne" in 2000. But as I said earlier, I'm not here to toot my own horn. Or . . . what the heck. Maybe this time I am.

The other thing happening around that time that helped "Songbird" find its way to listeners was the rise of the music video. VH1 started playing my videos a lot and having me as a featured guest on their broadcasts. At first, I didn't put too much value on the videos— they were something the record company said we should do—and for me nothing was more important than my songwriting and sax playing on my albums, so I was putting my entire focus on the music. But very early on, I saw the advantages of getting that kind of visual exposure, so I was more than happy to go along. I think the video for "Songbird" came out pretty good—if you like seeing me in jeans and a tank top walking on the beaches of Malibu with my horn.

I said it was pretty good. Not great.

I honestly didn't love the video, but I also didn't hate it either. The gang over at VH1 sure loved it and played it a lot! In fact, one of the first "VJs"—video jockeys—at VH1 was a wonderful guy named Roger Rose. He was funny and smart and charismatic, and he had a wicked sense of humor. Right up my alley. He used to invite me on a lot, we had a great time doing crazy little gags and stunts, and we became the best of friends. After almost forty years he's still one of my very best friends. I'm very grateful that my music has brought great people like Roger into my life.

I'm also very grateful that people were reacting to my music in the videos. But I also know they were reacting to something else.

I'm talking, of course, about "The Hair."

Okay, you've been patient up until now, so I won't keep you in suspense any longer. I know you love me for my music. But what you really want to know is, What's the secret behind these luscious locks?

When you're Kenny G, every day is a good hair day. And everybody—okay, mostly women—always asks me my secret. And the answer is, Just lucky I guess. Lucky I had a very special grandmother who had these same ringlets and lucky that she passed them on to me. But as you know by now, I don't think luck is enough, and I put a lot of thought into things. So when my curly hair wouldn't lie flat like other kids', I had to start experimenting with what I could do with my unruly mane, which I did *not* like when I was a kid. I tried all sorts of products in the sixties that I thought might get it to straighten out and behave (can anyone say "Dippity-Do"?). But nope—wasn't meant to be. So in high school I decided to let it grow out and see what happened. And what happened was not the "aha moment" I was looking for. It kept getting worse and worse and uglier and uglier. But did that stop me? You know me. Of course not! I knew it just needed more time. And to say that I don't lack patience is an understatement. So I stuck with it through the ugly stage, and finally, the hair got long enough for gravity to do its thing with those stubborn curls, and they eventually started to relax, and finally, at long last—praise the Lord and pass the hair gel—it looked great!

Remember that this was the mid-seventies, which was, of course, a fantastic time to let your hair take wing. Honestly, a guy could do almost anything with his hair back then—a perm, bangs, a mullet.

Aside from that awkward in-between phase, I kind of rocked the long flowy look. As I said, the curls are courtesy of my paternal grandmother. She had great hair, which she passed along through my father, but curls were not destined for him to enjoy. Although he had them as a boy, he was balding most of his adult life. My mother, not to be outdone, gifted me with hair that genetically resists going gray or falling out. And the good thing is that I don't have to do anything to it on a daily basis. Only apply a little defining cream to damp hair, then step back and let the magic happen. Never blow-dry. You've seen Michael Bolton's hair from back in the day, right? Straw. Then he cut it off, and there went his career. Just kidding! Michael and I are good friends. He's one of those people I can kid and who kids me back. I love that.

Is it safe to say that I'm almost as well-known for my hair as for my sax? Ah, the eternal question. But in the eighties hair like mine wasn't that unusual. I mean, look at Weird Al, Richard Marx (another very close friend of mine), all those guys in Whitesnake. These days, Weird Al and I may be the last men standing, tonsorially speaking. And our careers are still going strong decades later. Coincidence? Not to me!

My bad hair days, I'm sorry to say, lasted longer than I like to remember. If you look at my earlier albums, I was sporting what we called a "Jewfro"—a kind of Jewish Afro—which is pretty much all you can do with tight curly hair like mine. Fun fact: curly hair doesn't grow very fast, so it took a while to get to where it started relaxing. And I decided, no pun intended, to go with the flow.

Any music fan would agree that for the longest time, flowing hair was practically synonymous with music-god status, especially in the heavy metal world. What seemed to stump people was that such luscious hair was connected to a smooth-jazz saxophonist. Oh, the cognitive dissonance! I can hear those metalheads chanting, "What a waste!" But I think I overcame those preconceived notions quite nicely. Pro tip for aspiring music gods: embrace your natural gifts. I certainly wasn't the first musician to have long curly hair, but mine might be the most conditioned. It's arguably the star of my Twitter feed.

As someone who's been in the public eye for more than fifty years, I'm immensely grateful for the gifts I inherited in the hair department. They kind of make me seem ageless. Or at least give the illusion of it. (Exercising every day doesn't hurt either, by the way, folks!) Can great hair be a superpower? If so, I plan to coast on that for as long as I can.

In keeping with my lifelong mandate to tinker with and refine almost anything and everything, I have found that I get the highest score on the hairometer if I don't wash my hair very often. Maybe once every week or so. I've found over the years that this works well for me. My hair just doesn't get greasy, and it stays clean, so why torture it? And the curls tell the tale. Rinse and repeat? Who needs that? And definitely no man bun! Yuck!

So there you have it. Holding nothing back here. As I said earlier, if my hair were ever to fall out, my career would go down the toilet.

I'm kidding, of course.

I hope!

CHAPTER TEN

Road trip!

In the last chapter I invited you into Studio G to see where the magic happens. But that's only part of the magic. What you do in the privacy of the studio is one thing—but what you do out there in front of the people is something else.

Let me tell you, after the success of *Duotones*, what started happening on the road was *really* something else! For one thing, guess who called and said he wanted me to open for him. Liberace! No, just kidding, although I would have loved that. As I said earlier, he's one of the guys I first went on stage with, and from whom I learned a lot about stage presence and performance. No, it was arguably someone as far from Liberace as you can imagine. One of the absolute pillars of jazz—some say the greatest jazz musician of all time.

I'm talking about Miles Davis.

Now I should mention, I guess, at this point, that it was around this time that some jazz critics started taking potshots at my music. Some said it wasn't "real" jazz, whatever that means. Some thought it was too commercial, that I turned my back on traditional jazz to go after commercial success. That one made me scratch my head. Some thought it was too . . . whatever. I didn't much listen, because I didn't much care.

I loved what I was doing, and a lot of people felt the same. What the critics said didn't bother me at all and certainly didn't influence me to change anything.

Some might find that hard to believe, but I think you've gotten to know me by now a little bit. You know that I've been fighting to make the kind of music I want to make since I first started. Remember that when *Duotones* came out, no one picked "Songbird" to be the break-out song that would achieve commercial success. But I went on *Carson* with it anyway—and then people accused me of writing it *just* to be a commercial success.

And if I hadn't learned it already, I certainly learned it now: You can't worry about what other people think. You just have to make your own kind of music.

I'm very happy that my music is successful. This should be clear by now. But that's a by-product of me creating what my heart tells me. So when it comes to the assumption that I make whatever music I think is going to be commercially successful—as if that's where my inspiration and motivation come from—that's just plain wrong. I can't control what the public thinks or what the critics think. I'm very good at knowing what I can and can't control. If people give me a chance to clear up a misunderstanding, I'll try, but if people want to decide for themselves what's going on in my mind and don't want to hear what I have to say about it, that's something I can't control. Therefore, it's something that makes no sense to worry about. So I don't spend much time thinking about it.

And look, the whole *Carson* thing could have gone the other way, right? I mean, when I walked off that stage, my record company could have said, You blew it, kid. You had a chance to promote our single. Now we're gonna drop you from the label.

And you know what? I would have been okay with that, because I knew that I had played the song that I wanted to play, not something that others decided I should play in order to be successful. I loved playing the music I was doing, but I also knew by then that I had an audience who would come out to hear me play—because they had for years. So if I'd been dropped by the label, I could have regrouped and found my place in the music world. And that was enough for me, whether I had a big-selling album career or not.

I tell this to any musician who asks me how I write music that connects with so many people. I always say, "Don't try to outguess the audience and do what you think will be successful. Do what *you* like, do what connects with your heart, and if they like it too, they'll find you."

So for the jazz "purists" who think I turned my back on traditional jazz and decided to do what I thought would get me rich and famous, all I can say is, "If only I were that smart." None of that was even in my brain. Those songs came from my heart, and that's the way I hear them. That's the way it is. My integrity is intact because those songs are my little babies. I hatched them myself, every note and nuance. They are who I am.

I only mention it now because a lot of people have asked me, "Hey, when Miles Davis, the king of jazz, invited you to open for him, wasn't that a great response to those critics? Didn't you feel vindicated?"

I know that would make a good story, but the truth is, I didn't think about it that way at all. Partly because, as I said, I didn't think about the critics that much. But also because no matter what they said, I didn't feel I needed any vindication. I felt like I belonged on that stage. I was part of the music scene—a very successful part of it. I didn't need to prove it to anyone. Least of all some guy writing in a newspaper.

Here's what did matter to me, though: listening to what Miles was doing. He showed me a lot. And I'll tell you, it was as far from traditional jazz as you can imagine. He had this young band, and he could play just a few notes and they would improvise around him, and the crowds loved it.

It was way beyond the "fusion" label they slapped on what he was doing in the seventies (because people love to put labels on things), but to me, it was just Miles deciding, I don't want to keep playing the same thing I did in the fifties and sixties and seventies. If jazz is about anything, it's about moving on and experimenting and changing. Think of how different Miles sounded in the fifties from the big band jazz of barely a decade earlier. Why on earth should he sound the same forty years later?

And that's how I felt about my music too. If Miles could do something so far afield from traditional jazz, why shouldn't I?

And then, a few nights into the tour, we were playing at Lincoln Center in New York, and Miles stopped by my dressing room. Let me bask in that for a second. *He* stopped by *my* dressing room. To tell me he liked my song. "You play that song the ladies like," he said in that deep, growly voice of his. "It sounds good. I like it."

Miles Davis likes "Songbird"! That was a pretty nice moment for me.

Right after he stopped in, I asked him if we could take a picture together. We stepped out of my dressing room and found someone with a camera—remember, no one had cell phones in those days—and when the picture came out, I was so proud! I passed it along to someone, and somehow it made it into the press, which ended up adding fuel to this idea that my music was an affront to traditional jazz. Because if you look at that shot, it looks like Miles is glaring at me.

But the photo was taken completely out of context. He wasn't glaring at me. I mean, two seconds earlier he had told me he liked my music! Never mind that I was opening for his tour, at his invitation. But you know, when you catch someone not ready for a photo, they might have a funny expression. (And Miles Davis was not one to stop and say cheese!) Well, the press had a field day with it—saying it showed the jazz giant scorning the smooth jazz poster boy.

But again, what can you do? The answer is, Nothing. I just went out the next night and did my thing again. Opening for Miles Davis. In front of huge crowds. And guess what? That Miles Davis audience, supposedly the most sophisticated jazz audience in the world? They loved it!

There was another funny story I remember from the Miles dates I played. I was opening for Miles on every show we did together, and sometimes we'd play two shows in the same night. One night, for our second show, Miles's manager came up to me and said, "Miles wants to open for you."

Miles Davis wants to open for you. How many jazz musicians have heard that? Not many, I'll bet! So I'm thinking, That's amazing. That's so cool. What a sign of respect! Or so I thought.

What actually happened was, our second shows started just a little after 10:00 p.m. This one was sold out, but by the time Miles finished up and I got on, it was after 11:30 p.m., and only about three hundred out of the three thousand people were left in the audience. I realized when I walked out that Miles had decided, Let me get out there and play and go home. Let Kenny take the late shift. And most of the audience did the same thing that Miles did. They went home.

Ha! Lesson learned. Don't get a swelled head.

In the summer of 1987 I was riding high. I guess you'd have to say I was a celebrity by this point, although that didn't mean much to me. However, I was getting to play for bigger and bigger audiences. The shows were successful from the business side, and that meant something important to me. It meant that I could keep playing my music, the way I wanted to, and there would be gigs for me.

That was a very comforting thing. Promoters and agents were happy, which meant they would continue to book me, which meant I basically now had a "steady job." And as a bonus, I was getting paid very well for it. And that allowed me to do something that gave me more pride than almost anything I'd ever done in my life up to that point.

I got to pay back my dad.

I had kept track of every penny I owed him, and I remember the day I handed him a check for something close to $125,000. It was one of the coolest moments for me.

I handed it to him and said, "Hey, thanks for the loan, Dad."

And he said, "Wow, will you look at that. Well, thanks. But I don't need the money, you know."

And I said, "Yes, I do know that, but I thought I ought to pay you back anyway."

And he said, "Well, thanks, son. I think this is almost better for you than it is for me."

And I said, "Well, thank you again. It is. It was important for me to know that I could do it. But I couldn't have done it without you."

So that's how we talked to each other—just joking around, not making a big deal about it. But truly, it was a big deal. When I think of the stereotypes of Jewish families you see in the movies, whether it's *The Jazz Singer* in 1927, *Funny Girl* in 1968, or *Armageddon Time* in 2022, it's always that the kid wants to go into show business or be an artist, and the parents are horrified because they want the kid to get a "real" job. So to be the poster boy for what a real-life Jewish family is really about—parents who love and support their children, come what may—means a whole lot to me.

And here's something else that meant a whole lot to me: I was about to start opening for Whitney Houston!

It had been six years since I had gone with Clive Davis to Sweetwater's in Harlem to see Dionne Warwick's cousin. I could still remember how I was absolutely floored by her voice, her presence, everything about her. I'd been so thrilled to see her rocket to stardom.

Now—thanks to the lovely marketing strategy of sending the top two Arista artists on the road together—I was going to open for her.

How cool was *that*?

So I have to tell you what happened our first night on the road. You're gonna love this one. I know I do. The first gig we played was at Tampa Stadium in Florida—where the Tampa Bay Buccaneers played—and it was probably the biggest crowd I'd ever played for. Maybe twenty-five thousand people. We did our sound check, and I did what I always do—took my sax out into the audience seats, to see how it would sound when I got out there later. Then, while Whitney was doing her sound check, I got called into her tour manager's office. His name was Tony Bulluck, and he was a huge, imposing guy, six feet five and probably 280 pounds, big and fearsome, kind of like a king-size mattress with arms and legs.

He sat me down and said, "Listen, I'm going to let you know something. You cannot go into the audience."

"Why not?"

"Our insurance isn't going to cover it. You can't go into the audience. That's how it's going to be on this tour."

That was a lot to process, but it wasn't all. "Also, one more thing," he said. "When Whitney comes out of her dressing room, you guys are not to be out in the hallways backstage. Don't talk to her. Don't make any eye contact. When she comes out and she's walking around, you guys stay in your dressing rooms. Okay? That's how it's going to be on this tour."

I left his office and went back into the band's dressing room. I told the guys, "I want to let you guys know something. We're going to get fired after tonight." I told them what Tony had said to me. The guys were as outraged as I was, which was good, because I knew they'd go along with what I had in mind. "Let's take first things first," I said. "Let's go play our music. The way we always do." Meaning, from the first song, I'd be out in the audience. Like always.

That night we went to play our music in that enormous stadium, and I was so far out into the audience, farther than I'd ever been, that if I went any farther, I'd have gotten my feet wet in Tampa Bay. When I got off stage, I was ready to get chewed out, but everybody was scurrying around getting Whitney ready for her gig. So I went back to the dressing room and told all the guys, "Let's go. Out in the hall. Stand right next to Whitney's dressing room door, and when she comes out, let's give her a high-five. 'Have a great show, Whitney.' All that stuff." The guys had smiles on their faces a mile wide—I could tell they were loving good old sweet Kenny being the bad boy—and out we went into the hallway.

Tony Bulluck was waiting for Whitney to come out of her room, and he was glaring at me. But no one said a word. Whitney came out of her room, and I said, "Whitney! Hey, it's so great to be on tour with you. Have a great show! We love you! Just know that we warmed them up for you! They're all ready."

She looked happy to see me and my guys there, which made me happy too. It was the most natural thing in the world—two performers on the same bill, one wishing the other a good show. She gave me a big smile, said thanks, and walked on by.

Now, it's appropriate that this was called the Moment of Truth tour, because I was about to face my moment of truth. Tony called me into his office and started yelling at me about going into the audience, about talking to Whitney. Words were said that I won't repeat here. The whole nine yards.

And here's what I said. "Okay, Tony, here's the deal. Fire me now, or know that that's what's going to happen. I'm going to play my set the way I want to, which means me going into the audience. And we're going to be in the hallway whenever the fuck we want to be in the hallway. That's the way it's going to be. So you probably should let us go now." I paused for dramatic effect—again, I'm a performer—and then said quietly, "By the way, also you will probably want to let Clive Davis know that you don't want me to open up for Whitney as well. I'll let you tell him, Tony. You're going to have to let him know since we're all part of the same team here. Arista is loving this pairing of its two top artists, but if you think I can't be out here, you let everybody know. Okay. Good talk. Let me know what's happening, hopefully before the end of the night, so I know whether we're going to show up tomorrow or not."

I think it's clear by now, especially with my upbringing, that conflict is not something I seek out. I really do try to avoid it. But ever since Roy Cummings knocked that sheet music off my stand, I've known, deep in my bones, that I had to stand up for myself when the time came. Also I knew we would be okay regardless of how this worked out because I was already playing for a sizable audience on my own—if not Whitney-size— and it wasn't like there were no gigs out there for me besides this tour.

So how'd I do? I think I did pretty well. In fact, I know I did pretty well. Because regardless of the outcome, I felt like I held my own, I didn't back down, and yet I'd found a way to do it respectfully and with a fair measure of kindness.

And it just so happens that it worked out fine. While me and the guys were having a few beers after the gig, celebrating both the start and possibly the end of the same tour, I got a message from one of Tony's assistants saying, "Hey, no problem, you can go out in the audience. And the hallway thing is a non-issue. It's all good. Happy to have you on the tour."

And not only that, but by the third or fourth night, Tony was out in the audience with me, making sure that no one messed with me! He was clearing the way for me, and believe me, I've never played football, but following that mountain of a man is what it must feel like to have one of those big fullbacks blocking for you. He parted the seas like Moses. And on top of all that, he was turning around and smiling at me and giving me high-fives between numbers. He was clearly, absolutely, 100 percent loving it!

Once again, it shows what I've learned ever since the first time I stepped off the stage. You gotta walk your own path. And to hell with anyone who tries to tell you that you can't.

By the way, on Whitney's latest album at the time, she did a great rendition of the Isley Brothers' "For the Love of You," which happens to be one of my favorite songs ever. I did the sax solo on Whitney's version, and I was really proud of it. When she did it in concert, the sax player in her band played my solo, and he did a good enough job, but of course the Xerox is never as good as the original. So after the first few nights I told her team, "Guys, let me come and sit in on that song. I mean, I'm right here, and I'm the guy who did it on the record. It'll be cool."

They said, "Thanks, we'll think about it." And true to their word, they thought about it. For forty-four more shows.

In early September 1987, we were in New York, playing Madison Square Garden. (Again, take a minute to let that sink in: little Kenny Gorelick is playing Madison Square Garden!) You cannot imagine what it's like to step out on that iconic stage and hear the mighty roar from the gigantic crowd and know they're cheering for you. I get goosebumps just writing about it.

Anyway, since it was New York, we all knew Clive Davis and the
Arista team would be in the audience. And lo and behold, finally, Tony's
people said yes. "We want you to sit in on 'For the Love of You' tonight," they told me.

Here's what I thought: You motherfuckers. I could have been doing
this since the Fourth of July. You're doing this because Clive is here and
is probably expecting it (and why would he not expect it?)—and you
know he is going to love it if we do it together. That's all fine and dandy,
but didn't it occur to you that maybe all the audiences would love it too?

That's what I thought.

Here's what I said: "Thanks, guys! I'd be happy to!"

See, there's the flip side. Stand up for yourself when you have to.
The rest of the time, be grateful for the opportunities and happy with
what you have. That's the formula that works for me.

Now you have to picture this scene: The Madison Square Garden
stage was set up in the round. I was up there with my musicians for our
opening set, but Whitney was up there all alone, with her band down
below. So when I went up to play sax on "For the Love of You," it was
just me and her. In the round. In front of nearly eighteen thousand
people. It was pretty overwhelming.

So Whitney started singing. I don't have to tell you what a beautiful voice she had. And how incredibly beautiful she was. And she was
leaning in close, looking right into my eyes and singing this beautiful
song to me.

I melted into a puddle on the floor.

It was amazing. When I started playing, I kept looking right at her
and playing just to her, the same way she sang just to me, and it was
electric. My sax and I were in the zone. Big time. Certainly, it was all
coming right from the heart, and you know that when it comes from
the heart, it sounds the best.

What can I say? Whitney and I had . . . a moment.

I know Clive was out there going crazy—his top two artists, together
and making magic in front of a sold-out Madison Square Garden. I was
certainly happy! I thought, Hey, I'm gonna get to do this every night for

the rest of the tour! Except I didn't. For whatever reason, they only did it that one night. But oh, what a night. A moment I will never forget.

And now, ladies and gentlemen, take a deep breath, because we're about to get on board this rocket ship (or maybe it's a souped-up tour bus) and take it up to the stratosphere. Ready? Because this is when I stop opening for other acts.

This is the moment that the Kenny G Tour begins. It's a tour that's been going strong for more than thirty-five years now!

It was really, really exciting.

And really, really hard.

Not that I'm complaining for one second. Look, this is what I've been working my whole life for. It's just that when you're the head-liner, there's a lot more pressure and responsibility. The phone never stops ringing. There are all kinds of decisions to make, and suddenly, Oprah wants you to come on tomorrow, and let's be clear, *you do not say no to Oprah*. Not that I would have. I mean, what an honor. And the record company, now that they've decided they have a good thing on their hands, wants you to do a ton of promotion, so they set you up on *Leno*, then *Arsenio Hall*, and then *Good Morning America* wants you on tomorrow even though that means getting on a flight from Los Angeles that lands in New York in the wee hours of the morning, grabbing a couple of hours of sleep, then going straight to the studio for a 6:00 a.m. sound check, sitting around for a few hours, doing your thing for two minutes, and flying right back home again. Or flying to wherever the tour was headed that night.

But again, I am not complaining at all. I mean, I've been given the opportunity that every musician prays for. That very, very, very few in-strumentalists ever get a tiny whiff of. So you know I'm gonna make the most of it. Which means that I know every show I do has to be the very best it can be. That's a whole different kind of pressure—but the kind I really like.

The very best part of this for me was that, as the headliner, I had all the time in the world to do what I wanted to do. When you're opening for someone, you know people aren't there to see you. No matter how well you do, you know they're going to start getting impatient after five or six songs, so you better wrap it up and get the heck off that stage. But now, the audiences were there specifically to see me. Imagine that! I finally had the time to explore all the things I wanted to do with my music. To take detours, to try different ideas. To be inventive, or subtle, or to reach back to old jazz, or reach forward to something new. Now I could be as cold and as bold as I wanted without worrying about if I had it all together. I could do all that because these weren't someone else's audiences. They were mine.

And oh my God, what audiences! We were playing big sheds like the Garden State Arts Center, Wolf Trap, and the Jones Beach Theater—big outdoor arenas that hold five thousand, ten thousand, or even fifteen thousand people!

That's great stuff, right? I mean, there should be nothing but smiles, right? Well, we all have our ingrained hard-wiring, our childhood conditioning, and mine was from a typical Jewish household that wanted to make sure I wasn't *too* happy about all this. I could hear my grandfather. "Oy vey, Kenny! Such a crowd! Don't mess it up!" And "Are they paying you enough?"

"Ha ha! Thanks, Grandpa, I won't. And don't worry!" (Two words that fall on deaf ears in a typical Jewish household.) "They're paying me *very* well."

"In dat case," he would say, "you *really* better not mess it up!"

As things started taking off, I thought back often on my grandpa's humor and the way I was brought up, the values I learned from my family. And when it came to my relationship to success and money, I had learned so much from watching my dad and his brother Hunsy. These lessons in family values helped me a great deal once I started doing well financially. I didn't go to junkyards looking for retread tires anymore, but I certainly wasn't living the champagne-wishes-and-caviar-dreams lifestyle. I'm proud to say that I maintained my perspective when it came to the value of the dollar, and I'm also proud that that is part of my DNA. Now don't get me wrong; it doesn't mean I don't spend money on myself for things that one would consider discretionary or luxury, like an expensive video projector or a marble cold-plunge tub. It means I do everything without taking my eye off the bottom line. And I'm not gonna let that bottom line get lower than where I need it to be in order to feel secure.

Remembering where I came from is my way of staying grounded, of staying myself. I am still Kenny from the Franklin High School hood.

I didn't have as much time to hang out with my friends as I used to, and that made me sad. But I did make a point, whenever I was back home, of taking a night off and hanging with the guys I grew up and went to school with, with all of us making fun of each other exactly the way we used to. My accounting degree came in handy as I started to make more money, and I kept everything in line. We stayed at nice enough hotels, but I wasn't wasting money on the big penthouse suites. We didn't fly first class—a bus tour was definitely good enough for me before, and it still was.

I've had a good track record with opening acts and finding potential super-headliners just before they became super-headliners. I think the right opening act is very important. Sometimes, when you add one and one, you get a million.

And that's from a guy with an accounting degree!

I have a long history of touring with Michael Bolton—more on that later—and after we toured for a couple of years together, Michael started to break out on his own and have big hit records. At this time, he was still my opening act, but it was more like a one-two punch with two headliners.

We would sell out ten-thousand-seat venues, yet I was still getting the lion's share of the money because he was still technically the opener.

"You know," he told me one day, "that's not fair."

"You know," I said back, "you're absolutely right."

"So you'll give me a bigger cut?"

"No, but I'll agree that it's not fair!"

Ha ha. Actually, I did give him a bigger cut as time went by and told him that the next set of dates would be done as co-headliners.

I truly had a great time watching the acts who opened for me become stars in their own right. A few years later, I invited Toni Braxton—already a big rising star—to be the featured guest on my tour. She was an absolute pleasure to work with. *Most* of the time. But there was this one time . . .

There was some kind of argument between her people and mine about the lights she wanted to use. I didn't care at all about that, but I did hear that her folks were being nasty to my people. And that's not okay with me.

You know by now that I like it when everybody gets along. And I can be pretty easygoing—it's my preferred state of mind. But also, when somebody steps over the line, I'm not gonna let it go. I'm fine with somebody being a bit of a diva, but I'm not happy about my people being treated shitty.

My team is made up of great people who are very experienced and talented at what they do, and we always treat people with respect. It doesn't matter that you are the opening act. You are still going to get our respect, and we'll help in any way we can. But that said, we expect that same respect in return. Especially from some much less experienced people.

I decided the best thing to do would be to talk to Toni, person to person. I was sure she'd feel the same way and that she wouldn't want to hear that my folks thought they were being treated badly. I figured we could clear the whole thing up in no time.

I went to her dressing room to talk to her and ended up waiting outside her door for forty-five minutes. And even with that show of disrespect, I started on a positive note. "Listen, I'm happy to get you your lights. We're all here to work together."

She couldn't have been more friendly and appreciative.

Then I told her, as gently as I could, that my folks felt like her team had treated them pretty disrespectfully, and could we maybe make sure that both teams feel as though they are being treated with respect?

That's when this sweet young woman came at me like thunder and lightning. She got extremely upset and started yelling at me. She processed what I was saying as me telling her what to do and said she wasn't "gonna take this kinda stuff" (I promise she didn't say "stuff") and that she couldn't wait for this tour to be over.

I was shocked by her reaction and hurt by the disrespectful way she had just treated me. And let me be clear. Being hurt by someone does not indicate weakness. It's a real feeling, and there is nothing wimpy or weak about admitting that something hurts you. It doesn't mean I'm going to cower away and not deal with things. Just the opposite.

So I told her I was sorry she felt that way and wished her a good performance that night. Strength is knowing when to not waste your time talking to someone who isn't receptive.

I left it at that. For about a minute. I don't hold grudges. But when someone goes off on me, I do like to get even. But not in a mean way.

Well, not too mean, anyway.

Here's what I did. Every night, during her show, Toni invited a man from the audience on stage, took out a big box of cigars, handed one to him, and said, "I wanna show you how I treat a man." Then she'd light the cigar and sing while doing a sexy dance in front of him the whole time.

So I scoped out where that box was at various times during the day, and I discovered that there were a few minutes when no one was watching it, and no one would touch it again until she opened it on stage during her show. The next night, I swiped the box and took out all the cigars. And replaced them with 150 condoms.

Now I should say right away, I know that in this day and age this would be seen as wildly inappropriate—and it probably was. But those were different times, and to a much younger Kenny G, it seemed like a brilliant little bit of revenge.

So I carefully put the box back, and that night, when she called a guy up on stage and said, "Let me show you how I treat a man," and opened the cigar box, all those condoms came pouring out onto the stage.

She was incredibly embarrassed, but like any professional, she managed to stumble her way through the rest of her set. Afterward she was fuming, and came up to me and said, "That was not cool!"

I said, with a perfectly straight face, "I know! Who would do such a thing?"

We looked at each other, and it was clear to both of us that we both knew it had been me. But then I saw what I swear was the slightest smile on her face, and I felt like she was maybe planning a way to get even.

Turned out I was right.

The next night, when I was on stage, she walked out—with a big Kenny G wig on! I didn't notice at first until I heard a big laugh from the audience, and then I turned and saw her, and I nodded like I was saying, Well played, Ms. Braxton.

But I was also thinking: Hey! Two Kenny Gs on stage—what's wrong with that! Ha!

CHAPTER ELEVEN

So should I tell some more road stories? I hope so because there are lots of them. But they're not the kinds of stories I bet some of you are hoping for. I'm a sax-and-hugs guy, not a sex-and-drugs guy. So you're not gonna hear about any wild orgies or broken-up hotel rooms.

But I am about to get naked with a bunch of guys from a different country. Control yourselves! It's not what you think.

We are now officially taking a road trip to Japan.

I think learning to relax is a discipline, just like learning to practice every day is a discipline. And if you're going to work as hard as we were working, you need to learn how to relax. I learned this in Japan.

On my first trip to Japan, I went to the gym in the hotel I was staying in. Working out is part of my daily ritual; even on the road—especially on the road—I make sure to stick to that regimen.

After my workout, I went into the spa area to take a shower. That's when things got strange for the American who had never been to a Japanese spa before.

First of all, all they had were sit-down showers. I'd never seen anything like this. There was a wooden stool and a showerhead on a fairly long hose. There was a mirror that you sat in front of so you could watch yourself while you showered. I felt awkward about doing this, but remember, I'm a jazz improvisationalist, and we're trained to improvise, to go with the flow and go off on tangents. So trying something new is right up my alley.

So I sat down and immediately thought, Wow! Where have you been all my life?

This was so much better than a regular American-style stand-up shower. It was so comfortable and relaxing. I looked around and started to copy what I saw everyone else doing: I gave myself a nice shave, trimmed my nails, the works. It was super fun and a squeaky-clean good time. I loved it.

Then I saw some of the Japanese men in what I thought was a hot tub, but when I stuck my foot in, I realized it was a cold plunge! Ice cold, in fact.

When in Rome, right? So I stepped in and couldn't believe how bone-chilling it was. These guys were frolicking around in there like they could stay in there forever. Me, on the other hand, I only lasted ten seconds. (I'm not gonna make the obvious joke here. I'll let you do that for yourself. Ha!)

Anyway, I didn't want to be the dumb tourist who doesn't understand the local customs, so I took a minute to figure out what was going on. Then I realized that everybody was going into the hot sauna first. So I did that, and it was *so* incredibly hot, but you know how competitive I can be, so I decided I'd outlast everyone in there. And I did!

The next step in the routine I was observing was to go into the cold bath, but first, I noticed, the Japanese guys would rinse the sweat from the sauna off their bodies with a couple buckets of water so the water in the bath would stay clean. Very smart. This I like. So I did that too.

Then I went into the cold plunge. After the initial shock to the system, it felt fantastic. (I lasted a few minutes this time, thank you very much.) After getting out, I stood there, enjoying this feeling that was very exhilarating and, at the same time, very calming. I was hooked, folks. Seriously hooked!

I continued my bath tour of Asia when we got to the Peninsula Hotel in Hong Kong. This time it was the hottest bath I ever took. It was in a wooden bathtub made of the softest wood. The water was so hot you had to get in inch by inch. (Too easy to insert a joke here! So I won't.)

When I finally got in, I relaxed and closed my eyes. When I opened them again, there were two Asian businessmen in suits and ties looking down on this naked sax man, and they said, "Excuse me, but may we please have your autograph?"

Such is life on the road!

Despite the interruption, after discovering the wonders of the hot-and-cold baths, I became a bath guy. (I know that some people hear the words "warm bath" and instantly think of Kenny G music anyway, so maybe it's fate!)

I was so inspired by this newly discovered bathing protocol that a new nighttime ritual was born for me at home. I begin every night with the hottest bath I can stand. I truly love a really hot bath. And I stay in there a long time. Because it's a great place to do something that I think most of us don't do enough—I know I didn't until recently: Contemplate. Sit quietly. Be alone with your thoughts. Just sit.

There's always something going on in life—our screens, or TV noise, or music, or someone talking to you, or you're getting something done, or trying to get something done, or spending three hours practicing the saxophone or whatever—so that moment, when I get into the bath, is like a signal to my mind and my body that it's time to just . . . stop.

Some people call it meditation; I call it contemplation. What do I contemplate? I try to think mostly about things that might improve my quality of life and the lives of those around me. How I can be more grateful for the wonderful life I have. How I can be a better performer, a better father, a better friend, a better partner. How I can be nicer to the people I meet in the world. How I can find more peace. These are the things I think about. But sometimes it's good to think about absolutely nothing at all.

So I have my hot bath every night, and then I go as cold as I can get. And I put a small sauna in my bathroom at home as well. Why not! I wanted to recreate my Japanese spa experience. When I'm on the road, I don't have time for all this, so it's my great pleasure when I get home to be able to take that time to be hot, to be cold, to contemplate, to find peace.

All I can say is, *Aaaaaaahhhh.*

Okay! Break time is over, gang. Time to get back on the road. And I was on the road a *lot* in the late eighties.

It was not just concerts. In addition to the big gigs, artists had to do a lot of promotion to get our records up front in the record stores. If you're old enough to remember Tower Records and stores like that, remember when you'd go in and see a big cardboard cutout of yours truly, with a bunch of albums where my belly button was supposed to be?

Yeah, that didn't happen on its own.

My team at Arista would set me up to go schmooze—shake hands, mingle, and sometimes play one of my songs—at what used to be called the National Association of Recording Merchandisers. Or, "As long as you're in such-and-such town," they'd ask me, "can you go by the warehouse of this record store and take some pictures with the employees and, again, maybe play a tune or two in the office?"

I mean, it wasn't like it was a quid pro quo: If you do this, we'll put your records up front. But it sure wasn't *not* like a quid pro quo. We all knew it was kind of, If you wash my back, I'll wash yours. I can guarantee you that nothing like that went on in the Japanese baths! But it sure did in the record business.

Before I get off this subject, I have to say one thing I really valued in those days was my relationship with the field staff at Arista Records. Everything started at the top with the man running the promotion department under Donnie Ienner. His name was Rick Bisceglia, and to this day Rick says that helping to launch "Songbird" was one of his most gratifying achievements ever. He did it with the help of his amazing field staff, who also went way beyond to make "Songbird" a hit. This included people like Linda Alter in Atlanta, Johnny Powell in Baltimore, Greg Feldman in the Northwest, June Colbert in Texas, Jeff Backer, Bruce

Schoen, and Mark Rizzo. When I think about the success I was having at this moment in my life, I never go a day without thinking of all the hard work that so many others did on my behalf. There wouldn't be a famous Kenny G without these people.

Speaking of famous: People ask me a lot about what it felt like to have the kind of fame I was starting to have. As I said before, it wasn't the reason I got into all of this. It was all about the music and still is. The fame part wasn't what motivated me at any point in my career. But that said, it did represent the fact that a lot of people were supporting what I was doing musically. And this allowed me to do things like play the kind of amazing venues I was playing and reap all the benefits of that. And successful shows and happy promoters meant that I could continue to make my music, explore it in all kinds of new ways, and have places to perform it. *That* was important.

I can tell you that it's fun, and kind of flattering, when I find that I'm on someone's radar that I wouldn't expect to be. For example, I was walking around New York City a little while back, and if you've ever walked the streets of New York, you know you can come across some pretty interesting characters. So I'm walking down the street, and this guy is walking the other way and is about to cross my path, and he's shouting, "Motherfucker . . . goddamn ficking-facking mother . . . son of a bitch," and this goes on and on, and he is very loud. And honestly a little frightening. I don't want to engage him, so I try to not make eye contact, but we do, and he immediately smiles and says, "Hey! Kenny G! How you doin', man?" He gives me a fist bump and then continues on his way, and without missing a beat, he goes right back to his rant: "Mother-frigging franking goddamn mother-jumping son of a bitch . . ." It was a moment I wish I could have recorded!

That's what being famous means. Everybody recognizes you. As I said, for me that part never mattered all that much. But sometimes you get to share a smile with someone who under normal circumstances would never look at you twice, and that's the kind of connection that means everything to me.

You never know what effect your music can have on people. After one of my concerts in New York City, a guy came up to me, looked me right in the eye, and said, "Hey, man, I want you to know, I listen to your music when I have sex."

I said, "Oh, really, bro? Tell me about that."

He said, "Yeah, man, when you play, I play. You start slow, I start slow. You hit your high note, I hit my high note. You hold your note, I hold my note. You finish, I finish."

Not exactly what I have in mind when I write my songs, but hey, whatever works for you is cool with me.

So anyway, between the promotional appearances, people recognizing you on the street, and Asian businessmen asking for your autograph when you're naked in a hot tub, it's almost a relief to get back on the road and do your thing. And that's what I was doing. Concert after concert, bigger venue after bigger venue, we were building one of the biggest tours in the country. And loving it.

Now the challenge is to put on a great show. Fortunately, by this point, I've done so many shows that I've developed a concept of how to do just that. How to build a show, piece by piece. I've learned what works and what doesn't.

Want to know how it's done? Okay. Here's how I go about putting together a Kenny G show.

There are so many factors that go into deciding what songs to play, what order to play them in, and what goes on during those songs. Over the years, I've figured out which songs work live and which ones don't. Some songs sound great on a recording but on stage just aren't exciting for some reason.

Discovering which songs work in concert is trickier than it sounds. Was it the song itself or where we placed it in the order of things? Those are tricky decisions, but after thousands of concerts, I know how to make that call. And the key to putting together the set list begins with figuring out how to start the show in just the right way, then looking at how the dynamics of the songs that follow relate to each other. And that determines which songs follow which songs. That's the heart of how to build a concert.

It starts, as you already know, with me in the audience. I know that's a great icebreaker. You want to wow the crowd right from the start, and also, it's my way of dissolving the usual separation between performer and audience. So I start with a beautiful song that's not too slow and not too fast. Something that tells the audience that they made the right call by coming to the show, because they are going to hear the kind of song that motivated them to come see us live. And while I'm out there, I make sure to do one of my famous long circular-breathing notes. Even though people may have heard or seen me do this on record or video, it's not the same as watching it live, and people go absolutely nuts over this. I can tell they're going, Holy cow, how is he doing that? And for a couple of minutes they are completely awestruck. But then the laughing and cheering start to take over the room, and everyone starts to get the clear message that the evening is going to be a lot of fun.

I feel the electricity and excitement from the crowd that first time I do it. It makes me proud and gets me excited too! If you ever wonder if performers react to how much you're cheering out there, wonder no more. It's definitely a two-way street, so if you are enjoying it and you let the artist know it, the artist is absolutely going to feel it, and it's definitely going to add to the dynamics of the performance. I think I'm pretty objective about this and can speak for most performers: if you're loving what we're doing, please let us know.

I finish the song on stage with a flurry of fast runs and impressive sax stuff, and it's my way of showing that the concert will be more than just beautiful melodies and long notes. There is going to be some shredding going on up here! And I have the heavy metal hair to back that up.

The next song is one that I would call a filler. It's a feel-good song that keeps the vibe going and lets the crowd catch their breath—even though I'm the one who needs to do that! But I'll catch mine later. We have many songs to choose from that can fill that spot. I keep that one a little short. But should it be a slow-tempo filler or an up-tempo one? Oh, it's got to be an up-tempo song, because you don't want to lose the momentum. You want the crowd to keep that happy-go-lucky feeling that we all just created together.

After that song ends, it's time for me to say hello and let people start to get to know me a little as a person. So I take a few minutes to talk to the crowd. I don't understand performers who never speak to their audience. People come not only to listen to music but also to feel like they've met you and, hopefully, gotten to know you a little better. And how can you meet someone and get to know them without talking to them?

I want people to feel the connection with me and the band, so I use my little talking space to create this connection. I like to give them a little information about myself, some info about the guys so it's not all about me, and a little something to make them laugh. Like I might say, "Do you see this saxophone? This is the same sax I played in high school." I wait a beat, then say something like, "Unfortunately, it represents the only long-term relationship I could make work."

That always gets a good laugh, but then of course I correct myself and point out that the band and I also have decades of history together—something, I might add, that can be pretty rare in my business and is something I'm both very proud of and very, very happy about.

There you go. I've talked a little about myself and the band and made fun of myself a little; the audience members know they can relax and don't have to be intimidated by the music and that we're going to have fun together.

Then what happens? It's time to change things up. I've already played one of my fancy cadenzas, and I've done my circular breathing, and I've played some fun sax songs, so I feel like we have to do something different, or the crowd might start to feel like the night will be just more of the same. Yes, even great sax has its limits. It's time to feature one of the great musicians in the band.

I might start by introducing my percussionist Ron Powell, then stand back and let the audience watch him as he does his thing. Ron is a force of nature—he's an amazing percussionist who has incredible technique on his instruments; he also works out in the gym every day, so he is in amazing shape and not the least bit shy about showing off his muscular build. He also has a perpetual smile and more energy than the sun. He brings a huge tambourine out front and gets the crowd going while the band backs him up. He rolls the tambourine behind his neck and spins it on his finger like a basketball, then plays the most amazing one-handed percussion solo in the middle of it. You've never heard anything like it! Words cannot do justice to how fabulous he is or how much fun he is to watch.

The crowd goes bonkers.

Okay, now what? Well, I know that people came to hear my famous instrumentals, and now I've just teased them by going in a whole different direction, so it's time to bring in one of the big guns. (It seems unlikely that anyone has described one of my romantic ballads as "a big gun" before, but I think it's appropriate.) So I'll do something that I'm sure they have heard like "Forever in Love" or "Sentimental." It should be something from my *Breathless* album because that was my most successful album, so I'm confident they will have heard this one. The crowd loves it, and I'm feeling fantastic, because I know we are all really feeling the great vibe that's going on here. We're like one big family now. The crowd and the performers. All in sync.

Then it's time to change things up again. We go back to our jazz roots for this next part. I pull out the big tenor sax, and we do some old traditional jazz standards. I always take a couple of songs to tour the history of the jazz greats and share some of this treasured music with folks—some of whom, I'm sure, are hearing it for the first time. I tell the crowd we're all being transported back in time to a Greenwich Village jazz joint in the fifties or sixties, and I'll do a Coltrane number, then off to a snazzy uptown club in the sixties to hear a song by my personal favorite, Stan Getz. When we're doing our sound checks, we love to groove and improvise and go wild on those songs. We do a more controlled version in concert, because it would be too much for the crowd to digest if we played these jazz songs for twenty minutes each, but I know it still conveys the power and the magic—the heart and soul—of those great, great masters of jazz. And I try my best to do them proud.

Then we'll feature another one of the great musicians in my group. This solo will have a whole different feel than the powerful theatrics of Ron Powell's percussion solo. We are going to get further into our jazz roots on this one. So I introduce my piano player, Robert Damper, the guy who's been with me since high school. I give Robert room to do a real old-school jazz piano solo. I know some people will appreciate it and go, Whoa, this is so nice, and yet I also know that others will say, Hey, this isn't what I came to hear, or This song is too jazzy for me, and they'll get up and go get a drink or something. That's cool—I don't care. I know musically it's the right thing to do at this point, to show the audience some traditional jazz. And also, I get so proud of Robert during his moment to shine because it gives the audience a chance to hear what an incredible musician he is. It's also one more chance to fulfill what I consider is our duty to share some old-school jazz standards with the crowd. And we feel honored to be in a position to introduce them to folks who may never have heard them before.

By now it's time to get the party rolling again. We break into something really funky, like the 1970s R&B hit instrumental "Pick Up the Pieces." And on this one it's time for my bass player, Vail Johnson, to blow everyone's mind with his incredible technique. He does a super funky solo, and after he's done I often joke that he is the funkiest white bass player in America. I love playing this song, because it gives me a chance to see and hear which members of the audience remember the funky music of the seventies with the same fondness that I do. And by the way, when you start shouting out the title of the song when it comes around, trust me, we hear you loud and clear. And we love it!

So now we've done pretty much a whole concert, and we're only halfway through. Time to take a break and introduce the band. The rest of the band includes my guitarist, John Raymond, who plays a killer solo earlier in the show and adds amazing parts to all the songs. And last but certainly not least there's my drummer, Danny Bejarano. I always tell the audience how important the drummer is, and it's true. It's a tricky role. We need someone who knows how to play with enough power to drive the band but not so much that it would overpower the stage and not be musical. It's a fine line, and Danny walks it beautifully during every show. He is an incredible musician, and he gets his moment to do his killer drum solo—and he nails it every night.

I'd be remiss if I didn't mention another key player in all this: our sound man Monty Montfort. He has mixed our sound for almost forty years. It's the sound you hear when you come to our shows. He's sitting in one of the most important chairs in my organization. We may be playing amazingly on stage, but if you aren't hearing the sound right, the concert is a failure. How many concerts have you gone to where the sound was out of balance, or something was off, and it spoiled everything? We don't let that happen. Our gang is in the venue at ten the morning of the show, setting up. This includes our amazing monitor engineer, Elliot Nielsen, and our drum tech, Bobby Mertz.

I get there about 1:00 p.m. and do my two to three hours of practice before we even get to the sound check. First we make sure the sound on stage is perfect so that we can play our best. I also spend time out in the house checking everything with Monty so that when you come to see our show, I'm confident that we have done everything we can to make sure that everything is set where it's supposed to be and that you will have the best experience possible.

Introducing the band is a fun part of the concert for me. I like to tell jokes about each of the guys and give them a chance to show off a little something for the crowd. But then comes the hardest part of the concert: How do we keep it going? It's like you shot a seven under par on the front nine, and you took a lunch break, and now you have to go back out there. (Have I told you yet how much I love golf? We have a lot to get to. I better wrap this concert up!)

So how do we start it up again? You usually can't go up-tempo. It depends on the vibe of any particular night, but usually, the crowd's not ready for it again. You have to build up to it. So you find something midtempo, something romantic. It's got to be heartfelt and soulful, something they can groove to. And something I can groove to! I believe that when I'm really feeling it, the audience can sense that. So I'll play a song like "Going Home" or "Heart and Soul"—something that's full of feeling, a song that says to the audience, Sit back and enjoy this. We are starting the final chapter of this concert, and we are doing it together.

After that I can do something a little bit more up-tempo and build some tension before I do my biggest cadenza. I know that this cadenza is going to go over the heads of most people—it's fast and furious solo sax playing like they've probably never heard before. Hopefully they're awed by the technique enough to stick with it and maybe even love it a little. It's not easy listening by any means—despite what the critics say, that's not my goal and never has been—but it's super challenging, and it's my way of seeing if I can bring all the technique that I practice every day in my three-hour practice session to the stage. It's something that gets my attention, and I do this mostly for me. But I also try to present it in a way that lets the audience absorb the experience, the excitement and the frenzy of all those notes and patterns. I have to say that after thousands of cadenzas, I think it works, and I think this is the right time for it during the show.

After that we can coast home. I'll do one of the other big crowd-pleasers—like the song that started it all, "Songbird," if I haven't done it yet, or "Over the Rainbow" or the theme from *Titanic*—and we're done.

So there you go. That's how you build a Kenny G concert. Warning: don't try this at home. These are professional drivers on a closed course. It's tougher than it looks.

But seriously, I do think a lot about all that, and I think about it for one reason. I want people to walk away feeling like they had an incredible musical experience. I'm sure that after the show is over, a lot of people probably leave and can't remember a single song I played, but they walk away knowing they loved the *feeling* of being at my concert. Maybe they came expecting to hear "Songbird" and hold hands in the dark with their boyfriend or girlfriend and have a quiet romantic time. Of course we gave them that, but we also got them excited and happy and moving and grooving and took them on a whole bunch of musical journeys. And we all had fun doing it.

We laughed together and maybe shed a tear or two together, and I think a lot of the people who came were pleasantly surprised, because they didn't expect all that. We took them on a journey of what I truly believe is the highest level of musicianship, and I say that as a proud tribute to all of the people who join me on stage and who have dedicated their lives to being the best on their respective instruments.

If you are looking for the reasons that we're having the good fortune to be able to still play and attract an audience after forty years, I believe the way we deliver an exceptional concert experience is certainly an important one. And when people tell me that that's the experience they had at a Kenny G concert, nothing could make me happier.

I can't talk about the concert experience without discussing one other part in a little more detail, and that part is my audience. There is one element of my audience that I'm particularly proud of and that I think makes our concerts special. And that is, it's a very *everything* audience. Here's what I mean. We have Black people, and white people, and young people, and old people, and people who think they're hip, and people who know they're square and don't care, and everything in between.

The multiracial makeup of our audience is particularly important. People ask me about it all the time. I've been told that in the early eighties, I had by far the most multiracial audience around. I think it's different now—the music world isn't quite as segregated as it was then—but in the eighties, it was much more uncommon.

I was first made aware of this in Birmingham, Alabama, around 1987. After the concert, the promoter came up to me, and his eyes were really wide, like he'd seen something he'd never seen before, and that's exactly what he told me.

He said for years at that venue, concerts were either a Black performer with a Black audience or a white performer with a white audience. He said he'd never been to a concert in Birmingham with such a mixed crowd.

I guess I hadn't noticed it because I've been around that kind of crowd all my life. Actually, as I said before, all our earlier gigs were in front of mostly Black audiences because our music was mostly played on Black stations. So when a concert in LA was put on by the Wave—that's

KTWV, the "adult contemporary / smooth jazz" station that was one of the first to play our music—it was mostly a Black audience because that was a major segment of their listenership. But when we started hitting the pop charts and that audience would show up, we'd have a half-Black and half-white audience.

Watching how the power of music was affecting the makeup of my audience and bringing people together was humbling, and it made me feel extremely proud. I mean, of course I was just happy that more people were coming out to see us, but the makeup of the audience made me feel that I was bringing cultures together a little bit, cultures that didn't usually go to the same concerts together, and that's something to be proud of, I think.

Because I grew up in a multiracial environment and had been welcomed into Black venues as a white performer, I felt like I could relate to all the members of my audience and speak to them all with the proper respect. I'd make jokes that everybody could laugh at together, and make sure I didn't cross certain lines. It was around this time that I started giving away a Kenny G–model saxophone at every gig, and I remember once in Hampton, Virginia, out of an almost entirely Black crowd, a white guy won the sax. As he came up on stage and I handed it to him, I turned to the audience and with a deadpan look on my face said, "Of course, of all the people to win the saxophone, it has to be the white guy." That got a big laugh, but I patted the guy on the arm to make sure he was feeling comfortable too.

From my perspective, it was a very funny moment, and I felt very connected with everyone in the crowd. It's like talking about the elephant in the room in just the right way that makes everyone feel acknowledged and respected.

Including the elephant.

Acknowledgment and respect: two very important, very powerful ideas.

The age range of my audience is something I first noticed later, when I began doing shows in Asia. From what I've seen, Asian families generally go to concerts all together more than American families do.

Kids in America, from my vantage point, don't seem to like to go to the same concerts as their parents. But in Asia, there was much more of a sense of the family doing things all together, and the kids seemed to feel that if their parents and grandparents were going to go see this American sax player, then they wanted to come too and be part of the family experience.

When I got back home, I noticed that the crowds at my concerts were breaking that American stereotype as well. So many moms and their sons, and dads and their daughters, would come up to me after the show and tell me how my music was one of the few things they liked to listen to together. How wonderful to know that my music was part of a shared experience bringing families closer together. I can't tell you how much that means to me.

As you can see, a lot of thought goes into putting on our show. From the songs and the dynamics to the sequencing, from the tempos and solos to the talking points—it's all really important. And equally important is my wonderful audience, because without that support, we wouldn't be able to keep doing the thing we love to do more than anything else in this world. Thanks, everybody!

CHAPTER TWELVE

Okay, time to take a short time-out from the music world to talk about the two things I love most in the world.

Flying and golf!

Just kidding. I do love those things—and I'll get to them in a bit—but it was around this time in my life that I got married; it was a marriage that ultimately wouldn't last, but which gave me the two greatest gifts of my life.

My two sons, Max and Noah.

Like a lot of guys, I wasn't sure I was ready to be a dad, but at thirty-six years old I thought I was old enough to figure it out and not mess it up too badly. As you've seen by now, I like learning how I can become the best I can be at whatever I do. I enjoy the learning process in general, but especially when I'm learning about things that interest me. So I consider myself a perpetual student about almost everything, and that includes parenting. I think I have pretty good instincts, so my mindset about parenting was that if I didn't know how to do something, or if I needed to improve something I was doing, I thought I would be able to learn along the way. And I had confidence that I would be a great father.

I always assumed that I would have boys. My dad has three brothers, and I have a brother, and he has two boys. So I guess I figured we were a boy kind of family. Turns out I was right.

I wasn't worried about all the little things that went with bringing up a baby, like holding their heads right, changing diapers, dealing with crying, and so on.

Some things were pretty easy right off the bat. For example, I think it's safe to say that I'm pretty handy around the house, and as it so happens, if you can change a tire, you can change a diaper just as easily. Besides, the lug nuts are a lot looser.

I think you all know by now that I wasn't going to leave anything to chance and just hope the good ideas would come, so I started doing research. A lot of it. I read a lot about parenting and the different approaches to things like where babies should sleep, what to do if they cry, how to talk to them, and so on. I took what I wanted from my research but also let my natural instincts come into play. I was fairly sure that if I was able to create beautiful songs, the same creativity would help me figure out how to produce a beautiful and nurturing vibe for my kids and make a place where a wonderful and long-lasting relationship with them would form.

But I also learned a lot more useful things from my research too. I want to share a few key things that I learned about parenting that I think worked really, really well.

Let me say this: I want to share this because I feel I have such a very close and wonderful relationship with my two adult sons, who are leading healthy and happy lives of their own, and I don't think all of that happened by chance. But in no way do I think I know better than anyone else about parenting, or am I taking full credit for how everything turned out. Okay, disclaimer done. Here's my parenting story.

Let's start off with the concept of sleeping. When you talk to new parents, you always hear one of two things: I'm not getting enough sleep, and it's driving me crazy; or, The baby won't go to sleep, and *that's* driving me crazy.

I focused on the second crazy first. How do you achieve the magical, mystical ability to get babies to actually close their eyes without them crying for an hour first?

One of the books I liked a lot talked about not leaving your baby alone. It's part of human history. And it made sense to me. Years ago, when a baby was born in a village, they wouldn't put the child in a separate little hut in the nighttime. The baby was always going to be close to somebody. This concept really resonated with me, and I wanted to try it with my kids.

So when my kids were little, they were never left alone in the nighttime. When they called out, I wanted them to always feel like someone was close by.

I wanted them to feel that the universe is a caring place, that if you reach out for love, you'll find it. And that Dad's there for you. That felt right to me.

It also meant that I didn't get a lot of solid sleep during these early years, but that was okay because I wasn't a really sound sleeper back then anyway. I woke up a lot in the night, even on my own. So I thought, Hey, this is cool! Now when I wake up, there will be something to do. I can look at or play with my baby boy! Fun!

Now, when my boys got older, it was different. I was now able to talk with them, explain things, and that changed the equation. So now I could explain to them why, for example, it's better to not suck your thumb, or that it's not good to eat too much chocolate. Or that everyone will benefit from a really solid night's sleep, so it's time for you to sleep in your own room. But before that, I felt they were just too young to comprehend these concepts, so what was the point of trying to teach a lesson that was unteachable? It didn't make sense to me.

And eventually, they did start sleeping in their own rooms. And there was no trauma or drama about it. I'd sit with them for a while as they were falling asleep, then come back and check on them often enough that they always knew that Dad was close by. That made them feel safe, and that made them calm. And that made them fall asleep feeling peaceful, which gave me a warm feeling too. For me, that was better than having them cry it out on their own.

And it was even more satisfying because I got to feel the sweet pleasure of figuring out how to keep my kids from enduring any unnecessary trauma.

All that said, I have to also say that I was very lucky I didn't have a regular nine-to-five gig. There's no way I would have been able to do all that if I had to wake up early and be ready for work.

The other thing I made sure to do—starting when the boys were very little—was to keep a work-life balance. When I ask my kids now, "When you were growing up, did you feel like I wasn't around enough, because I had to go on tour?" they look at me like I'm crazy.

"You were *always* around," they say (with a little more annoyance in their voices than I care to admit, but let's let that pass). I'm proud of the fact that when I was home I was fully present. That made a huge difference.

It's true that I was touring about 90 days a year. But for the other 275 days, I was all in. I mean, *all* in. I did laundry, I cooked, I played games, I focused on them totally. Even when they went to high school, I was the one to drive them to school every morning. That made me very happy. I loved being a dad! And still do. Every day.

As time went by, I realized, Hey, maybe I am ready to be a parent! I started developing my own philosophy. As I said, some of it came from books I read, but most of it came from the way I approached anything, from playing the sax to fixing a toaster: Pay attention. Have patience. Figure it out the best you can, try it out, and tweak when necessary.

So as I kept doing my research on improving my parenting skills, and as I kept asking smart people for their opinions about it, it became clear to me that there is one skill that a lot of kids never get the chance to develop on their own during their childhoods: decision-making. Kids don't often get the chance to make their own decisions, because grown-ups have told them what to do, and even how to feel, all of their lives.

"Don't cry about that."

"Pick that up."

"Go do this."

"Eat your vegetables."

"Do your homework."

"Hang up your towel."

It's all orders. And kids will follow those orders because they are kids; they want to please their parents, and they usually aren't in a position to oppose what their parents say anyway.

I started thinking about how I could help them develop their decision-making skills but still get them to do what I wanted them to do. I also wanted to support their feelings without shutting them down. And try to figure out how to give them information but let them make their own decisions.

The thing I had going for me was that, as a jazz improvisationalist, I wasn't afraid to try new things—assuming they weren't going to cause any permanent harm, of course—and just see what worked.

And some of them started working pretty well.

For example, their stuff is lying all over the floor, and I want them to pick it up. Option one, of course, is, "Hey, guys, go pick that stuff up before we do anything else." But here's what I tried instead: "Oh God, there's stuff all over the floor again. I hate seeing stuff on the floor. It makes me so mad. I sure wish that stuff would get put away." Now, did I say I was angry at them? No. I said I was angry because there was stuff on the floor. It was my problem, not theirs. I don't like it when things are messy. And I didn't tell them to pick it up either; I just said I wished it would happen. Inside, of course, I'm as calm as could be. But outside, I'm looking pained. ("And the winner for best parent actor in a dramatic role goes to . . .")

Guess what? Right from the first time I tried it, they started scurrying around, picking stuff up. Because they didn't like seeing their dad upset.

So I started thinking about that—about giving information instead of orders—and the more I tried it, the more it worked for us. So when I wanted them to go to bed, here's how it went:

"It's bedtime."

"I don't wanna go to sleep."

"Yeah, I know, but it's bedtime."

"Dad, I hate going to sleep."

"I know! Me too! I love it when I get to stay up late. I wish it wasn't bedtime! But it is. Darn it."

This would go on for a while—but at some point, they'd realize, there's no escaping bedtime. Because it's simply a fact that it's bedtime, and no one, not even Dad, can do anything about that. And they'd decide to go to bed.

Let me say that one more time for emphasis: *they* would decide to go to bed. I kept giving them the disappointing news that in fact it was bedtime. That I wasn't happy about it either and I hate bedtime sometimes too, but lo and behold, there is nothing we can do. It's just bedtime.

The idea of helping them learn to make their own decisions led me to something else that was important: letting them learn to deal with their own feelings. If they were upset about something that happened, I'd make sure first, of course, that they weren't physically hurt, and then I'd cuddle them, and hold them, and soothe them, but I wouldn't try to make the tears stop right away.

Believe me, I recognized in myself the powerful urge to try to make them feel better—I think all parents experience that—but I wanted to give my kids a chance to deal with their feelings themselves, without shutting them down. I'd say, "I know it's hard." Or "I know it's not fun." I wanted them to feel that I could relate to why they were angry or why they were crying. I wanted them to feel loved and cared for. And I would leave it at that. I wasn't trying to fix anything.

And it worked, because they felt valued and heard. They felt like their experiences and feelings mattered—something everyone wants, no matter what age they are. And as a result—even though it was hard for all of us in those moments—my boys grew up to be men who can handle it when times get tough.

When I look back on it, I know I did everything I could to give them the best chance to be functioning adults who are not afraid to make decisions. And who aren't afraid to deal with their feelings. And when they do have a problem, guess who they come to? They come to the person who was always nurturing to them. Who listened to them. Who was their comfort place. Good old Dad (who is getting old, and I wish I had a fix for that; I'm working on it and will share when I solve it!).

People ask me what it was like for my kids to grow up with a celebrity dad. I have to say I'm extremely lucky—I have a unique career in that I have had a lot of success, but I'm not the kind of guy the media was very interested in. Other folks in the so-called top twenty-five have their entire lives dissected by the media—from the Beatles to Barbra Streisand—but for some reason, I guess I was never that interesting. I'm not insulted! It means I get to live my life, go to Whole Foods and do the shopping, without it showing up on Page Six of the *New York Post.*

I guess some of that had to do with achieving fame before the era of social media, so there weren't a thousand folks with cameras posting about me all the time. Clearly that didn't stop the paparazzi from going crazy over other members of my generation, but I got a pass. The best part of it was that my kids could live a normal life. When I showed up for back-to-school night, it wasn't like there was a big clamor. I brought them to school just about every day anyway, so people were used to the skinny guy with the long (beautiful!) hair hanging around.

When they were old enough and it worked out with their school schedules, they'd come on the road with me too. Max came on a tour of Russia with me once when he was in his teens, and we all went to China when I played at the opening of the Special Olympics in Shanghai. The three of us performed together at one point—we did "Over the Rainbow" at Orchard Hall in Tokyo. I was very proud because they both played their parts as well as any professional, even though they were still under eighteen years old. The audience gave us a very warm round of applause, which I think was as much for my family as for the actual performance itself.

I am so happy and proud of the fact that my relationship with my boys remains great to this day. And I'm very, very proud of the men that they have become. I know that I tried my best to keep them grounded and not too entitled. And that was challenging, given the fact that they grew up with a celebrity dad and the lifestyle that goes with that. But I can tell you that they turned out to be nice, hard-working people.

I support their careers in the same way my dad did. As long as they're pursuing something they truly love and believe in, I'll help them along the way. And guess what? For both of them, that something is music!

That's right. They went into their dad's business. I hope they are grateful I didn't become an accountant or take over the plumbing-supply company (not that there's anything wrong with either of those).

I didn't push them into it. I try to stay out of the way and let them find their own paths. Max started on sax, but he didn't like it. He's a phenomenal guitarist now. I'm grateful he didn't stick with the sax, because knowing how good he would have gotten, well, I don't want the competition! Max has a heavy metal band and is making his own records now. I help him where I can, but he knows that I can't make it happen for him. I can open some doors, but his success will be dependent on his own skills. There is no shortcut to success in the music industry. I think he has what it takes, and I believe that if he sticks with what he is doing, it will work out for him.

Noah's more into the composing side. His passion is doing film scores, and he's working with one of the top composers who do music for major films. He got that position on his own, and with his skills developing and his experience growing, it's only a matter of time. He definitely has the talent. So just like with his brother (and father), the lesson is, stick with it, keep developing your skills, and keep working hard, and things will work out. I'm grateful that I can provide them both with the space they need to develop their respective skills. I'm very proud of that, and of both of them.

Would it matter to me if they weren't in the music business, or if they weren't on their way to becoming successful? Not one bit. The main thing is that I raised two really nice, solid guys. And *that* matters to me more than anything in the world.

CHAPTER THIRTEEN

Okay, back to the late eighties, everybody. When we last left off, I was having a great time on the *Duotones* tour. But now it was time to get back to the studio. And to break another stereotype.

Historically, instrumentalists get one big hit, and that's it. Herb Alpert had a huge success with "A Taste of Honey," which wasn't hurt by having a naked lady covered in whipped cream on the album cover. He then went on to have many number one albums, and another number one hit with a vocal version of "This Guy's in Love with You." But after "A Taste of Honey," he never had another top instrumental hit. Chuck Mangione had his one hit with "Feels So Good." Then there was Spyro Gyra's "Morning Dance" and my hero Grover Washington Jr.'s "Just the Two of Us"—all fantastic songs, all big hits, and all the only big mainstream hit each of those guys had. And so that's what everybody figured was going to happen to little old me. Kenny's had his hit with "Songbird," he had a big tour based on its success, and that's it.

Wrong!

There wasn't any question in my mind, not because I thought I was any better than the guys who came before me, but because I knew I hadn't set out to write a hit record. I hadn't gotten a big-time producer to take my stuff, add their input, and produce the hell out of it in order to make it a hit. I had sat alone in my small, improvised studio and let my heart guide what was going to flow out through my sax, and with very little modification, that's what went out on the air. I hoped that if I stayed true to that, then whatever magic connected "Songbird" to an audience could—and would—happen again.

So my plan after the *Duotones* tour was to do basically the same thing. My plan was to tune out the negativity about how hard it is to have a second instrumental hit, as well as any advice about what made "Songbird" a hit, including all the well-meaning suggestions on how I could duplicate that success. (And believe me, a lot of people tried to share their thoughts on all of this with me.)

Come hell or high water, I was going to do it again, my way. To listen to what was in my heart and let it come out of my sax. I went into my studio to do just that. Except it wasn't exactly a studio. More like a bedroom. In fact, exactly like a bedroom. Because it *was* my bedroom.

By this point, I'd moved to a small apartment in the Sherman Oaks area of Los Angeles, on Dickens Street, right off Ventura Boulevard. Now, you might be wondering why I was renting a small apartment after having had such a big hit with "Songbird." Well, even though my records were making a lot of money, I hadn't seen any of it yet, and I don't like to live beyond my means. So even though I knew the money was coming—or at least, I hoped it was—all I could afford at that time was a small apartment, so that's where I was living. And my bedroom turned into a makeshift studio.

I decided to record my first song for my new album the way I did on the *Duotones* album—all alone, with no one looking over my shoulder, giving me the thumbs-up or thumbs-down.

My bedroom seemed like the perfect place, except it was a wee bit smaller than good old "Studio G" at my old place. So I improvised. I put my keyboard on top of the bed and used that as my desk. I started with a little synthesizer arpeggio again.

Then I had to set up a way to play my sax along with it. I dangled the microphone by its cord off the bed and knelt down on one knee to point my sax at it. I didn't play too loudly, because I didn't want to

disturb the people in the apartment next door, and I think that contrib-
uted to the sound that I was starting to create. Softly, I began playing.
And what came out was "Silhouette."

It was a very different melody than "Songbird" but, to my ear, just
as beautiful. And most important, it sounded the way I felt inside. That's
all that mattered to me. I felt like I was speaking in a language I'd been
learning since high school, the language of the sax—my sax—and I was
writing poems in that language and talking to people in that language
and commenting on life in that language, and the more I stayed true to
what it was letting me say, the more I wanted to say it. And the more
beautiful it sounded to me.

The rest of the album was recorded all over town. One of the songs on
that album was "Pastel," left over from my sessions in Sausalito—a beautiful
melody that I love, although it never wound up getting much attention.

Another one of those songs turned into a funny favorite. I wrote
a funky song called "Against Doctor's Orders." I called it that because
of what had happened a little while back, when I'd broken my thumb.
I was sitting in my old Datsun 240Z with my thumb hooked into the
little spokes of the steering wheel when someone backed into my car,
and the wheel jerked and broke my thumb. So I had a cast on, and the
doctor told me not to play sax until it healed. But Clive Davis and Burt
Bacharach called to say they were doing a song Burt had co-written for
Dionne Warwick called "Love Power," and they asked if I would play on
it. Of course I said I would, even though it was against doctor's orders.

That phrase was in my mind, as I still had the cast on, when I wrote
this funky number for the new album. So I called it "Against Doctor's
Orders." When we did the video for that song, we based it on that idea—
only we took it to hilarious extremes. Dudley Moore played the doctor,
and he was absolutely hysterical. He looks at my x-ray and tells me I'm
dying and to stop playing the sax. I say, "But Doctor, sax is my life,"
and he looks at this big buxom nurse and says, "*Sex* is my life too!" He
makes some boob jokes to the nurse, who is played by his wife, Brogan
Lane; they seemed very funny at the time, although today, of course,
they'd be extremely offensive. But those were different times.

Just when I'm trying to figure out what to do about the doctor's orders, an angel appears and says, "Go forth, Kenny! Play that funky music, white boy!" And the rest of the video is all these funny things happening in the hospital while I'm playing my sax. For example, my best friend, Roger Rose (who, as I said earlier, was one of the original VJs on VH1), is in it doing silly stuff like taking a bubble bath. My sax music brings people back from the dead, and Dudley Moore is hamming it up all over the place. It was super fun, and funny too.

I have to say that one of the biggest highlights of making this album was the chance to work with one of the all-time greats, Smokey Robinson. "We've Saved the Best for Last" was a cool song that a friend of mine named Lou Pardini co-wrote. I had met him in Los Angeles, and he sat in on keyboards with me a few times, and somehow Clive got Smokey involved.

If you watch the music video of that song (don't you love YouTube?), it looks like Smokey and I are having a ton of fun together. And there's one simple reason for that: we were! And here's a bit of trivia for you: it was the one and only time I wore glasses in a video. I got contacts after that and have had LASIK since then, so that's some rare archival footage right there.

Smokey was a super awesome guy. One of the biggest talents on the planet, but so down to earth. He was gung ho to do it, and I was gung ho to do it, and we had the best time. There's a lot of down-time when you're shooting a video, so we got to hang out and talk, and it was a pleasure. He is truly one of the nicest guys in music.

My favorite video from that album was the one we did for the song "Silhouette," which became the big hit from that album. It's a simple video—it shows me walking down the street after a gig, going into a fancy restaurant, playing my sax, and then walking home alone—but there's something so sweet and beautiful about it. Very cinematic. The director understood the music and got the look that matched the vibe of my melodies. This was the first time I saw myself playing my sax and actually liked what I saw, because it captured the vibe of what I feel in a lot of my songs. It was very romantic, and a little playful and funny, and warm and beautiful and melancholy all at the same time. That's what I feel when I hear this song, anyway, and when I see the video.

If you want to know my least favorite video I ever did, check out "Hi, How Ya Doing?" On second thought—please don't! It's so embarrassing. It was from my second album; I was just starting out, and I thought that I had to do whatever the record company thought I should do, which for some inexplicable reason included singing and breakdancing. It hurts to even think about. So let's move on.

By the way, if you want to know why I called the album *Silhouette*, it's because I'm superstitious. Remember how I called the earlier album *Duotones* because it was the name of the process the photographer used to make the cover art? Well, when we took the back cover photos for this album, you can see that it's a shadow. I looked at it and said, "That's a nice silhouette," and then I said, "Hey! There you go! That's the name of the song. And the album."

Sometimes these things are pretty easy.

And in the end, the song "Silhouette" did what I was basically told was impossible—it broke the one-hit-wonder jinx that had befallen so many instrumentalists before me. People liked it, it ended up being a bona fide hit, and it did extremely well on the charts. It may be my most requested song that we play live.

Let's backtrack a little bit so I can explain why Dudley Moore was someone I could call a friend (and someone who would make a video with me). How the heck did that happen?

Dudley Moore and I became good friends after I recorded some of his songs with him at his home studio in Los Angeles. Imagine getting a call out of the blue from one of the biggest movie stars in the world. (And how did he get my number?) But that's what happened, and I went over to his house to hear his music, and I was blown away by his musicianship and melodic touch. I actually hadn't known he played piano. Anyway, that's how we became connected and how he came to be part of my "Against Doctor's Orders" video. He was one of the nicest, funniest, and most interesting guys I've ever known.

People know him as part of the English comedy boom in the early sixties, doing the kind of thing that led to *Monty Python's Flying Circus* a few years later. And of course his big role as Arthur in the movie of the same name. But a lot of people (like me) didn't know that he was a terrific piano player—somewhere between classical and jazz, although he did a number of great jazz albums in the sixties.

He had his own way of composing, and he created these memorable melodies and captivating songs. I played on six or seven of the cuts on the album he was working on, which was called *Songs without Words*, but then Clive Davis put the kibosh on it. He said it wasn't going to be good for my career because there was already too much of my stuff out there, and he didn't want to flood the market. "If people want to hear you," he said, "let them buy your records." I understood his reasoning and it made sense, but I'd promised Dudley that I would be on his record, and when I promise something, I keep my word. Period.

So I simply said, "Clive, I'm playing on this record."

His response was simpler: "Okay, but you can play on just one song."

My response was a little more complicated: "Clive, there's no way I'm playing on just one song. How about four?"

We continued in that vein until we compromised on two. I was very apologetic to Dudley but also glad I could work it out with Clive to do the two songs. This is why you hear me on only two cuts of that album. (I wonder where the other mixes that I played on are!)

It broke my heart, in the nineties, when Dudley was diagnosed with a degenerative brain disorder. At first his symptoms weren't terrible—he couldn't remember his lines, he had difficulty playing—but they made him more and more depressed. The disease progressed rapidly. The friend who was with him when he died said his last words were, "I can hear the music all around me."

I hope so, Dudley. I hope the music carried you through. I hope I made you smile one-tenth as often as you made me smile.

Rest in peace, my dear friend.

Right after *Silhouette* came out, I was invited back to my old synagogue with my mom. It was Yom Kippur—the holiest of Jewish holidays—and I had been invited back to come blow the shofar. The shofar, which is usually an actual ram's horn, is blown during the service, and it's kind of a big deal. One of the key moments in the Yom Kippur service is when someone gets up and plays a certain series of notes on the shofar. You don't play it like a saxophone—it's more like a trumpet—but I was able to figure it out. I was honored to be doing it, and happy to be doing it in front of my mom.

At the end of the series of notes, the person blowing the shofar is supposed to hold the last note for a long, long time—it's called *tekiah gedolah*, the "great blast" that signifies the end of the Yom Kippur fast.

Now, of course, I have the circular-breathing technique, and I decided to use it for this big note! My back was to the congregation, so they couldn't see my face. I held the note, and held it, and held it. Could this be the longest anyone had ever held it in the history of this synagogue, or maybe in the history of the Jewish people? Who's gonna argue?

After holding the note for a very, very long time, I turned around and looked at the congregation. They were looking at me like it was some kind of miracle, like God had given me the breath the way he gave them the light that shone for eight days on Chanukah. It was sweet and funny, a wonderful light way to end the seriousness of the holiday. The perfect moment.

Or so I thought.

As I walked from the pulpit back to my seat, everyone was shaking my hand. Touching me like they were trying to get a second-hand connection to God through me. It was very touching to see so many people so moved by what I had done. It truly was a spiritual connection that everyone was feeling together.

Well, not *everyone*.

When I got back to my seat, my mom looked over at me and said, in a very condescending tone (and I quote), "This is not a show."

Ouch! That hurt. But despite her downer vibe—or maybe because of it—I came away that day with a very valuable lesson that I've repeated time and time again: when you do things from your heart, with the right intentions, for the right reasons, and to the best of your abilities, you don't need to get anyone's approval to feel good. It's about knowing your own value, as a person. It's not about needing to get that from outside. You don't have to wait for someone else to tell you your worth. You just have to know it yourself.

I know how hard I work at my craft. I know I have talent, I know I treat the people around me with respect and kindness, I know that sometimes my music inspires, and I also know I don't need anyone, including my mom, to tell me those things.

Despite what happened that day, I walked out of that synagogue a happy man.

And I've pretty much stayed that way ever since.

My mom passed away not too long after that. It was a terribly hard experience for me and my family, but at least I felt that we'd come to respect each other in the end. She had a terminal condition, and we all knew she was going to pass away in the near future, so as we spent time with her in those final days, I took the lead and talked to her about things that I had held inside, since I knew this would be my last chance to do so. We ended up having some real heart-to-heart conversations before she passed, and that helped me so much.

I asked her directly why she never said "I love you" to me, or told me that she was proud of me and my accomplishments. When I got to play Carnegie Hall, she was there, and even then I didn't really hear it.

She looked away for a second, then turned back and said, "You were always a happy and confident person. You didn't need it. And it's a given that a mother would feel that way about her child, so it didn't need to be said." When she said that, I thought, Well, that makes sense. I can see now that her coming to see me at Carnegie Hall was her way of "saying" it without actually saying it.

Well, I accepted that answer, and I guess it made me feel slightly better, but I also know that I completely disagree with that whole way of parenting, and I tell my kids daily how much I love them. I think this way is *way* better. I know it is.

As I think about my mom, I have to say I'm grateful to her because I know what I have achieved was due, at least in part, to her pushing us to work really hard, to accomplish the most that we could, to not being so warm and fuzzy with me, to expecting me to get straight As, and all that. Sure, this also created other issues for me—issues that I worked hard to overcome later in life—but it also created in me the drive to get as far as I could in whatever I tried to do.

For all this I say, Thank you, Mom. I love you.

My circular-breathing technique had become pretty famous around that time, largely because of Regis Philbin. I was on his TV show when he asked me, "I hear you can hold a note for a long time. Is that true?" I explained to him how it's done, holding air in your cheeks and pushing it out while you're breathing in through your nose. I demonstrated it, and of course his audience went wild—people love it—but by chance, the people from *The Guinness Book of World Records* happened to be in the green room at that very moment. They were going to appear later in the show to talk about some records that had been set, and when I ran into them afterward, they said, "You should try to set the world record for the longest note ever held on a saxophone."

I thought it was a funny idea, so I asked them what the current record was, and they told me it didn't exist. "Well, then," I said, "it won't be hard to set the record, will it!"

We joked about it for a while, but I agreed to do it. I told them I could probably go ten minutes, and their response was, "Whoa, that would be awesome!" A little while later, we set it up at a music store way downtown in New York called J&R Music World. When I showed up, they had a whole audience of people who had heard I was going to perform! I said, "Guys, I'm just gonna play one long note. Don't pay any attention, because it's gonna be incredibly boring for you." But they stuck around anyway.

The *Guinness* folks had set some rules—I had to play the same note the whole time, they had a meter to make sure the volume stayed the same, all that stuff. I actually didn't know how long I could go for—and please, no sax jokes here!—but I was about to find out.

So I stood up and started playing an E-flat. And ten minutes went by. And then twenty. And twenty-five. And I thought, Seriously? And then thirty, and thirty-five, and I thought, Oh my God!

And at forty-five minutes and forty-seven seconds, I finally stopped. Here's the thing: Try not swallowing for forty-five minutes! Eventually, saliva's going to build up somewhere, and it finally got between my reed and my mouthpiece. The sound broke for a split second, and so I was stopped by the *Guinness* folks. (I actually could have kept going!) But I was still very happy with the end result.

And the first thing I did afterward was go and put ice on my lips. It ain't easy setting records!

The other wild thing that happened around this time was that my music became insanely popular.

In China.

I'd played there first in 1986, and from the start, I was stunned to find out how popular my music was over there. Budweiser sponsored my first tour, and it was in two of the major cities—Beijing and Shanghai—and there was an enormous amount of publicity. Budweiser put up these gigantic billboards on the highway with my big face and a big beer can that said, "The King of Beers—and the King of Saxophones." People were recognizing me and coming up to me in restaurants—in China! Where I'd never been! It was absolutely surreal.

I started going back there just about every year. But it was during the time that we released a collection of performances called *Kenny G Live* in 1989 that things got *real* surreal. (Is that a thing? Real surreal? Why not!) That album included a song of mine that I had been doing in concert but hadn't put on a record until now. It was called "Going Home."

Well, the next time I was in China, that song was everywhere. And

I mean everywhere! Shop owners started playing it at the end of the day to tell the workers that it was time to close up shop. They took the title literally and ran wild with it. It was their song for the end of the workday, the signal for everyone to go home. "Going Home" became ubiquitous in shopping malls, at gyms, at the end of the school day, at the last stop on a train, and as the last song at wedding celebrations. Insane! But super cool too.

I hadn't realized it during my first concert back. I played that song in the middle of my set, and when I finished and looked up, the place was empty—the audience had all left and gone home! (Okay, that's not really true. But I tell this joke a lot when I'm asked about how popular that song is in China, and it always gets a good laugh.)

In the documentary *Listening to Kenny G* by Penny Lane (yes, that's her real name, and she is a fantastic filmmaker—you should check out her brilliant films), she interviewed some music experts in China who tried to explain why my music is so popular there. One of them talked about the absence of certain notes in certain Chinese music and how songs like "Going Home" also skip those notes.

I don't pay attention to that approach to music. If someone says, "I love the way you left out the fifth in that chord and then went to the sharp nine," I always smile politely, but it goes in one ear and out the other. That stuff doesn't matter to me. Here's what matters to me, and why I think I'm so popular in China: it's all about the way something sounds, not why it works in theory or on paper. One day, I was sitting in the Four Seasons Hotel in Shanghai, having dim sum, noodles, vegetables, and rice—man, I love that stuff, so good and so much fun to eat—and I was listening to the music that was being piped out in the hotel. It was Chinese melodies, Chinese songs, and as I sat there, I thought, Wait a minute. This is why I'm so popular here! Because the music sounded so beautiful to my ears. Precious and lilting and uplifting and soul-satisfying. It was music that spoke to my sense of melody. These were melodies that I felt I could have written. I truly loved what I was hearing. So if I liked the traditional Chinese melodies and they felt to me like my own songs did, I figured that my melodies were connecting with the Chinese people in the same way. I sensed a deep connection to the emotion in that music, and I believe that people there sensed that deep connection to the emotion in mine.

Each time I go back—and I play for audiences throughout Asia—I see how deeply they seem to be relating to what I'm playing. It gives me great joy.

As, I hope, my music does for them.

By the way, I do want to take a moment to say that I had a wonderful time working on that documentary with Penny Lane. It was also a big learning experience for me because I had to give up creative control, and I think you know me well enough by now to understand that when it comes to my music and my art, that doesn't come easily to me. So I had to have an incredible amount of trust in Penny. If I had been in control, I don't think the documentary would have even gotten finished, because I would have gone into the minute details of, How did the sax sound in that clip? Did I like the words I used in that part of the interview? And more importantly, how did my hair look?

Penny made all the decisions, and I learned to be okay with things that I didn't think were perfect. Thanks, Penny, for the great documentary, and also for the great lesson in not missing the forest for the trees.

After *Duotones* and *Silhouette* had sold like ten million copies in total, and then we put out a live album that sold millions more, I felt like, Well, I don't think it's the best idea to put something out too quickly right now. It would feel like we were flooding the market with my music, and I know that's not a good thing to do, even though I'm sure we could have put out another record quickly and it would have done quite well. But after the success of the last three albums, I wanted to take my time and do something special. And I think I did.

It only took four years.

I started working on the new album as soon as I got off the road. I was excited because I was entering a brand-new realm. My work on this album coincided with the birth of digital recording. I had graduated from my eight-track machine and was up to twenty-four tracks now, but I was still laying everything down on big reels of analog tape, and the editing capability was still limited by the technology. But with digital recording, we had a lot more editing capability. I was able to work on my sax parts and tweak them like I'd never been able to tweak before. I could get melodies to be exactly the way I wanted, rather than "close enough" because that's the nature of the recording process. I could literally drop out a note I didn't like and replace it with one I did, with the press of a few buttons. For a perfectionist like me, that's like catnip.

But I don't like to use the word "perfectionist." As I said earlier, I do know that perfection is impossible to achieve on a regular basis. It's a nice goal to strive for, but you have to know that it's not something that you should measure yourself against.

That's why I talked earlier about "best efforts." If I can make something better by giving it my best effort, then I'm a happy guy. If my best efforts don't result in a better outcome, then so be it. I can walk away happy, knowing that I could not have done any more than I did. Because how can you do better than your best efforts? I wish I had known this a long time ago, but the truth is that I didn't. I was focused more on results. The good thing is I know I've evolved, and although it's taken a while to feel good about efforts rather than results, I've found it to be a much better and healthier way to live.

So anyway, that's what I was doing with this next album—tweaking and playing and giving everything my very best efforts, and because I had the new technology literally at my fingertips, it made everything a lot better.

I had moved into a bigger house at this point and was setting up a real cutting-edge studio for myself. I decided I wanted to work on a Sony 3348 digital recording machine—so-called because it had forty-eight tracks of digital recording. I mean, forty-eight tracks! How crazy could I go with one of those?

So I bought two.

They weren't cheap. But I bought two so I could have ninety-six tracks that I could use to do whatever I wanted. I could take a sax part and play it again and again and put those takes on fifteen or twenty different tracks. Then I could combine the best of each track and make it into one great sax performance. I learned how to do it from my engineer Steve Shepherd, who is one of the nicest and most talented guys I know. He showed me how to use this technology so that I could sit in my studio all by myself and experiment with parts and then edit and "comp" the parts—a music term that's short for creating a "composite" track, where you combine pieces from different takes—so that I could end up with what I wanted. And that is super fun and very satisfying. I never had a chance to comp different takes so freely before that machine was invented, and this allowed me to be more creative than I ever had been before.

The other great thing about the new technology was that I could mix the album right at home. I'd never done that before either, and I loved it. When everybody went home, I could sit and listen to what we'd done. These innovations were very much a part of what made my album *Breathless* so special for me. So if that album sounds a little different from what came before—and a little better, if I do say so—I have to give some of the credit to the birth of the digital age.

It came out in 1992, and the first song that was released as a single was "Forever in Love." I did all the writing on that and played all the instruments. And that was extremely satisfying—you know how I love to be in control as much as possible!

Saying the album did well is a huge understatement—it sold twelve million copies in the States and probably twenty million worldwide.

That meant so much to me. I felt like the world was truly acknowledging my process and my writing. Like I would never have to ask anyone anymore, Hey, is it okay if I put some of my own songs on my albums? In truth, I'd already won that argument with "Songbird" and "Silhouette," but it didn't hurt to keep proving the point.

At the same time I was always afraid that if the vocal songs the record company wanted me to put on the albums did really well, then I'd be pressured into doing more of those and possibly fewer of the instrumentals that I wanted to record *my* way. And in fact there were two vocals on this album, one by Peabo Bryson and one by Aaron Neville. They were great songs by two great artists, and come on, who wouldn't want those two on their album. They were magnificent. And they definitely added to the success of the album.

But once again the most successful song on my record was an instrumental that I wrote and performed myself. So that meant a lot.

I think the big question that *Breathless* answered was this: Now that I was recording differently than I had before, really tweaking things, was it going to make my music sterile? Was it going to take away the vibe that I had with "Songbird" and "Silhouette"? Was I going to mess everything up by being so meticulous with every note, now that I had the technical capability to do so? In short, recording *Breathless* that way was very different from the way I had done it in the past, but was it better?

My answer? Yes, way better. I had the control I wanted, so the end result was way closer to what was in my head and heart when I was imagining how the song would sound. Thank you, technology, for providing these super creative tools. They were invaluable to me, and when the world responded in such a positive way to my album, well, it solidified and justified this whole process for me. And that support meant the world to me.

So thanks, world, too!

There's one other thing about this period of time that I should probably mention.

My uncle had become an investor in a one-store coffee company in Seattle. The company was trying to expand, and he said to me, "You know, you've had some success. You should invest some money in this company."

So I said, "I don't know all that much about the coffee business, but okay, who else is investing?" It turned out that many of the well-known names in the business community in Seattle were, so I looked at how much they were investing and said, "Okay, I'll match what they are all doing." There were about ten of us.

So yes, I was one of the first investors in Starbucks. Good timing, right?

To help bring attention to the company as they opened at other locations in other cities, I would play at the openings. And to make it even better, a few years later, Starbucks came up with the idea of selling CDs at the counter in their stores—something that had not been done before. And the rest is history—a history I'm proud to be a part of.

And by the way—that first CD they sold?

Well, that's a story in and of itself.

CHAPTER FOURTEEN

So what was next for the Jewish guy from Seattle who gets called in to blow the shofar at his synagogue?

A Christmas album, of course.

It came about in the funniest way. Two things converged like two sticks you rub together to make a fire. The first happened at one of my shows around Christmastime. We were playing at the incredible Universal Amphitheatre. Remember how the first time I played there I was opening for George Benson? By this point I was headlining and had multiple sold-out shows. Crazy how life works.

In the early nineties, playing Christmas songs was not something most artists did. But I liked an arrangement for "White Christmas" that I had worked out with my old high school friend Robert Damper, who was playing keyboards with me (and, as I've mentioned, still is). It was simple and beautiful.

The second thing that happened was after the show. The famous actress Dyan Cannon, who I knew through mutual friends, came up to me and said, "You know, you should do a whole album of Christmas songs." As much as playing a Christmas song was not something most artists did on stage, doing a whole Christmas album was considered totally un-hip. Not like today, when everybody and their sister has a Christmas album out, in every genre. Back then, Christmas albums were traditionally done by folks like Elvis and Frank Sinatra and Johnny Mathis, veteran artists who had been around forever. Doing a Christmas album was kind of like doing a gig in Vegas. (And at that time doing a gig in Vegas was considered *really* un-hip. Now everyone from Lady Gaga to Drake is happy to play there. Boy, have times changed. In fact, if anyone has any connections for a residency in Vegas for me, please let me know!)

There were certainly not any jazz guys doing Christmas albums. Some of the jazz greats had done one or two Christmas songs at some point in their careers. But they were few and far between.

So I didn't give it much thought when Dyan suggested it. But then, by chance, Clive Davis suggested the same thing. I don't know if he also got the idea from hearing us do "White Christmas," but one day I was in his office, and he brought it up. The enormous success of *Breathless* meant there was a lot of attention on us, and I think it gave us the chance to do something a little different. But *this* different?

"Clive," I said, "what do you and I know about doing a Christmas album? We're both Jewish."

"Irving Berlin was Jewish," he said, "and he wrote 'White Christmas.'"

"Well," I said, "when you put it like that. If you're giving me a thumbs-up, then I guess I don't mind being in the company of Clive Davis and Irving Berlin."

And that's how it started. I didn't mind that no one else was doing Christmas albums—certainly no jazz instrumentalists—because, as you have probably figured out by now, I like doing things that other people aren't doing, and all I care about is how the music sounds to me and whether it feels like it comes from the heart.

We decided that the best way to approach this album would be to honor the songs themselves. Up until now, the recorded Christmas music I had heard didn't excite me at all. Artists were always trying to get cute and do ridiculous arrangements of these beautiful, classic melodies. Why is Nat King Cole's version of "The Christmas Song" the greatest one? When you hear "Chestnuts roasting on an open fire," why is it his voice you hear in your head? Because he made it classy and kept it simple. He's not putting a polka arrangement on "The Little Drummer Boy" or doing a salsa version of "God Rest Ye Merry, Gentlemen." I remember one artist doing an arrangement of "O Christmas Tree," and suddenly there was a big rock guitar solo in the middle. Yuck! We weren't going to do that.

Instead, we took each song on its own and thought, What is the classiest arrangement we can do? Arrangements that will stand the test of time. We already knew "White Christmas," and so we went with the version we were doing live, which was just a matter of staying true to that beautiful, beautiful melody. What next? "God Rest Ye Merry, Gentlemen." Okay, that almost sounds Jewish, because it's all in a minor key. So we let that be a sad song. We weren't going to soup it up and make it fun and happy. I wanted to let that melody sing on its own, and maybe it would even bring a tear to someone's eye, because it's so melancholy. But that's what it is, as a song, and we wanted to stay true to that.

How about "The First Noel"? Okay, a beautiful happy melody in a major key. Let's let it sound as sweet and pure and pretty as we can. "Silent Night"—a perfect gem of a song. All you have to do is not screw it up. If you're going to do a key change, make it the right key change.

We took that approach with each song: If you're going to make it build, how are you going to make it build? Kettledrums or strings? We broke down each song and tried to make each one a priceless little jewel.

There are two original songs on the *Miracles* album. One of the songs was dedicated to my baby son, Max, who was born a few months earlier. We wrote this little lullaby as an ode to the miracle of birth. That's how the album became *Miracles*.

The other original was "The Chanukah Song" (not to be confused with Adam Sandler's song of the same name!). We wrote that because I wanted this to be a holiday album, not just a Christmas album, and because there are so few Chanukah songs out there—and the ones that exist are, well, pretty terrible. I mean, up against all of the incredibly beautiful Christmas melodies, you have the six-note "Dreidel Song." The big news about the dreidel is that it's made of clay, and that's all you can think to say about the holiday? We can do better.

So it was important to me to write a Chanukah song. And that's why it's included on the album. It's a sad melody, but to me it's so heartfelt and pure, and it's the sound of the songs I heard growing up in a Jewish environment. That eastern European sadness is something that to me sounds absolutely beautiful. I think this song came out great, and I was proud to include it.

One of the biggest fans of that song, by the way, was Barbra Streisand. When she heard it, she also thought it was beautiful. She got in touch with me and said she wanted to write lyrics to it and make it a real vocal Chanukah song. This never happened, but the fact that she said that made me feel really proud.

Speaking of lyrics, I was happy that we were doing an all-instrumental album. But guess who wasn't? You got it. Clive Davis. As usual, he wanted a few vocals on the album.

I'd given in to him every time he asked that—which, of course, was on every album I'd done up until now—but this time, I fought him. And fought him. And fought him. And he fought me, and fought me, and fought me.

Now I want to say right away that we fought with smiles on our faces. It was frustrating, but I also knew that Clive was a wonderful guy who only had my best interests at heart. He cared so much. He saw me as a son, like he saw all of his artists as family. And the feeling was mutual.

Remember how I talked about giving my kids room to make their own decisions? Yeah, Clive might have thought of me as a son, but he wasn't that kind of dad.

Our argument dragged on until late October, when finally I said, "Okay, Clive, somebody's got to win this argument because the album has to come out in a couple of weeks."

To his everlasting credit, Clive said, "Well, if you insist on doing it your way, you'll be making a huge career mistake. But it's your record. You have to have the final say," which I thought was wonderful. I mean, I didn't like the part about the big career mistake. But I loved that he was saying it was my decision. He did tell me that if it was going to be all-instrumental that it was too long, and I had to take two songs off it, which I did reluctantly (but a few years later, when we made the second holiday album, I was happy to have two songs already in my pocket).

It's hard to go against the head of the company. If you do it your way and the album is a flop, you're going to get all the blame. But I've always been okay with that. Look, I'm a pilot. I'll tell you more about that in a bit, but for now I'd like to tell you about a well-known rule in aviation, which is that once you're up in the air, the pilot's always in charge. When you're flying the plane and air traffic control tells you to turn right but you don't think you should because there might be a mountain hiding behind those clouds, you don't turn right. You simply say, "Unable." Because as the pilot, you have the decision-making power. No one else. If I made bad decisions in my career, at least they'd be my own. That's why I never blame anybody else for anything. I'm never the victim—because I know I always had the choice to do it my own way.

So that's what we went with, and all that was left was to shoot the photos for the cover. The cover of the album features a beautiful little naked baby boy, which I guess evokes an image of the baby Jesus; but the truth of it is, it's the baby Max. I don't think my son ever minded my showing his little tushie to the world. It's a beautiful picture, and we've always both loved it, and loved that it's on the cover of an album that's in millions and millions of homes.

Miracles did really well—and it became the first CD sold at the counter of Starbucks. I'm sure that helped propel it to great heights.

Years later, when *Miracles* had become the number one Christmas album of all time (some charts say it's Elvis's album that tops the list, but I'm okay with being in that company!), I said, "Clive, you have to admit, I was right about keeping it instrumental."

He said, "Nope. Would've sold more if you would've listened to me." That's Clive!

Around this time, I started getting recognized for the work I was doing by my peers in the music industry. I had been nominated for Grammys a bunch of times in the 1980s, but now I started actually receiving awards. And as much as I don't do my music for awards, I have to say, it felt pretty nice.

One of the first awards—one I'm particularly proud of—was the NAACP Image Award for Outstanding Jazz Artist. I got the first one in 1994, for my album *Breathless*, and another four years later. Just to be in the company of those who've won the award—Miles Davis, Quincy Jones, Grover Washington Jr., Ella Fitzgerald, Wynton Marsalis, just to name a few—well, it's appropriate that I won for *Breathless*, because looking at that list takes my breath away. One of the reasons I'm so proud of that achievement is that I'm the only white guy on the list. The fact that I was honored twice by this prestigious organization is absolutely humbling.

A lot of other awards followed around this time. I won a Soul Train Music Award twice, was nominated for *Billboard*'s Top Pop Artist, and was the Favorite Adult Contemporary Artist at the 1994 American Music Awards, which was kind of stunning to me. I mean, I was up against Whitney Houston and Michael Bolton, and I didn't think for two seconds I would win, so when they opened the envelope and said my name, I was so flummoxed I kind of stammered my way through a totally lame speech. Oh well.

In 1994, I won my first Grammy for "Forever in Love." It also turned out to be my last Grammy. And I'm perfectly okay with that. I really didn't worry too much about the awards. Sure, they help a lot with album sales because of the worldwide exposure you get, and of course I care about that—but beyond that, you can't get too hung up on awards because they start to get you focused on what other people think of your music. The only way to keep making good music is to focus not on what they think but on what you think. That's what I think, anyway.

Of course, the awards ceremonies themselves are a lot of fun. One of my favorite moments was at the inaugural RIAA Diamond award ceremony in 1999. Those were the awards for albums that had sold more than ten million copies—a very elite group—and they had everybody there who had won the award, as well as all the record company icons. It was a big bash. I had won for my album *Breathless* and MC Hammer was there, along with Billy Joel, Boston, Elton John, Journey, and more, as well as record company executives like Clive Davis and Ahmet Ertegun.

I was posing for a picture with all of the other winners who were in attendance, when suddenly I felt somebody pinch my ass! I looked behind me, and there was Elton John with a big smile on his face. So when it comes to the awards I've won, I guess we have to add the "Elton John Thinks Your Ass Is Pinchable" Award to the list.

Just as I was not paying too much attention to the awards, I was paying even less attention to the critics. I was getting some great reviews, but some snarky reviews also started piling up along with the record sales and the awards, and I'll share a story about how I look at that, a story that pretty much sums it all up.

I was playing the Saratoga Jazz Festival in upstate New York in June 1987. "Songbird" had recently come out, and I was a fresh face, brand new, playing alongside greats like Dizzy Gillespie, Dave Brubeck, the Marsalis brothers, Roberta Flack, McCoy Tyner, and lots more. How cool is that? And there must have been about nine or ten thousand people in the audience.

The reviews came out the next day, and they were wonderful. Of course I was very pleased. So the next year, when they invited me back, I thought, Well, that went over pretty well last time. Let's do a pretty similar set. I didn't have a new record out, so I decided to stick with a lot of the same songs. Now, when I play those same songs night after night, there's still a lot of improv involved, so it still feels fresh every time, but the set list was close to the one from the year before. The only difference was that by now I had sold a lot more records.

Someone showed me one of the reviews from the same guy who the previous year had called me "innovative" and praised my "great musicianship." What did it say this year? "He's gone commercial" and "His music is full of fluff."

Now, I am positive I was a better saxophone player than I had been the year before. About one thousand practicing hours better. I also know the music and performance was better than the year before, when I had received good reviews. But I think this particular jazz reviewer was angry that I had sold a lot of records. We played the same basic set but better, and the same guy who had loved me a year before gave us a shitty review this time because in his mind I'd become a commercial artist. The fact that I appealed to a lot of people must have meant that there was something inferior about the music.

That's when I learned, early on, not to worry about what the guy typing away behind his desk thinks. No matter whether the review is bad or good. In other words, don't get worried about the bad reviews, and don't get too pleased with the good reviews either.

There is one other thing about jazz critics I should probably mention, though. Because I believe it's likely that a lot of their criticism of me boils down to this: Because my music is so popular, they are convinced that for a lot of kids today, Kenny G is their only connection to jazz. And that upsets them. They believe that somehow I'm getting in the way of people listening to guys like Charlie Parker or Miles Davis or Stan Getz or any of the great masters from the fifties and sixties. I think that is such a lame point of view. Here's why. They are missing a much bigger picture. I believe that what happens way more often is that people who didn't know they liked instrumental music discovered that they did through my music, and because of that, they then went on to discover guys like Coltrane and Miles and Getz.

I want to point out that, in fact, I know that a lot of kids *do* hear about Charlie Parker and Miles Davis and Stan Getz. And you know who they hear about them from? They hear about them from me.

As I mentioned earlier, at my concerts I take a moment and change the mood of my live show and figuratively bring everybody back to a jazz club in Greenwich Village in the late fifties and early sixties. I do a song by one of my heroes, Stan Getz. And another by John Coltrane. I play them in my own style, but I stay as close as possible to the feeling and spirit of the giants whose footsteps I'm following in because I want my audience to feel the greatness of the music of those jazz masters. Sometimes people come up to me after a concert and say, "Hey, I've been listening to Stan Getz, thanks to you." Or Coltrane, or Miles, or Dizzy Gillespie.

That makes me really happy.

I'll tell you what I did love the most about the awards shows: performing at them. It was always a great chance to get my music out there in front of millions of viewers, and whenever I got to perform, it was special. If you asked me whether I'd rather perform at the Grammys or win one, I'd pick performing every time. I'm not going to lie to myself. We all know that no one's watching the Grammys sitting on the edge of their seats waiting to see who wins Best Instrumental Album. When they give out that award, if you listen closely, you can hear the sound of a million toilets flushing all across America.

But the musical numbers? Those, for me—and I think, for a lot of people—are the highlight of the show. I thoroughly enjoyed the time I performed at the Grammys with Michael Bolton. We did a duet on the song "How Am I Supposed to Live without You" at the 1990 Grammys. That was truly epic.

Michael and I toured quite a bit after that. I first met Michael after I saw him on the TV show *Showtime at the Apollo*. I was in a hotel room, and here was this guy at the Apollo in Harlem with long, stringy hair who looked like a heavy metal rocker but had an absolutely incredible, soulful voice. I contacted him, and he started doing a few songs during my concerts, and when he did his first album, *Soul Provider*, I played on a few songs.

We had a kind of falling-out a few months later when the two of us had eight sold-out shows together at the Universal Amphitheatre in Los Angeles. The first show went fine. I was driving my car to the theater for the second show when I heard on the radio that Kenny G's show that night had been canceled. I started shouting at the radio, "How can it be canceled? I'm headed to the theater right now!" I found out that Michael had canceled it. He had flown in from the East Coast on a red-eye, and he was run down and his throat was sore. After doing the first show, he felt he had to cancel the second one. But he never bothered to call me or talk to me about it, and he made the decision to cancel the concert without any input from me.

I was pissed. And so were the six thousand people who showed up that night only to get turned away at the door. I am tenacious about never canceling a show, so this was a very sensitive issue for me.

When I finally got a chance to talk to Michael later that evening, I told him in no uncertain terms that I was extremely upset about canceling a show for the first time in my career. I said he should have been more responsible when it came to being prepared to do these eight sold-out shows; Michael insisted that he had to do what he had to do, and that was just the way it was. So I got even more pissed. Michael and I managed to make it through the rest of the shows but probably didn't say two words to each other and didn't talk for a long time after that.

Time heals all wounds, though, and a few years later, we ran into each other and started talking. He was on his way to Europe, and I said, "Hey, you know, I used to have you open for me when you first started out. How about returning the favor? You're big in Europe and I don't have a big following there. How about letting me open for you?"

The next thing you know, the two members of the Long-Haired Jewish Jazz-Pop Society were headed to Europe together. It saddens me to tell you that we had another disagreement of sorts. It all stemmed from me playing nine minutes too long during our set in Paris—not something that should have turned into a big deal, if you ask me. But it did turn into a big deal, and after that tour we stopped talking for another couple of years.

But once again, time healed the wounds, and a few years later we started hanging out together again and doing a few shows here and there. And guess what—no problems! It was great. I see now that doing a full tour together didn't work for us, but doing a few concerts now and then works really well. It's better to figure out what works instead of concentrating on what doesn't work and complaining or gossiping about it. But the most important thing I can say today, when I look back at my relationship with Michael, is this:

No matter who was right or who was wrong, just one thing really matters.

Only one of us still has great hair. Ha!

CHAPTER FIFTEEN

I did my next album, *The Moment*, back in Seattle in 1995, which was cool for me. I had moved back there for a while and set up a studio for myself. I'll always have a particular love for that album because it reminds me of returning to my roots.

But it was my next album that was the real departure. Clive was pushing me to do an album of the old classics—putting my own spin on the old tunes. This time, I didn't fight him on it at all. The reasoning was, we'd put out so much original material, I agreed with Clive that it would be better to not crowd the field or overstay our welcome. So we decided to try something different.

The Arista folks and I all worked together to pick the songs, and most were pretty well-known choices, like "Summertime" and "Over the Rainbow." But as always, I tried to invest them with my own sound. The result was *Classics in the Key of G*. I wish I could take credit for coming up with that name. I can't remember who thought of it, but I love it.

One of my favorite cuts on that album was "Body and Soul." That's a song that's been done by a million people (including Stan Getz, whose version is one of my favorites). I started by listening to as many versions as I could. I thought about what I liked and didn't like about each version, and something started to gel for me. With a standard like "Body and Soul," a lot of classic jazz versions start by playing the melody once and then kind of abandoning it, doing improvisational riffs that are brilliant if you're a jazz aficionado but that don't spend enough time establishing and honoring the melody itself before the improvisation takes over, in my opinion. Coleman Hawkins, for example, does a great bebop version, and as a saxophonist I really love it, but for my record I thought it would be better to respect the melody more as I was starting to figure out how I wanted to play it. What I wanted to do was to try to channel all the great jazz versions I'd heard but still give my own personal touch to "Body and Soul," while making sure to keep respecting that incredible melody. If you know those brilliant lyrics and kind of sing along when you hear it—"My life a wreck you're making, you know I'm yours just for the taking"—I didn't want you to lose that feeling of the melody while listening. Then, when I did get to the improv section, I tried to extrapolate off that melody and see what kind of ideas it led me to. Later I'd reestablish the melody and then figure out an ending.

What you're hearing there is basically the whole library of "Body and Soul," a version that hopefully honors the best of the improvs that came before me. Throughout, I kept hinting back at the melody—the way Stan Getz did—using a little piece of it here and there. So in a lot of ways this cut is a good example of the way I think about jazz—remembering everything that came before me and putting my own sound and feel into it. I like that cut a lot.

In working on that, I focused on the purely instrumental versions that preceded me, so I never listened to Louis Armstrong's famous version. But speaking of Louie, there was another one of his songs that created quite a brouhaha for me.

What happened was, I was sitting in my driveway listening to the incredible duet Natalie Cole did with her late father's version of "Unforgettable." She took the Nat King Cole recording and sang along with it, and it was so brilliant and beautiful that I thought, I wish I could do something like that. Then it hit me. I've always loved Louis Armstrong's version of "What a Wonderful World," both his vocals and his great trumpet work. What if I did a duet like that?

Natalie Cole's song was produced by the great musician and producer David Foster, who is a friend of mine, so I called him up and said, "Hey, what about this idea?"

He said, "That's great! Let's do it!"

The first thing we did, of course, was contact the Louis Armstrong foundation and run it by his family to get their blessing. We assured them that we would give all the proceeds to charity. We wanted to honor this great song and this great performance, and we wanted to do our best to make a beautiful and respectful tribute. They all thought it was a great idea.

David did an amazing job with the production. The song was successful, so I guess a lot of people thought it was a great idea too. But at least one person didn't.

The famous guitarist Pat Metheny took to the internet to write some truly mean-spirited things about me and about how I did the song. I didn't really even want to mention this, but it got a lot of attention at the time, and I'm often asked about it, so I also didn't want to ignore it as I talk about this track. I won't repeat the things he said here, but needless to say it didn't make much difference to me, and the song was universally well received. Whenever I have the right video playback system, I try to do that song live with a video of Louis Armstrong on the big screen as I play my sax along with him. I think it's quite an exceptional thing to see. When I look up at the big screen and see Louis Armstrong right there as I'm playing my sax "with" him, I get a very warm feeling—a real mixture of gratefulness and humbleness and pride.

Another song on that album that people ask me about a lot is "The Girl from Ipanema," which I did with Bebel Gilberto. Stan Getz made that song famous. He first recorded it with the great Portuguese guitarist João Gilberto, and it featured an English verse by João's wife, Astrud Gilberto. Of course, it became one of the most well-known and most-recorded songs ever. So to be doing that song with João and Astrud's daughter was quite an honor. It was fun to do a song that had become famous because of one of my sax heroes.

I'm proud of the way all these classic songs came out, but if you want to listen to the one I think we did the best, it would be "The Look of Love." I think we found just the right feel for this one and added just the right little nuances to make this song very special, and to toot my own horn one more time, I think that one's just about perfect.

But there is one song that is extra special for me: "Stranger on the Shore." That was a big instrumental hit for the clarinetist Acker Bilk in 1961. There's a reason that means so much to me. "Stranger on the Shore" was one of my dad's favorite songs. And to get to do that song, for my dad, was like a special present I was able to give to him. It's a beautiful melody in its own right, but the connection between father and son makes it all the more beautiful. I know it made him very happy.

Welcome to the 2000s!

We started the millennium with two more Christmas albums, which sold incredibly well, sandwiched around an album of original material that went gold as well. After that, I had ideas for a whole bunch of new songs—I was feeling very creative—but Clive had other ideas.

This time, not only did he *not* want me to do any original material, but he didn't even want to do an album of instrumentals. His idea was to get me together with some of the biggest names in the business and have me do an album of duets.

It wasn't my favorite idea, but I was open to it.

This is something that takes place a lot between artists and their record labels. Agreeing on the concept and direction of one's next album can get tricky, especially when the record company is gung ho on ideas that aren't exactly what you have in mind. You have to walk the fine line of keeping their excitement and support while making sure that your musical integrity isn't compromised.

On this one, while I didn't love the concept, I did feel like it was going to be cool—especially because they were contacting some incredibly talented people. So I said okay and reassured myself that it would turn out fine.

And it did. Most of the duets were with vocalists—and again, how incredibly lucky am I to have such greats as Chaka Khan, Barbra Streisand, and Daryl Hall (from Hall & Oates) on my album. But my favorite song on that album is the one I did with the incredible Cuban trumpet player Arturo Sandoval. He's an amazing musician, so I was honored that he wanted to do a song with me. When you listen to it, it feels like we're riffing off each other back and forth. But here's the secret: We weren't in the same room. Not even in the same state. We sent him the music, and he played his part, and then I put mine on later.

Actually—more secrets—I wasn't in the same room with any of the people on that album!

It was all about trying to take what other folks had laid down, hearing the spaces they'd left, and thinking about what would make sense in those spaces. It's kind of like they had given me a jigsaw puzzle with some pieces missing, and I had to figure out what shapes those pieces were and how I could fill in those blanks. All that said, it was still my album, so I wasn't just going to be a sideman for their vocals. (And there were times when I had to edit out some vocals to allow for more sax. Sorry, guys!) So there is a lot more of me than there would be if I were playing a song for their album. And that's how I thought it ought to be.

There wound up being a number of really fun cuts on that album. The duet with alto sax superstar David Sanborn on "Pick Up the Pieces" took me back to my old Cold, Bold and Together roots. And getting to play—virtually—along with my old heroes Earth, Wind & Fire was a real treat. As I said earlier—can you imagine how cool it was for me to do a song with them after having idolized them when I was in high school and college? They were so huge, and here I was having them do a song with me, *for* me, on *my* album. Unreal.

My process was the same on each cut: Find the right notes to play for the melody. Do the same for the solo parts and for the parts that go back and forth with the other artist. And so on. It was fun, and it was challenging.

In the end, I was proud of what I achieved on *Duets*. I was able to find the right balance between my saxophone parts and the performances of the other artists—where to stretch out and improvise, where to lie back and let the other player's track come forward, how to play something that anticipated what they were going to do next so it all flowed together smoothly. This goes back to what I always talk about: if you practice long and hard enough and if you develop the tools you need and hone your ability to use those tools, you can approach new situations with confidence and succeed in ways you never succeeded before. It's not just what being a professional is about—to me, it's a philosophy that extends to all aspects of life.

That skill, the ability to listen to someone else's work and find the right way to complement it and add to it without getting in the way or being too showy, while still maintaining my musical integrity—the skill I honed on *Duets*—is one I continued to work on. And work on. And work on. And I think it's because of that skill that the guest appearances I occasionally do on other people's music turn out so great. Recently—and I'm bragging here—the Weeknd and Jon Batiste both called me up and asked me to play something on their respective albums. I'm proud of the solos I did on their songs. I don't think a lot of people can do what I do. And I say that with no disrespect to other players. I'm sure many musicians could put in a fabulous solo, but there's an art to making your solo become an integral part of the whole. It comes from a certain place in one's heart, and I don't think it's something that one can simply learn to do. It's an intangible feeling, a skill that started to develop more strongly in me during the making of the *Duets* album. So I guess that's another thing I can thank Clive for.

That ability has allowed me to have the great good fortune of being asked to play on the recordings of some of the greatest artists of all time—from Frank Sinatra and Gladys Knight to the amazing tenor Andrea Bocelli, just to name a few. I'm always honored and humbled to play alongside these legends.

Soon after that, I was getting excited to get back into the studio and do my own material again. Apparently, I was the only one.

Because Arista Records told me my days of doing original material were over. "The next thing we want you to do is an album of songs from the 'Great American Songbook,'" they said.

Now, let me take a second to talk about that phrase. I don't like it. In fact, I hate it! I don't use the word "hate" a lot. In fact, I hate "hate"! But the term "Great American Songbook" sounded so pretentious to me. I mean, who decides what songs qualify to be great American songs? Plus, an album of songs from the so-called Great American Songbook has been done so many times in the past by so many artists. The fact is, nothing about this idea seemed special to me. I wanted no part of it.

But that's what Clive and Arista Records wanted. Rod Stewart had just done *The Great American Songbook*, Barry Manilow had a big hit with *The Greatest Songs of the Fifties*, and Clive wanted me to ride on their coattails.

But I'm not a coattails kind of guy. Things came to a head. I held firm that I wasn't going to do it. Clive held firmer and said, "If you don't do it, we are going to have to let you go."

Let me go!? I was totally taken aback and deeply hurt when I heard this. It was a serious shock to my system. I honestly couldn't believe my ears. I mean, after all these years and all the success we shared together—a success which, in fact, was a direct result of my original music—and now they are saying that my original music is not worthy of their support? And they won't let me decide what music is best for me to do? And it's either do it their way or I'm out?

What the fuck?

Is this 1982 again and I'm just about to make my first record? No! I've sold seventy-five million records. That's seventy-five million reasons that the right answer is to just let me do what I do.

We both figured, Something's gotta give (oops, did I just quote a line from the Great American Songbook?). And well, something did actually give. And I'll give you a hint at what happened next: that's the last line from that songbook you're gonna hear in this book.

CHAPTER SIXTEEN

As you've probably realized by now, I don't back down from something just because it's hard. This approach has worked well for me in my career, and it's not something that I turn off when my work is done. It's just part of who I am.

When things take a tough turn in my professional life, there are a few things that especially invigorate me, even if (especially if) they're difficult, too, in their own way. I believe it's good to have balance in your life and do other things so you gain perspective when you start to refocus on your professional life. Those other things, for me to be interested in them, need to be challenging too.

I don't take myself too seriously (this coming from the guy who approved the Keepin' It Saxy board game!), but I *am* a serious, disciplined guy. If I'm interested in something, I try to become good at it because, generally speaking, I only like doing things I'm good at, and I like to be good at the things I do.

Which is why golf appeals to me so much.

I actually picked up three things in the same year when I was ten years old: the saxophone, a golf club, and a pair of skis. (Hard to hold them all at the same time!) I got very good at skiing. And my brother took me out to the golf course with his friends, which was nice of him—who lets their little brother tag along like that?—and I started improving at that too.

When I got to college, I actually made the ski team but not the golf team. I loved skiing, but I didn't like the competitive part of it. That's because I wasn't great when it came to racing—and racing is pretty much what competitive skiing is all about.

But golf was different. Golf satisfied that part of me that loves to practice, that loves to learn, that loves things with very specific ways of measuring right and wrong.

Spoiler alert: I've won my fair share of golf awards. And you know what? On a certain level they mean more to me than the Grammys and the other music awards. Because, as I said earlier, golf is an objective victory, and music is a subjective one.

Winning a Grammy doesn't mean you're the best, just that a small group of people decided they liked you or your music at that moment in time. But you can't say that at a golf tournament. If I get to the end with fewer shots than anyone else, then I *was* the best that day, end of argument. As I said earlier, I like the clarity of that. It appeals to my sense of fairness. And besides, I like numbers.

The better I got at golf, the more I realized that I could get even better, so the harder I practiced. Do I play golf for fun? Sure. But does the fun come from just being out there or from the vibe you get when you put in the hard work and see it pay off? For me, it's both. The discipline and commitment to practice are a big part of the fun. Just like when I practice my sax. Same basic idea. (Starting to see some consistent personality traits here?)

As I got to play in bigger tournaments, I never had the problem with nerves that a lot of people have. If I can stand up and play sax in front of ten thousand people, I can certainly stand up and swing a golf club in front of a few hundred.

But learning the mechanics was something else. I got to a certain level and then felt like I just wasn't getting any better, no matter what I did. I was winning, and people always had great things to say about my golf swing. In fact, I was voted "best musician golfer" by one of the golf magazines at one point. But I wasn't improving, and that meant it wasn't making me happy anymore.

I started taking lessons from some of the best teachers in the world. I was trying to understand the "definitive" golf swing. I spent years going down many rabbit holes looking for it. I've recently come to the conclusion—and boy, I could have saved myself a lot of time and aggravation if I had just listened to the great golfers and teachers who told me this all along—that there isn't a definitive swing after all. Each of us has a unique set of skills and comes into the game with our own tendencies, our own pros and cons, our own advantages and disadvantages. The real challenge is to find what it is that *you* have to feel in order to make the golf ball do what you are hoping it will do. So it's not a particular swing that one should try to master, but instead, it's about trying to find out what you personally need to feel in order to accomplish your goals. That's why there are so many different swings that all seem to work. Each person is trying to feel what's right for them to feel when they swing.

I thought to myself that learning to play golf can't be all that different from learning to play the sax. They are both individual skills that require practice. And so for a long time I tried to use the exact same approach to golf as I do with my sax: I'll just go to the golf range and practice and practice until I master the swing, and then I'll worry about where the ball actually goes.

I did that for years, but as I said, I stopped getting better. And I think I know why. I'm convinced that my mistake was forgetting to apply an essential element of my learning process in music: I didn't just stay in the practice room. I got out there and played actual gigs. You have to get out there to see what works or doesn't with what you have been practicing, then adjust as needed and practice some more. With golf, I stayed on the range way too much and didn't get out on the course often enough to see what really works and what doesn't. I wasn't giving myself a chance to develop the feel that I needed to feel to make the ball do what I wanted. I was just too focused on the swing on the range, instead of what I needed to do to get the ball on the fairway or in the hole.

I practice golf a lot differently now—and I'm having a lot more fun too.

There's another thing I carried over from music to golf. Every morning when I practice my sax, I'm still a student. I still think, How can I get better? And even on days when I'm struggling, I know that I'm putting in the hours, and that's the process that *will* make me get better. It's that simple. The question isn't whether you are going to get better if you practice consistently; the question is, How long will it take to get to a certain level? And that second question has no answer. You have to trust the process. It works, and it will work. It's that trust in the process, a trust I learned from music, that gave me the patience to know that I would eventually get better.

I've had some fantastic experiences through golf. I'll share a few with you, not because I want to name-drop or brag but because I'm proud of the experiences and also very grateful to have had the opportunity to play golf with some amazing individuals. And I know that for avid golfers, there is nothing better than getting inside the ropes and hearing the details of a round of golf with a celebrity or with one of the guys on tour.

I have to start with what I consider my greatest accomplishment in my golfing career (written with a smile because I know I don't actually *have* a golfing career!). I'll begin at the end—my tee shot on the eighteenth hole at Pebble Beach on a Sunday in the final round of play in the final group of the 2001 AT&T Pebble Beach National Pro-Am.

My partner is Phil Mickelson, and we have a one-stroke lead as a team going into the last hole. It's one of the most famous par fives in golf. Set against the Pacific Ocean on our left.

It's been a magical weekend. I've been hitting the ball well and keeping up my "Am" side of the Pro-Am. I'm making birdies and eagles on holes that Phil made par. (And, I should add, he's doing the same for me, but a lot more often.) So by Sunday, on that final hole, after we've team-birdied the last four straight holes, we're in the lead by one over Tiger Woods and his amateur partner, Jerry Chang.

Okay. I'm super nervous and end up in the sand trap near the green in three, with my ball buried in the sand. I'm an amateur, not a

pro, so I end up bogeying the hole. But so does my partner. We drop
back into a tie with Tiger and Jerry. I'm not sure how to feel at this
moment—I'm thinking, How are they going to decide who ends up
winning the Pro-Am? Did our bogey cost us the tournament? Will we
have to go into some kind of tiebreaker, and will my nerves get in the
way?—until Clint Eastwood runs out and announces that they're going
to declare co-champions.

Now, I'm feeling pretty happy—co-champion with names like Phil
Mickelson and Tiger Woods at Pebble Beach is very cool—and then, as
I'm drinking in this moment, my cell phone rings. It's a flip phone—
remember those?—and when I flip it open, I hear, "Hey, Kenny. It's
Tiger." (Wow! Tiger Woods is calling me. How the hell does everybody
get my number?)

"So, Kenny," he says, "man, you really choked on that last hole."

I start laughing my ass off. I mean, when Tiger Woods is calling you
up to rip on you, you've made it!

"Hey, Tiger, fuck you!" I say with the biggest smile on my face. Because hey, when do you get to say *that* to the greatest golfer in the world?
And I know he'll enjoy the back-and-forth. He's very cool that way.

He laughs and says, "I'm just calling because I'm proud that we will
share this trophy together."

I was speechless after that. Despite everything I said about golf
achievement being an objective thing and not a subjective one, the fact
that the great Tiger Woods was calling me up to make me feel like part
of the golf community in that way was awesome. And it started a relationship that included many more rounds together.

I did observe something during one of my rounds with Tiger that
I'll share. We were on the sixteenth hole at Sherwood Country Club in
Los Angeles, and he had a very short eagle putt. It was a very easy putt,
but he missed it. I asked him if he flubbed it on purpose. He said, "Yeah,
I don't like to make too many eagles in a practice round before a tournament." I didn't realize it until he said it, but I'm exactly the same way
with music. When I'm doing a sound check, and all of a sudden, I hear
myself playing something better than I've ever played it or I'm doing

some complicated riffs that are coming out absolutely perfect, I'll cut it short. It's the feeling of, I want to save that for the gig. I don't want to leave it all here in the sound check. Something like that. Not sure if it actually works this way in the end, but it was cool to see another professional feeling something similar in his own field.

So maybe golf and sax are similar in more ways than I knew.

President Bill Clinton was another fun guy to play with. His office called one day and said he was going to be in Los Angeles and wanted me to take him out at my golf club. I guess I learned a thing or two about being a smart-ass on the golf course from Tiger, because I said, "Well, okay, but tell him I have some conditions."

Now if you don't think it takes some balls—and I'm not talking about golf balls—to tell the president of the United States he has to meet your conditions to play golf with you, you don't know what it's like to get a call like that. I was somewhat joking around, of course, but his people took me dead seriously, so I pressed on.

"Tell him I'm not gonna hide out with just him and me and the Secret Service. He's gotta say hi to my friends at the club and be available so that if someone wants to say hello, they can."

And guess what? They agreed, and he did!

I was the most popular guy at the club that day. All the famous guys who play at my club were suddenly my best friend, coming up and saying, "Hey, Kenny, my friend, how are you doing? Oh, Mr. President! Didn't see you there!" Ha! Of course President Clinton couldn't have been more gracious, saying hi to everybody in that way of his, where he makes everyone feel like the most important person on earth.

We did our round, and President Clinton was telling stories the whole time. Just like when he was in the White House. On the third hole, out of nowhere, he said to me, "You know, Osama bin Laden was trying to kill me for years." Now *there's* something you don't hear every day. I mean, what do you say when somebody tells you that?

I think I said, "Did he come close?"

Okay, so sometimes I'm not the most articulate guy. I played a better round than he did, though!

I did get to play at the Presidents Cup a number of times. I never played golf with the next president, but I did play sax for him at a Presidents Cup tournament in Korea. George W. Bush was a really funny guy. What a personality. Really knows how to make people feel at home. My sound engineer Monty is from the Washington, DC, area and had done the sound at some of the president's speeches. When President Bush saw him in Korea, he motioned to him and said, "Dude! Dude! Come over here!" I thought it was so nice of him to make my sound guy feel so welcome.

When I was playing that night, I got to the point in the show where I was doing my circular breathing—that long, sweet note—and I went over to President Bush and was playing right at him. Then and there, he asked me, "Hey, Kenny, what's your handicap?" Right in the middle of the concert! I kept holding my sax with one hand, and with the other, I held up four fingers, because my handicap was four at the time. While I was still playing, he said, "Hmmm, not bad for a guy your age."

Afterward he invited me to Texas to play golf with him. I haven't made it down to Texas yet, but that one's definitely on my bucket list.

A lot of celebrities play golf in Los Angeles. Two of my favorite guys to play with are Ray Romano and George Lopez. I like to think that I'm a pretty funny guy, but these guys are really, really funny. *Seriously* funny. And smart and fascinating to talk to. They both love golf the way I do. We all connected at the Pebble Beach Pro-Am over the years. I've played it about seventeen times, and Ray has played it over twenty. Not sure how many times George has played it, but they both love the game and respect the rules. So we all have a lot in common. Ray in particular is such a stickler about the rules that he won't even give himself the shortest of putts. And he'll punish himself if he doesn't achieve whatever goal he is aiming at. For example, he'll say, "If I don't shoot the score I'm going for, I don't get to watch TV for a week."

I'll say, "That's nuts, you know that."

And he'll say something like, "That's just the way I am." More often than not, he'll shoot that score or better.

At heart, Ray is just a guy from Queens who still hangs out with his old buddies. Even though we saw each other every year at Pebble Beach, our friendship developed slowly; I think it's the best way for a friendship to develop, because it's real and honest, not a showbiz schmoozy kind of thing where everybody becomes "best friends" overnight. I respect him enormously and I like him a lot. I'll play golf with him anytime, anywhere, and when you factor in our handicaps, the game is always very close.

With George Lopez, there is an ease about him that makes him very fun to be around. He's also super smart and always keeps things real. I love my time with him. He knows that at any point he can make anyone laugh, and I enjoy the mix of deep, heartfelt conversations about life and show business, and him hitting you with one-liners that are so funny you can't help but laugh out loud!

Another one of my favorite guys to play with is Michael Douglas. I've had the pleasure of getting to know him over the years, and I have to tell you that he is a truly great guy. He used to arrange a celebrity golf tournament that was an event to help those in the motion picture and television field, and the list of celebrities who would be there—and lucky me to get the chance to hang with these fun people and get to know them—was unbelievable. The list includes Sly Stallone, Samuel L. Jackson, Mark Wahlberg, Catherine Zeta-Jones, Joe Pesci, Matthew Mc-Conaughey, Don Cheadle, Thomas Gibson. I mean, can you imagine?

I've been around celebrities for a long time, but I still kind of get goose-bumps in a situation like that. And let me tell you, it was sheer fun!

It was team play, and for some reason, very often it would come down to my having to make a putt in order for my team to win the tournament. And, ahem, I don't mean to brag, but basically I made it every time. Sinking a putt under pressure is one of the hardest things to do in golf. But loving the position of having the chance to win is some-thing that some people are lucky enough to thrive on. And I'm one of those lucky ones. I have that confidence, and it always—well, *almost* always!—gets me through. It got me through that night, years ago, on *Carson*, when I decided to play "Songbird." It gets me through when I step out on stage in front of ten thousand people, and it gets me through on the eighteenth hole when I have a putt to win. I have to say again that I'm very lucky that I'm wired this way, and it has really helped me in my life. It helped me make that putt even though Sly Stallone, who was not on my team, was trying to distract me by going, "You're going to choke, G! You're going to choke!"

And I stood up and looked at him and his team and said, "Sorry to do this to you guys, but this is going in." And it did.

Another highlight of the AT&T Pebble Beach Pro-Am came as part of the celebrity shoot-out that happens on the Wednesday before the tournament officially starts. You play for money for charity, and you play as teams of two. One of the teams was Bill Murray and Justin Tim-berlake; another would be Clint Eastwood and Huey Lewis—that sort of pairing. I was paired with Toby Keith.

Here's how it worked. You played five holes, and each one was worth $20,000 for charity, but if you tied the first hole, then the second one was worth $40,000, and so on. One year it came down to the last hole. We'd tied all the way, so this hole was worth a hundred grand, and we tied that too. So now it was down to a chip-off, and Clint Eastwood chipped his to like six inches from the hole. Everyone was roaring be-cause he was such a fan favorite, and everyone wanted him to win.

Then I hit my chip. From the second the ball left the ground, I knew it was going in. I didn't even watch. I hammed it up—turning my back to the hole, taking off my hat, and giving a big bow to the crowd. If I'd missed it, I would have looked like a horse's ass, but the ball came to a rest right on the rim of the hole, and the crowd went bonkers. That was one of the most fun times I had at those events.

I have to say that I like playing with the pros way more than the celebrities. The part of me that wants to improve and improve, that relishes the challenge of playing with the best of the best, is stronger, in the end, than the part of me that gets a huge kick out of being heckled by Sly Stallone or Samuel L. Jackson.

I have been lucky to play with the best of the best. The great Arnold Palmer called me up one time (again, how the heck does everybody get my number?) and asked me to play sax at his tournament at Bay Hill. I was so honored, of course, but I said, "I'll do it on one condition: I get to play a round of golf with you. Not in the tournament, just a nice round of golf."

He said, "I'll go you one better—let's play two."

I said, "I'm there!"

We played, and I found out that what everyone says about Arnold Palmer is true. He was about the nicest guy on the planet. What a great day that was.

I've gotten to play many rounds with Jack Nicklaus too. We got paired up at a Pro-Am for the Honda Classic down in West Palm Beach, and I guess we took a liking to each other, because we made a point of always getting together during the many years I hosted the event. I do a lot of charity things for him and his wife Barbara's children's hospital, and we always make time to get away and have dinner and relax. His personality is more serious on the golf course than Arnold Palmer's was—and that's not a criticism at all because I like serious conversations—but off the course, he's about as easy to be with as anyone you've ever known. How lucky am I to get to know him and Barbara!

But as much as I've loved golf—the challenge of it and the camaraderie of it—there's one part of the game that is the hardest for me. A lot of people say there's a Zen to golf. That true success comes from clearing your mind, dismissing all thought, and being one with the moment. And letting go.

That's really hard for Kenny G.

Sometimes I'll tee up and think, On the last shot, there wasn't enough right-side bend. The club was coming too much from the outside. My right shoulder was too high, so I was going left. My hips didn't rotate enough through the hitting area. I'll focus on those details and try to compensate. And that simply does not work. Period. As much as I want to force my body to make the "right" moves, the golf swing doesn't work like that. This has been, and continues to be, a very hard thing for me to accept and even harder to change. I'm smart enough to know what I don't know, so I'm trying to embrace the idea of working on the mechanics on the range and then letting go and actually playing the game of golf on the course.

I can honestly say that I'm currently having more fun on the course than I've ever had, so I know there is something to this. I've taken some time away from the game lately because I've been traveling a lot and working on a new record, but when I get back to it, I'm going to try to experience that Zen-golf state. My goal is to not think about any of the mechanics except on the range. I know that won't be easy for me, but I also know that with my best efforts over time, it will start to sink in. (Like all the putts I'm going to make!) On the course, my plan is to just hit the ball and try to imagine how I want the shape of the shot to look.

But it's like the sax. In order to do that, I need to have the muscle memory of the right moves, a memory so ingrained in me that I can trust my body to do the same thing it did in practice. My hours and hours of practice on the saxophone have given me confidence in the mechanics, so I can let it fly. With golf, I know that I need more work and more practice on the correct mechanics of my swing in order to get there. Someday I hope to achieve the Zen of the game.

Speaking of Zen, I should add that the most enjoyable and connected experiences I have on the golf course don't come when I'm playing with other people or in big tournaments. I actually play golf alone more often than I play with others. When I'm walking the fairway all alone and hit a great shot or make an amazing putt, it's very much like being in the studio and recording something beautiful or technically perfect when no one is watching or listening. It's a feeling that's for me alone, and it reiterates the same theme that seems to keep coming up in my life. I know when something is special and don't need anyone else to tell me. I never have.

My other love, flying, is like that for me as well. As amazing as a great golf shot is, there's nothing on earth—literally—that compares to the pride, peace, and solace I find up above the clouds.

There's something about flying that's like golf and the saxophone for me—and I bet no one's ever said *that* before!

If you think about it, it makes sense. Flying is a skill you can take a lifetime to learn but never master. It involves a huge challenge—learning a language and a set of skills that most people don't have. I have music to thank for my love of flying because, like so many songs from back in my R&B days, it all started with a bass player.

I was always intrigued by flying, and curious about how a person could learn to fly an airplane. I never thought about taking flying lessons. But one day back in the eighties I was talking to a very dear friend of mine, Nathan East, who's actually a very famous bass player. He's Eric Clapton's guy right now, but he's played with everybody—Michael Jackson, Phil Collins, Stevie Wonder, Herbie Hancock, and on and on. We were talking, and he happened to mention that he was getting his pilot's license.

A little light clicked on in my head—in that part of me that loves a challenge—and I asked Nathan to give me his instructor's number. Fast-forward thirty years, and that guy, Harry Murlowski, still holds a very special place in my life. He's the guy who taught me (and my son Noah) how to fly. Harry is a wonderful, quirky guy from England with a very pleasant British accent and a knack for teaching. He's all about problem-solving and teaching you how to stay calm in tricky situations. Sometimes, we'd be up in the air, and he'd cut the power and say, "Okay, you've lost your engine. Now what do you do?" The first time he did it, it took all I had to not panic, but I guess that was the point. Over time I developed the skill to stay calm in an airplane no matter what.

That came in handy about ten years ago. I had fueled up my vintage de Havilland Beaver at an airport in Arizona, en route from Los Angeles to Toronto, and was in the midst of my initial climb when I realized something wasn't right. My rate of climb was much lower than usual. I didn't think that the plane was likely to go down, but it wasn't going up much either. I was maybe three hundred feet up, and the plane actually stopped climbing. Not good! I knew the altitude and temperature were at play here, but I still felt like the airplane should be performing much better than it was. Had I miscalculated the weight of the plane? The density altitude?

That's when my training—and my natural instinct to be curious, to take problems apart and put them back together—kicked in.

I thought, Is the gear still down? Are the flaps in the wrong position? Nope, gear's up, flaps are at climb. And then I realized that not only was I not climbing, but I was starting to drift downward. And my oil pressure was really low.

Very not good!

In a situation like this, at low altitude, nothing good comes of trying to turn around and head back to the airport. The reason is, when you go into a turn, you have less lift—the thing that keeps planes in the air—than you have when the wings are level. So some pilots who try to turn back in this situation wind up crashing, because they lose what little altitude they have by making the turn.

I did not panic. I thought, I'm going to be fine. I'm going to live through this. I can always find an empty stretch of highway or something to land on if worse comes to worst. Even so, I was sure that something mechanical was definitely wrong. That was not a good feeling. I wanted to learn from it. What could the problem be? Let me think about my options. Let me think quickly, of course!

This is where another long-time philosophy of mine kicked in. Never be afraid to ask for help. Don't let pride get in the way of improving. Learn from the masters. From the cockpit, I texted a picture of my instrument panel to my friend Shane Carlson in Seattle, an expert in the type of plane I was flying. I didn't have much time before the situation was likely to go from bad to worse, but I wanted him to see what I was seeing. I started tweaking the mixture and power settings and tried a few different flap settings as well. At that point, I called Shane and he talked to me while I was teetering on going up or down. Fortunately, the tweaking got the plane to climb ever so slowly, and the oil pressure stabilized, so I was able to climb little by little and continue my flight. When I landed two hours later, it turned out that some oil hoses were loose, and oil was leaking a bit. Not the end of the world, but unsettling nonetheless.

On the ground, I thought about what had happened and how I handled it. And I was very pleased about the fact that I didn't panic but instead had more of a level-headed curiosity, a feeling of wanting to figure things out, as well as the strong desire to improve my skills to just be better at whatever I was doing. Both traits were instilled in me early on by my parents—and boy, did they come in handy that day.

Thank you, Mom and Dad.

I got my pilot's license in 1989 up in Seattle and bought my first plane, called a Glasair III—a very fast little single-engine fiberglass plane—and started zipping around the country with it, flying from gig to gig. My friend and instructor Harry came with me on tour. They say a good pilot is always a student, and I am always interested in learning, so having Harry along meant I could keep learning all the time. While I was on tour, I trained for my instrument rating. An instrument rating means a pilot has gone through intensive training that's focused on flying solely by looking at your instrument panel, not out the window, which is essential if you're going to fly in the clouds. It's truly a remarkable skill and a great challenge—and have I ever mentioned that I love a challenge?

That, in the end, is why the saxophone, golf, and flying are so similar for me. They scratch that same itch, allowing me to take a very complicated concept, pull it apart into its various pieces, learn the mechanics of each of those pieces one at a time, and then practice each of those mechanics over and over again until the muscle memory kicks in and they become as natural as tying your shoe. I take great pride in the achievement, but I also derive enormous pleasure from the doing of a difficult thing I couldn't do before.

Years later, Harry and I started flying around in a Learjet. It was an older model, but it was still very, very fast. One time I finished a gig in Atlantic City, and just for the hell of it, I turned to Harry and said, "Come on, let's go back to Los Angeles tonight." Just because we could. Getting to go coast to coast, on our own, at night, was about the coolest feeling in the world. We were up over forty thousand feet, and I looked to my right—and there were the northern lights! It was an incredible sight.

There are so many things about flying that I love. There's a peace and solitude up there that's not like anything else in the world.

When I'm in the act of flying, and I'm all alone in the cockpit, that's when I get that same satisfying feeling as when I'm in the practice room with my saxophone. Or sinking an eagle putt when I'm playing all by myself. No one's watching me or listening to me there, and it doesn't matter, because it's a great feeling to be good at something and simply do it. Just for yourself.

The plane I fly is a pontoon plane, the de Havilland DHC-2 Beaver, and I think it is a very safe plane to fly. It has a big, long wingspan, so if the engine were ever to quit, you'd have a lot more glide time to figure out what to do. And it can touch down on land or sea.

The decision to switch to the Beaver came as sort of an epiphany. I was flying back from Pebble Beach in the little Glasair down along the coast. I was flying over Big Sur and looking out at the ocean, and the seas were really rough that day. This plane had a short wingspan, which results in a short glide path, and I thought, If I lost my engine right now, I don't know if I'd survive, because I'd have very little time, and there's no place to land. You've got those big cliffs on your left and the ocean on the right. I don't know what I'd do.

I saw the Pacific Coast Highway, which is very curvy on that stretch—no long strips you could land on if you had to, even if there were no cars on the stretch, so that wasn't an option. And I thought, You know what? This is my last flight on this airplane. The engine never quit on me in all the years I owned it, and there was no logical reason to think that it would quit in the next thirty minutes. But I knew that once I touched down, I would never take it up again.

I think that decision probably stemmed from good survival instincts, but it also had to do with being a new dad. Max was probably just a year or two old when I had that epiphany, and when you become a dad, your survival instincts get heightened. Not only are you protecting yourself—which is pretty good incentive to not do anything crazy anyway—but you're making sure you're staying safe for your child as well.

There's a lot to keep track of when you're piloting a plane; but there are times, when the radio chatter has abated, when the weather's just right and all the instruments are saying exactly what you want them to say, and I know the safety factor of my plane is very high, that I am able to just take in the moment and appreciate the breathtaking views in front of me. My favorite place to fly is up in the Great Lakes region in Canada.

I'll mainly fly over smaller lakes, but sometimes I'll edge out over Lake Huron when the water is perfectly calm. I'll crack open the window and stick my elbow out like I'm driving an Oldsmobile 88 down the Pacific Coast Highway, and I'll bank over and fly toward the sunset, and it's the most beautiful thing I've ever seen. It's like looking at the face of God—the awesome beauty around you, the majesty of mountains and water and an endless expanse of sky—when you have that bird's-eye view and can see sixty miles in every direction. I know a lot of people never get to experience that, and in that moment, I feel so grateful, and so blessed.

CHAPTER SEVENTEEN

The standoff between Clive Davis and Kenny G never made the papers. No one except our inner circle knew what was going on. As I mentioned earlier, I've been lucky that the paparazzi and the press have never been all that interested in me. That's made life a whole lot easier in a lot of ways. It certainly makes things very comfortable for me when I'm grocery shopping and no one is making a big deal about it—and it was really helpful in this particular situation. Because things were getting pretty tense.

Clive dug in his heels on the idea of "Kenny G does the Great American Songbook."

And so did Kenny G.

Here is where I made one of the biggest career mistakes I've ever made. And I have no one to blame but myself. I should have talked to Clive directly about these things, but I let my manager handle it. And not just any manager, I should say. I had met Irving Azoff socially at a few different events, and we were friends. He's a major, major player—at one point *Billboard* magazine named him the most powerful person in the music business. Not a bad guy to have on your side. One day we ran into each other, and Irving said, "You know, you should let me manage you," and I jumped at the chance like I was diving off the diving board when I was ten years old.

But I'm also a very loyal guy, and my manager at the time, Dennis Turner, to whom I owe a whole lot, was someone I didn't want to hurt. I was torn, so I came up with the idea of being co-managed by both of them, which I thought would be a great way to keep my loyalty and still get a very powerful ally on my team. I used my old accounting-degree skills and calculated that we would all make more money with Irving as a partner compared to what was happening currently, because of all the new opportunities that would undoubtedly come. Unfortunately, Dennis wasn't interested in that, and I had to part ways with him. It was sad for me, but I had to do what I felt was best for my career. There are times when opportunity knocks and you have no choice but to open the door.

As things started to get heated with Clive and Arista, I let others do the talking for me. That wouldn't happen today, as I have no problem with confrontation and conversations about things that might get challenging. But back then I did. I would withdraw and not want to deal with anything that was uncomfortable. I'm not proud of this trait, but it was a part of me then; it's something I've had to work very hard on, and I can happily say that I have fixed this and it's made my life way better.

The issue remained that Arista was not interested in a record of original material, and that's all I wanted to do. They said it wouldn't sell enough records to justify making it. As I said earlier, I was caught completely off-guard by this. Because I thought, Come on, after all, I've sold seventy-five million records. Seventy. Five. Million. That's plenty for a lifetime. We don't need to sell one more record. At this point I should be the guy that the company keeps around no matter what happens because we have had so much success in the past. Like a legacy. That's what I thought, anyway.

Boy, was I off base. Arista gave me an ultimatum: either I did the record they wanted me to do, or I was off the label.

I couldn't believe this was happening, but I knew in my heart that I needed to make a record of originals. I would be betraying my integrity if I did another cover record.

So I left my Arista family. I was in uncharted waters. But I knew how to swim.

Now the big question was, Where do I go next?

This might seem strange, but the answer to that question came from my long-time association with Starbucks. Starbucks had an exclusive deal with a label called Concord, and they would only release records on that label.

As I mentioned earlier, back in 1994, my *Miracles* album was the very first record they sold at Starbucks, as a kind of test to see if they would be able to sell music. It did really well. After *Miracles*, Starbucks started releasing all sorts of CDs. And now, a dozen years later, I was talking to Concord Records about being one of their artists, and of course my music would be sold at Starbucks. It seemed like the stars were lining up for me once again. This is going to work out great, or so I thought.

But it turned out that I was about to make another big career mistake.

I signed a five-record deal with Concord and had a terrific time making the first album for them. With original material! *Rhythm & Romance*, which was all samba, salsa, and bossa nova songs—things I'd been wanting to experiment with for a long time—was released on February 5, 2008, and Concord/Starbucks took a huge ad out in *The New York Times* to promote it. I thought, This is gonna be fantastic!

Sure enough, we sold about five hundred thousand copies—not the millions I was selling with Arista, but not too shabby. Things were going really well. For a while.

Six weeks later, I walked into a Starbucks, and my record was nowhere to be found. I was confused. Where was it? I learned that this is how they do things. They have a six-week window, and then they switch the CD out for another one.

Um, you think maybe you should have told me that up front? Or maybe I should have asked?

Yeah, you'd think.

Too bad I didn't.

Yikes! The whole reason I signed with Concord was that Starbucks was going to be my point of sale, at all the stores worldwide. As a worldwide artist, I needed a company that had field staff that would help me promote records in Atlanta, Chicago, Detroit, Miami, Houston, and all the other major US cities. Concord had only one office in Beverly Hills, but I had thought, Well, Starbucks is everywhere, so that will make up for it. But without my record at their stores, I wasn't going to get the exposure I needed to reach the people around the country who connected with my music. What the heck was I going to do?

I was in complete shock. I knew that I had made a huge mistake here, but I had signed a five-record deal, and now all I could do was fulfill that deal and hope for the best.

Of course, I still put my heart and soul into every record. In fact, my next record was called *Heart and Soul*. I'm super proud of the music I was putting out, but as you can probably guess, my record-selling career went downhill after *Rhythm & Romance*.

If I wasn't feeling bad enough about my decision to leave Arista, here's the kicker: I finally talked to Clive about our breakup. And it brought home a very valuable lesson in maturity.

Here's what happened. I ran into Clive, years later, and worked up the courage to ask him to lunch to finally have the conversation I should have had back when we were splitting up. I said, "Clive, why did you and I get a divorce after twenty-five years? I never wanted to get a divorce."

"We never wanted it either," Clive said.

What? Okay, Clive, you've got my attention. I asked him, "Then why did it happen?"

"Your team insisted that you be able to record an album of original material but didn't want the budget to change for it," he said. "We felt like the record budget you wanted was too big for the record you wanted to put out." In other words, they figured my original compositions wouldn't sell enough for the big budget that I had earned with my past record sales.

Here is how it worked for me and my record deal with Arista. For each record, I was given a finite amount of money with which to record and finish an album. For my very first record, it was a rather low amount, but as I sold millions of records over the years, the budget grew to a very large amount. Here is how the accounting part of making a record works: Whatever it cost to make the record came out of that budget, and if there was any left over, I got to keep it. As the budget kept getting larger, the amount left over also grew. Good deal, right? Well, at this point in my deal with Arista, they didn't think I could keep earning enough to justify it if I did the album of original material that I wanted to do.

So apparently, Arista decided that in order to make that much money back, they had to go with something safer than my originals, even though my original music was the music that had sold the most over the years. *That's* why they were asking for the "Great American Songbook" stuff and all that. It wasn't just a creative argument, after all—it was also very much about the bottom line.

I actually felt queasy when he told me that. I could barely believe what I was hearing. Again, there was that big part of me that felt like seventy-five million records should be enough for a lifetime pass. But okay, there is an accountant's brain under all these beautiful curls after all, and I can understand that no matter what, a record company isn't going to put out a record they think is bound to lose money for them. Even a Kenny G record. But still—the fact that it was just a bottom-line question, with no consideration of our long and lucrative history, was making the old anger rise up in me.

But much more than that, what I was feeling, in that moment, was shame.

I was ashamed that I hadn't been mature enough back then to be part of the conversation. I would have easily been able to work out a compromise on the budget. I could have come up with a deal that made everyone happy—I could have made the record I wanted to make for a quarter of the budgets we'd been working with—and my place with Clive and Arista Records would have remained intact.

Don't get me wrong—I'm still pissed off that it all came down to a bottom-line question, but looking back on it, I'm kicking myself for not taking part in the conversations personally.

I wanted to make 100 percent sure I was understanding what Clive was telling me. "So, Clive," I said, with more than a little lump in my throat, "do I have this straight? If I had taken a smaller budget, you would have let me do what I wanted to do?"

"Of course!" Clive said. "That's what we wanted."

"Oy vey!" I said. "Of course that would have been what I wanted too! I didn't care that much about the budget. I just wanted to make the record I wanted to make."

We stared at each other for a moment. Neither of us knew what to say.

Then, finally, I realized what I *had* to say. "I'm sorry, Clive. I really am. This is not on you. It's my fault. All of it. I apologize. I wasn't mature enough to have this conversation with you back then. I had others talk on my behalf, and it hurt our relationship. I'm sorry I didn't have the maturity to get involved, because we could have resolved this in a heartbeat."

Clive reached out and put his hand on my arm. And then he said something that brought me to tears. "We're still family," he said.

It's not easy for me to admit my mistakes. (I can admit that!) But I learned an important lesson that day. Work hard to fix the things you need to about yourself. Sooner rather than later. And it led to me learning a lot more lessons in the years to come.

The next album I did, *Brazilian Nights*, was very special for me. Once again, it didn't sell very well—which is a shame, because I think *Brazilian Nights* is one of the best albums I've ever done.

The album was inspired by my love and admiration for Stan Getz and his bossa nova music. He and Charlie Byrd introduced bossa nova to America with their album *Jazz Samba* in 1962, but it's my favorite album of his—*Getz for Lovers*—that inspired me to do my own. I was also inspired by Cannonball Adderley, who did a nice bossa nova version of "Corcovado (Quiet Nights of Quiet Stars)," one of the more well-known bossa nova tunes of that era, and Paul Desmond's album *Bossa Antigua*. You should definitely check those guys out.

I worked hard to learn the licks and study the vibe and nuances of those great bossa nova players. And I'm happy with how everything turned out.

It was not my normal way of playing. I felt motivated to do this record so that I could explore adding bossa nova flavors to my own style, but another big part of my motivation was sharing my love of those great saxophonists with people who wouldn't necessarily reach that far back into the jazz world. So if I inspired a few folks then—or inspire you right now—to go check out those amazing albums, then I'll feel like it was all a big success.

That album set off an idea in my head: What if I continued to explore the jazz greats of the fifties and sixties, beyond bossa nova, but combined that with my love of creating my own melodies? Could I do new material in the old style? I loved the jazz greats, but I didn't want to do another *Classics in the Key of G* because, well, I'd already done that. So I wondered, Could I take everything I'd learned from listening to Stan Getz and John Coltrane, to Miles Davis and Chet Baker, to Sonny Rollins and Dexter Gordon and Cannonball Adderley—but then use those lessons to create new songs?

I'd never tried to do that before.

I knew it would be hard. What I didn't know was that it would take me six years.

New Standards was truly a labor of love. But it was truly a labor. Composing the songs for *New Standards* took a long time, because they had to be up to the level of what I was hearing from the jazz masters of the fifties and sixties.

The first step was kind of an intellectual foray, delving into what makes that music so appealing to me. I love it when I hear it. Why am I loving it? What are they doing and how are they doing it? This is what went through my mind as I tried to analyze and figure out what was going on with that music. I wanted to create songs of my own in that style and do so without copying any of their licks or chords or arrangements. It had to be original.

The essence of what makes the songs on *New Standards* so different from my previous twenty or so albums is in the chord progressions. Okay, let's pause here. This might be getting a bit technical, so let me take a second to explain. Every song that we hear is made up of a series of notes, which are part of chords—chords are just groups of those notes—and the changes from one chord to another are called the progressions. Traditional jazz songs from the era we're talking about have a certain sound or vibe. That has a lot to do with the chords and the chord progressions. The great jazz ballads of the fifties and sixties were created by the jazz masters who added their own sounds to those progressions.

When I was writing the songs for *New Standards*, I wanted to try to recreate the vibe of those songs but add my own voice to them. I worked with a wonderful keyboard player named Sam Hirsch who truly knows his stuff when it comes to traditional jazz. So I'd play a certain fragment of a melody I was thinking about, and he'd play some cool jazz chords in progressions that would go along with that melody. And then back and forth—his chords would spark an idea for where the melody would go, and the melody would suggest new chords to him. I've told you I don't like dancing, but this was like two people dancing together, trying to find their rhythm. I love how it turned out.

When the compositions were finally done, the actual recording process took a long time as well. That had a lot to do with my established, deep-rooted feelings about recording. I know that any recording I do is going to be around for a long time, and that means that I will do whatever it takes to make everything as perfect as possible. And that simply takes time. I worked on every note until everything sounded just right to me. This is not a new process for me by any means, and it truly defines how I feel about recording music: do everything you can—and take as much time as you need—to make the music as great as it can possibly be.

These new arrangements meant a lot of new decisions too. Since we were recording songs that were supposed to sound like they came from a bygone era, we decided not to use any synthesizers, only real instruments. But there were a lot to choose from, so that led to a hundred other decisions: Should we have violins? Cellos? Woodwinds? Should I play soprano or switch to tenor for this song? There were lots of those kinds of creative decisions, and I had a lot of fun making them.

I loved that album. We didn't call it *New Standards* because I thought these songs would all become standards, of course. It was because I thought I'd done something new and special with the sound of the old standards. And some day in the future—who knows?—maybe one or two might be considered standards. I'm humbled to imagine it.

When it came out, a couple of the songs started to attract some attention. There's a song called "Anthem" that became pretty popular. I called it that because anthems are songs that tend to have bigger intervals—the pitch difference between one note of a song and the next—and when I wrote that one, it had those kinds of intervals, and so it sounded like an anthem to me.

"Emeline" was another song that was a big home run. That started with Sam. He played the first chord, an achingly beautiful chord, and I heard the notes that needed to be played with that chord. Unfortunately, the first note is my least favorite note on the soprano sax. My middle C-sharp. But it was the only note that was right in that space, and I knew it belonged there, and I knew I had to start with it. I also knew how hard it was going to be to make that note sound warm and beautiful. It took a while, but I finally captured the sound I was looking for. I have to say that I'm very proud of myself on that one. I think it turned out just perfect.

There was another song that was really tricky. Because doing a posthumous "duet" with one of my sax heroes, Stan Getz, was a big mountain to climb.

I put "duet" in quotes because it wasn't me playing along with an existing Stan Getz song, the way I did with the Louis Armstrong song. Sadly, Stan, may he rest in peace, wasn't around for me to ask him to join me. *Brazilian Nights* was my homage to his bossa nova years, and now I was determined to do a song *with* him. But I also knew that since this was an album of "new" standards, we couldn't include an existing song.

However, the technology that existed at this point allowed me to take the notes Stan played—in live recordings, in the studio, wherever—and arrange them in a different order. You could arrange them to play whatever you wanted; in this case, to play a melody I'd written.

It was an audacious plan, I know. And an incredibly challenging one.

And, to me, a perfect idea.

Of course, I wouldn't have dreamed of starting the project without the blessing of Stan's family, which they graciously gave me. I wrote what I thought was the right melody, and then my friend and incredible piano player Randy Waldman figured out the right chords to go with it. We took it all into the recording studio. I recorded my part, and then meticulously, one note at a time, we added Stan Getz's sound to mine.

I had written a melody for Stan, the way I would have if he were alive, and we found the right recordings to pull those notes from. We also had the help of an absolute genius mixer/arranger/producer/everythingist named Jochem van der Saag, who handled some of the exacting technical processes, along with my engineer Steve Shepherd. We got the most amazing musicians to play an incredible orchestration, which was written by another close friend, the great orchestrator Bill Ross. This was a group effort fueled by our love for Stan Getz. I think the result—and I make no apologies for saying this—is a masterpiece.

We called it "Legacy," by Kenny G, featuring "The Sound" of Stan Getz. This was true, because we were using his sound, and also a subtle play on words, because Stan's nickname was "The Sound."

Around the time we were done, by a fortunate coincidence, Stan's son Nick was starting to do a documentary about his father's life, and he asked me to appear in it. I met with Nick and Stan's wonderful loving wife, Monica, and they asked me if I would play the song for them.

"Kenny," Monica said to me, "I've always been honest with Stan. I'm gonna be honest with you. If I don't like it, I'm gonna tell you."

I said, "I would want you to do that." Inside I was thinking, You're gonna love this song so much, there's not even a question. You're going to absolutely love it. But I didn't say that, of course. I just hit play on the little boom box I'd brought along, and I watched her listen.

And she started to cry.

I knew she knew her husband's work intimately, and I knew she was realizing that here was Stan playing a melody she'd never heard before.

"It's absolutely beautiful," she said. "I didn't expect it to be this beautiful. That's just how Stan would have played it."

And as much as I thought I was expecting that reaction, that's how incredibly relieved I was to hear those words. I knew the jazz police would come after me for doing this: Oh, the blasphemy! How dare he bespoil the sound of the great Stan Getz! But here was the woman who cared so deeply for Stan, who knew his music better than anyone, and who was the most protective of his legacy. Here was the woman who, in fact, may have been responsible for his greatest popularity: she was the one who had goaded him into doing bossa nova, which he feared might be too commercial and tarnish his "cool jazz" image.

Here was the woman who loved him most of all. And the fact that she loved the song meant the whole world to me. Sitting in that room, I had tears in my eyes as well. It's a memory I'll never forget. How lucky for me to be able to share an intimate moment with the family of one of jazz's great masters.

When the album came out, I was hoping that the world would take notice and that the music community would be reminded once again about the amazing Stan Getz. But sadly, I didn't get the right exposure or promotion, and the "traditional" jazz world—whatever that is—still didn't want to pay attention to Kenny G.

I called up a friend of mine, who plays music on the SiriusXM station Real Jazz, and flat out said to him, "Listen, you have to get past my name and listen to this record. I think you'll want to play it." And he said he would. But nothing ever happened. There, or just about anywhere else.

I guess that's part of my legacy.

The jazz critics who did pay attention to the album knocked it, as I knew they would. But I knew I had done something special. As for "Legacy," I knew that I was going to be introducing Stan to a whole new audience and helping to carry on *his* legacy.

Those who said we were profiting off his name didn't bother to notice that we wouldn't profit a single penny off this song; whatever we made went to the Getz family foundation, and they were free to do whatever they wanted with it.

But here's what makes me smile: I was in the Apple Store a few months ago, and a few of the young guys recognized me. They came over to say hi. They were playing some generic music in the store, so I said, "Hey, guys, why don't you put on some good music?" One of them hooked up my iPhone to the sound system, and I played the Stan Getz song. I didn't tell them it was me on there too.

Then they said, "Hey, that's great! Who is that?"

"It's Stan Getz. *G-E-T-Z*. Go look him up and start listening."

So while a bunch of kids were repairing my computer, I was turning them on to The Sound. When I was checking out and paying for the repair, I thought, They should have paid me!

CHAPTER EIGHTEEN

So what next?

I'm writing this on the day after my birthday. Another trip around the sun. Another chance to think about what to do on the next trip. Not to quote Lou Gehrig, but sometimes I feel like the luckiest man on the face of the earth. Because no matter how many mistakes I've made along the way, including big ones like leaving Arista, I've learned from them. And you know how much I love learning!

It's the same as with anything else I've learned—saxophone, skiing, golf, flying, making a great apple pie (did I mention I make a great apple pie?)—there are no wrong moves. Only moves that you can learn from. Moves that give you a chance to correct and improve and do something even better next time.

So that's one part of why I feel so lucky. I learned that lesson early on. And it was the guiding force in letting me explore all sorts of new worlds without fear. I also feel lucky because I get to apply that lesson to whatever I want to do next. So after *New Standards*, what was next for Kenny G? Lots!

At the end of 2023 I finished my last album for Concord. I'm grateful to Concord for giving me a place to land when I left Arista, but I thought it was time to put that relationship to rest . . . with an album of lullabies!

Where did this idea come from? Well, look. A lot of people have told me that they put my music on when they're having sex. And a lot of moms have told me they listen to it in the delivery room to keep them calm. So I thought, Well, let's complete the circle. I made the music that made the babies and brought the babies into the world. Now let me make the music to put them to sleep!

Just kidding. But seriously, this music isn't only for babies. Just as people can listen to Christmas melodies all year round, these lullabies are heartfelt melodies. Some that you know and some new ones that I hope you will love. I'm extremely proud of the arrangements and compositions, and I feel that I've made an album that can be listened to by anyone at any age at any time.

After that, I think I might try a classical album. Not Beethoven and Brahms and Bach, mind you. I want to delve deep into those styles of music and, as I did with *New Standards*, find a way to write some songs in that manner. I've started noodling around with it a bit. The other day my sound man Monty walked into my dressing room while I was practicing and playing around with some classical-sounding riff, and he said, "Bro, what is that? Is that Bach?"

I said, "No, it's G!" We both laughed. But his sincere question was the greatest compliment he could have given me, and I'm inspired to keep experimenting.

I have also always wanted to try my hand (and my saxophone) at film scores. We all know that music plays a crucial role in the filmmaking process. It can make or break a film. With all the success I've had creating instrumental music, you would think that doing film music would be an easy transition for me. But for whatever reason, the studios and directors haven't exactly been lining up at my door, and maybe it will never happen, but I haven't given up hope. I think I'd do great at it because for me, the greatest film scores are the ones with themes that we all can remember. A melody that sticks with you long after the film has ended. And that doesn't happen very often. It happened for me with the themes from *Titanic* and *The Last of the Mohicans*, as well as the theme from *Schindler's List*. Truly memorable compositions.

I think I've already proven with my own melodies that I'm very capable of creating a memorable theme, one that people would connect with and remember as well as they remember the storyline of the movie. I know that's somewhat grandiose. But it's said with confidence, not conceit. I can't wait to give it a try. I hope I'm given the chance. And if it doesn't happen, I'll be happy with what I have, not unhappy about what I don't have.

I do get asked to do a lot of charity work, of course, and I try to say yes whenever I can. It's another part of the way I was brought up—you don't just live for yourself. When you have success, it's important to give back.

But if there's one cause that's nearest and dearest to my heart, it's having music available in the public school system. I often hear about schools that have had to dissolve their music programs, and I think, What if that had happened to my high school? There would be no Kenny G! One more Gorelick in the plumbing-supply business, and one less guy sending his heart out to the world through a saxophone. And one guy who never would have gotten to live the incredible life I've lived.

So any chance I get to help in that situation, I try my best to do it. And as I move forward with life, if my charity work can help kids get their start in music the way my dad's support helped me get my start in mine, then I'll have done what I set out to do. And, I hope, I'll have made my papa proud. He passed away in 2019 at the age of ninety-eight. He was at peace. No pain; he just ran out of gas and closed his eyes. I know he was content and happy with the life he lived. I was lucky to have him in my life for so long, as an inspiration, and I think about him each and every day.

As I pause and give thanks for my most recent trip around the sun and look forward to the next one, I get reflective and start asking questions like, What do all these moments mean to me?

They mean more than they used to, I can tell you that. These moments, and a thousand more, I've learned to appreciate in a way that the young Kenny G probably couldn't have. When you're swimming across a lake and you look back and realize there's a lot less lake in front of you than behind you, it makes you take stock and think about the swim. Think about the feel of the water and the sun on your face and how much you've enjoyed the chance to be out there in this beautiful world.

It's not that I haven't always been a happy guy. I have, and I hope I've made that clear.

I've stayed happy, by the way, without needing drugs or alcohol to aid the process. Not that I don't drink. I'll have the occasional drink if I don't have a gig the next day. Nobody wants to see me up on stage giving anything less than my best because I'm tired from a long flight or had one too many the night before.

So what is it that makes me happy, day by day? Well, practicing and doing my best, of course. Finding challenges. Playing a great round of golf. Playing music from the heart. Being with my family. All the things I've talked about so far.

But there's one thing, as I prepare for this next trip around the sun, that I haven't talked about. Something that has helped me improve the quality of my life in a way that has truly changed it for the better. Before we get to the last page of this book (and again, thanks for sticking with me and listening to my story!), I want to share it with you. It's something I don't talk about very often.

What's helped me learn to be happier—and, I think, to be a better person—has been to find someone to talk to about myself. We talk about my life—my goals, my fears, my successes, my failures, things that make me happy, things that make me sad, what triggers anger, my relationships, my kids, my parents, my friends, my family, everything.

I'm talking about therapy, of course, but I try to stay away from the term. Because most people, I think, consider therapy to be for someone who is unhappy and has problems they need to solve, and for many people that is indeed what therapy means. And it's wonderful that good therapists can help them. But for me, therapy isn't a place that's about problems. I think of it as a positive place to go for the great guidance that will help you improve as a person and lead a fuller and happier life. That's mostly what therapy means to me.

It doesn't always need to focus on problems you may have in your personal or professional life. Sure, you can get into that stuff, but I have benefited from moving beyond that. My goal with all this is to learn how to improve myself and have the best quality of life I can. It's like being on a journey to understand what makes you tick, to uncover the process that goes on inside of you that makes you do the things that you do, and to figure out how you can make it work better. What are my tendencies under certain circumstances that aren't working, and what can I do to change them? It's not easy, folks, because it takes a lot of reps to replace an ingrained bad habit. But it's so worth it when you know you are on a path to being better and improving your quality of life.

When I started on this, it reminded me of my dad taking apart ceiling fans and dishwashers and putting them back together. Only this time the thing I was working on was me. I knew it was not going to be easy—but I was up for the challenge.

It took me a while, but I found a fantastic guy to talk to. An absolutely incredible person. Robert is smart, he's compassionate, he's objective, and he challenges me. He's seen all this before and knows the path and how things will most likely end up when people stay stuck in the way they have always been, and he does his best to guide me to the path of awareness, because only through awareness can the healing process begin—the healing that leads to a better quality of life. And he explains *why* better is really better. Since you've gotten to know me, you know I want to be the best at whatever I do. So why not want to be the best at being me? I got very motivated when I first started this journey, and I still am.

One of the first things we started talking about was my tendency to withdraw. The way I did, for example, when things were going south between me and Clive Davis. He guided me through the understanding of why this isn't a good thing to do. It took a couple of years of getting my reps in, but I can honestly say that I am not a guy who withdraws anymore. And that's a great thing. Boy, I wish I could have learned this earlier. A lot of things would have been better.

The best lesson I've learned so far is one that on the surface might sound a little backwards, but when you look at it logically, it actually makes perfect sense. And in fact, it has everything to do with looking at things logically.

In a nutshell, it has to do with feelings versus wisdom. I think a lot of us have heard the phrase "Listen to your feelings." Well, I have to say that I am convinced that this is not the correct way to think. It's a bit more complicated than that. The first part is to understand that feelings happen without us knowing exactly why. We just feel something. Anger, fear, worry, depression, and so on. The first step is identifying the real feeling and not the surface feeling. For example, one could feel anxious, but the real feeling behind it is fear. Fear is causing the anxiety.

Once you identify the feeling, then it's time to call on your wisdom. This is your brain thinking logically and entering into a "discussion" with your feelings about whatever situation you're in. This wisdom is the intelligent part of you that can determine what will make you feel better. So if you're feeling anxiety caused by fear, it's the wisdom that can figure out what you need in order to feel safe and not fearful. This wisdom side is the one to listen to, and a lot of times it goes against your instincts and feelings.

The key is to use that smart voice to talk to your feelings, gently but firmly, and let the feelings know that you aren't going to be on auto-pilot and follow them down whatever path they take you. The hope is that with enough of these inner conversations, little by little, the feelings will actually start to change. And then the real goal is that one's behaviors will start to change as a result of all this. Thoughts lead to feelings, which lead to behaviors. To change the behavior, you have to identify the feeling. And then use the thought to challenge and change the feeling.

So I'll share one real-life example of how it works. The other day, a member of my golf club started yelling at me because he thought I was playing too slowly on the last few holes and holding up the whole course.

My training—from my mom and dad—would be to either suffer

in silence and walk away, or to yell back and say "Fuck off" and then walk away.

But my smart brain took over. I took a deep breath and thought, Neither of these moves is going to make me feel any better in the long run. And my goal is to feel happy, to keep enjoying my day. My goal is to have the best quality of life in every minute. So what's an intelligent way to deal with this situation?

"Listen," I said to him in the friendliest voice I could muster, "I don't want to be talked to in that tone of voice." Just because I wasn't yelling back didn't mean I was going to stand there and take it without setting healthy boundaries. "Is yelling at me really the best thing you can do right now? Is there another way we can deal with this?"

As if on cue, another member of my group who didn't like the way he was talking to me stepped up, said, "Fuck you, asshole!" to him, and stormed off.

We both laughed.

"You see, anger is not the right answer here," I said with a smile. "We're both members here. We're going to be seeing each other all the time. Let's keep it friendly. What is it you really wanted to say to me?"

We had a friendly, polite conversation after that, and we're still friends.

I teach my kids about using thoughts and wisdom to master their feelings (frankly, they're tired of hearing me talk about it). But they know what I mean, and they've learned to make it work for them too. It makes me very happy to share this wisdom with my kids and see with my own eyes how much it has helped them with their quality of life. As a parent, isn't that what we all wish for?

Your feelings are your feelings, but they are *just* your feelings. Your intelligence has to say to your feelings, "I hear you. But you are not the real me. You are the me that wants to stay stuck with my familiar automatic reaction, and that isn't necessarily good for me. You're not going to make me happier. You are not improving my quality of life. It's time to listen to the *real* me. The *wise* me. That will truly make me happier."

Another big part of my feelings that I learned to talk to intelligently was my perfectionism. That came from my mom, of course. All that scrambling to make sure I dotted every i and crossed every t so I wouldn't get yelled at had some good parts to it. It was a big part of what made me successful. But as I've gotten older, although being good at things still makes me happy, I also had to look at what is the real cost of working that hard on all the things I work hard at.

So I've learned to look at my work ethic and the feeling that if I work harder and harder at things, then that's the best thing for me no matter what. I do believe in hard work, but now I have my "intelligent self" helping me to work hard, but to do so in balance with all the other things that I have going on—my family, my friends, my health. And I have my "intelligent self" asking my "feeling self" great questions like, When does the work ethic become too much? When does working so hard start to interfere with your ability to appreciate where you are, not just where you're going?

And that brings me back to that lake.

Swimming across a lake, when you recognize that there's less in front of you than there is behind you, has helped me want to enjoy each moment more, and to not worry so much about every note. The music, in this moment or in any other moment, is like the feeling of the water on your skin, and the sun on your face, and the cool breeze blowing through your hair. The music, even with notes that aren't the perfect ones, is beautiful. And let's let that in. Because, in the end, it's all that matters.

And so where do I go from here?

From here, I'm going to stay curious and see where that takes me. I've always been a very curious guy. I never lost that trait as I grew up, and I'm so glad. It's kept me intrigued by the things that I put my time into. Yes, I'm still curious about music. And flying. And golf. And so much more.

That curiosity is what leads me into great new adventures. It's also, in a way, what makes every day so much fun. I've been spending time in Paris lately, and I mostly get around by bike. I love bike riding, and as I'm riding around that beautiful city, I keep saying, "I wonder what's down there? I wonder what's up this street?" And I get hopelessly lost.

Which is the best part. Because getting lost is how you wind up finding things you never thought you'd find.

Right now, that curiosity has led me to learn French. I've always spoken French a little—I learned in school, but never got really good at it—and now I've decided to try to become fluent. Or just passable would be great. It's hard. Sometimes it feels like I'm never going to get it.

But I can talk to those feelings. And I can say, That's all right. I know I can't change that sinking feeling right this instant. But I'm going to stick with it. And my intelligence says that if I stick with it and consistently work on it and put in a lot of reps, it will get better. I've learned that.

So tomorrow, I'll get up, and of course I'll practice my sax for three hours, and that will make me happy. I'm grateful, in the end, to my mom, for instilling in me that discipline, because it's what gave me this great career and allowed me to play my music for all of you. That has been the greatest gift of all, and you'll never know how very grateful I am, every day, for that gift.

I'm also grateful for all the wonderful family and friends I have in my life who seem to truly care about my happiness. That's humbling. I'm extremely grateful that I've been able to learn (with the help of some wonderful words of wisdom from a few amazing people) that I really do get to rule my life. And I get to do the things that maximize my quality of life.

And tomorrow, I've got a gig. I'll stand there in the dark, in the middle of the crowd, and someone will whisper, "Hi, Kenny!" and maybe someone will pat me on the back or grab my hand. I know I'll see a lot of smiles and eyes filled with joy and sentiment. I'll take a deep breath. The spotlight will kick on.

I'll hear you all show your excitement. I'll hear you roar. It's a roar that tells me you've enjoyed my music. A roar that tells me you've shared my musical journey, that we've walked it together, and that you're as excited about the next two hours as I am.

And that, my friends, is the sweetest music of all.

ACKNOWLEDGMENTS

Where do I even begin?

Before anything else I want to thank you, holding this book in your hand (or listening on your earbuds). When my managers, Steve Ross and Danny Nozell, came up with the idea of a Kenny G memoir, I didn't think anyone would care enough to read about my life; but they thought so, and I'm glad they won me over. It's been a pleasure and an honor to try to tell my story. So thanks for listening! Thanks, Steve and Danny, for your guidance on this and so many other projects. And thanks, guys, for bringing in the fabulous Jeff Kleinman and Steve Troha at Folio, as well as Jamie Chambliss, who really helped us with the writing; Katherine Odom-Tomchin; and Sophie Brett-Chin. They're great agents and a great team.

I want to thank the extraordinary team at Blackstone for believing in this book: Josie Woodbridge, Addi Wright, Anthony Goff, Sarah Bonamino, Rachel Sanders, Nicole Sklitis, Francie Crawford, Kathryn English, Stephanie Stanton, and Bryan Barney.

A special thanks to my partner in crime on this project, Phil Lerman. This book would not exist without you, my friend. You are a true talent. I am honored to have had the opportunity to collaborate with you. Thank you for helping me find just the right words; but even more importantly, thank you for the wonderful friendship we started.

Holly Rubino did a brilliant first edit; Riam Griswold did a meticulous copy edit. Thanks to both of you.

I also want to thank my amazing business team: Gary Gilbert, Todd Morgan, Lester Knispel, and Lee Blackman. You take care of business, and that means I can make my music with a peaceful mind and heart.

My other past managers, Dennis Turner, Mark Adelman, and Jeffrey Ross, have also helped me so much in my career, as have Abby Wells Baas at William Morris, Justin Hirschman and Dennis Arfa at AGI, and Steve Cook at the Cooking Group. Thanks to all of them as well.

I'll never be able to say thanks enough to the legendary Clive Davis, he of the magic fairy dust. I'm so fortunate he sprinkled some on me.

I'm lucky to share the stage every night with my terrific band: Ron Powell, Robert Damper, John Raymond, Danny Bejarano, and Vail Johnson; as well as my front-of-house sound engineer, Monty Montfort; monitor engineer, Elliot Nielsen; drum tech, Bobby Mertz; and tour manager, Tom Hudak. It's great to be on the road and do the things we do. This is as good a team as anyone could ask for. We count on each other every day and do fantastic things every night, and I'm so fortunate that we've been able to stay together this long. Our longevity is a testament to how great you all are at what you do, and how great you all are as people.

So many people are responsible for what you hear when you listen to a Kenny G album, and I wouldn't be here without their help: Bill Ross, who does the wonderful orchestrations you hear on those albums, as well as pianist extraordinaire Randy Waldman and my engineer and long-time friend Steve Shepherd. And thanks to the folks at D'Addario and Vandoren Paris, for my reeds, and for all the great products you make that help me and many, many other musicians around the world make the best music we can.

To my dear friend Nobu Matsuhisa: you inspire me because you make food the way I make my music—with your heart.

Rob Huizenga: For your extremely knowledgeable guidance that has kept me in good health all these years. I'm super lucky to have you in my life.

Forty-year friendships are hard to find: I'm so fortunate to have my lifelong friend Roger Rose in my life. Your support means so much.

As a pilot, I know that staying safe in the air is the number one priority. I have Shane Carlson, Curtis Warn, Jeff Whitesell, and Harry Murlowski to thank for that. Blue skies, guys. Blue skies.

Like the GPS in my airplane, it's also crucial to have direction on the ground. To my trusted guide and guru, Robert Strock: your wisdom has made all the difference in the quality of my life.

Shout-out to Penny Lane, the fantastic documentary producer who first got me to reach back and start telling my story for her film *Listening to Kenny G*. It was so gracious of you to share all of your archival research with us for this book; it helped me immensely in remembering so many things I'd totally forgotten about.

If I tried to thank all the great musicians I've had the absolute pleasure of performing with, or who've appeared with me on my albums, or who inspired me, it would take up another whole book. But I do think about them nearly every day as I reflect on how fortunate I am to have had the chance to make music with them and to learn from them. They are a big reason I have the wonderful life I do.

And to all the saxophone colossuses (colossi?) who came before me—to Stan Getz, and Charlie Parker, and John Coltrane, and Lester Young, and Paul Desmond, and Michael Brecker, and Dexter Gordon, and Grover Washington Jr., and the original saxophone colossus Sonny Rollins, and Coleman Hawkins, and Art Pepper, and all the rest—I stand on your shoulders, and I hope I have honored your legacies by trying to follow the path you laid out for me, even as I carved my own. Thank you for all the inspiration—it has been the greatest gift to me. And to the readers: Please, after you've read this book, if any of those names are unfamiliar to you, go to your Spotify or Apple Music or Pandora and check them out. That will be my greatest gift to you.

When I think about the long and winding road that led me here, I have to stop and give thanks to the wonderful musicians who gave me my first breaks, Tony Gable and Jeff Lorber. You both gave a chance to a young guy with a sax and a dream, and I'll never forget your faith in me. I hope I've lived up to it.

And going back a little further, thanks to my brilliant teachers, including Johnnie Jessen, Roy Cummings, and James Gardiner, who helped me learn, way back in the beginning, to make beautiful sounds come out of a beautiful sax.

And of course, to my mom and dad: You taught me patience, and you taught me the value of working hard, and you taught me to try my best, every day. I know that so much of what I have in life is thanks to you. I hope you're looking down, and smiling, and proud of me. I miss you both dearly.

To my brother, Brian, and sister, Paula: I hope you enjoyed walking down memory lane with me in this book. I think we make a great trio.

To Little, for bringing so much joy into my life. And to the Delicate Flower, for making me enjoy my life whether I like it or not. *Je t'aime toujours.*

And finally, to Noah and Max. No dad could be prouder than I am of you, or luckier than I am to have such wonderful, smart, caring, talented sons. (Not to mention musical!) I hope you liked your dad's book. Now go practice some more at whatever you're working on. Look where it gets you! Ha!

Me and my brother, Brian. Even though he was five years older, he never left me behind when he went off with his friends. I appreciated that a lot.

Brian; my sister, Paula; and me in 1974—the year I graduated high school. We called my hair a "Jewfro" back then. (This was the first year I actually started to like my curls!)

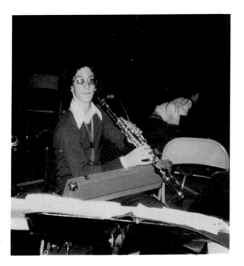

Jazz opened new worlds to me, right from the start. Here I am on a high school jazz trip to Paris.

Doesn't everyone have a story about pulling a dead opossum out of the wall, or is it just me?

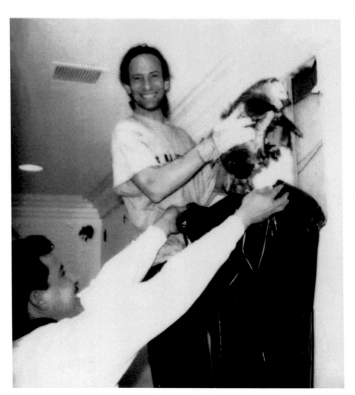

Lounging around my apartment in the early eighties.

Above: Cold, Bold & Together. Tony Gable (the tall guy in the back) was the leader. The other guys weren't sure about letting a white kid into the band, but Tony convinced them. It was a pivotal moment in my life.

Left: A simple music festival in a Seattle park. One of my very first solo gigs.

Below: In the studio with Jeff Lorber in the early eighties. (That's me on the left in my short-lived short-hair days!) My years with the Jeff Lorber Fusion were amazing—but we reached a point when it was time to step out on my own.

One of my mom's proudest moments—and one of mine—was when she got to see her son's sold-out concert at Carnegie Hall.

Me and my dad backstage at the Moore Theatre in Seattle in the eighties. He made it possible for me to have a career, and always loved seeing me perform.

Grandpa Harry. He hardly had any wrinkles on his sweet face even at one hundred years old.

My grandparents at my bar mitzvah, 1969. Such nachas! (That's what Jews call it when you're spilling over with pride for your kids.)

Four generations of G together for the first time! With my dad and Grandpa Harry.

Me and my dad in his later years. We were always at ease with each other.

After I became a pilot, I got to take Dad and Grandpa Harry on my plane. Afterward, Grandpa turned to my dad and said, "But he is so young! How could he control it? Did he go to college to learn that?"

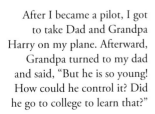

With my newborn son
Max, my first child.

Nothing makes me happier
than spending time with the
boys—and what adventures
we have! We caught this
twenty-eight-pound salmon
in Canada in 2007.

With Max (center) and Noah,
celebrating Max's twenty-first
birthday in New York City. We
never miss a chance to share
the big moments together.

Left: Me and my de Havilland Beaver. This photo was taken just before a flight where my landing gear wouldn't lower fully. I circled for two hours before I could get the problem fixed!

Right: Flying with the Blue Angels. I'm smiling here—but seconds later I was grabbing for the barf bag!

The first love of my life: a 1968 Oldsmobile 88, with Godfather whitewalls. (Confession: I couldn't afford the real ones. Those are fake add-ons!)

When I started making some money, I tried to stay pretty frugal but did buy myself a few presents—like my first airplane and this incredibly cool Corvette.

With my great friend Nobu Matsuhisa, sushi master. He says he makes his sushi like I make my music: with his heart.

Roger Rose was one of the first "VJs"—video jockeys—at VH1 and one of my early supporters. Forty years later, he's still one of my very best friends. Here we are at my fortieth birthday.

Photo by Robin Layton.

Budweiser sponsored one of my first trips to Asia. I've loved going back ever since.

At the Special Olympics in China in the nineties.

I was honored to
be asked to give
out medals at the
Special Olympics.

The day I got my star on the Hollywood Walk of Fame was a huge day for me. So glad I got to share it with my friends Sugar Ray Leonard (second from left) and Harry Hamlin (far right).

Celebrating *Breathless* going platinum—it would wind up going platinum twelve times over! —with Clive Davis, Roy Lott from Arista Records, and my manager at the time, Dennis Turner.

At a radio promotion in the nineties, I was joined by two dear friends who were inspirational at the start of my career: Robert Nesbitt (far right), a very well-known Seattle DJ who encouraged me in the early days; and Tony Gable (second from right), leader of Cold, Bold & Together.

With Barry Manilow at a Grammy party in the nineties.

With Michael Jackson and his brother Jermaine.

KG and the Bee Gees!

With Clive Davis. Clive was like a second father in my life: I owe so much of my career to his faith in me.

After I performed at a Hollywood party, Don Rickles came up to me and said, "Kenny! Get a haircut! You're making a fool out of yourself!"

With my dear pal Dudley Moore, at his home, working on his album *Songs without Words*. Most people know him as a comic actor; I knew him as a very humble and gentle man, and a brilliant jazz pianist (but still one of the funniest guys I ever knew!).

With the great songwriter
Diane Warren.

Me and Michael Bolton.
We had our ups and
downs over the years,
but our friendship always
rose to the surface.

The legendary
Smokey Robinson.
One of the great
highlights of my
career was getting to
work with him. As
sweet as his voice
is—that's how
sweet a guy he is.

Left and above: The great Arnold Palmer.

Above: Clint Eastwood. We always got along great because of our mutual love and respect for both golf and jazz.

Pebble Beach is a very special place to play golf. But even with the beautiful Pacific Ocean in the background, nothing gets in the way of my laser focus for each shot.

Left: Me and Jerry Chang holding up the shared AT&T Pebble Beach National Pro-Am championship trophy.

Below: Serenading the great Tiger Woods at a reception during the AT&T Pebble Beach National Pro-Am in 2001. I have wonderful memories of that tournament—including getting the championship trophy!

Bill Clinton asked me to play at the White House. I said I would—if he would come play golf at my club. And he did!

With George W. Bush at the Presidents Cup in Korea in 2015.

With the super talented Penny Lane, who directed the documentary *Listening to Kenny G.* It wasn't easy for me to give up creative control! But I think she did a brilliant job and told an honest tale.

GO FOR WHAT YOU LOVE
AND Practice, Practice, Practice
Kenny G

Right: Decades after I graduated, I was asked back to sign the wall at my high school. My advice was the same thing I did when I was there.

Below: Me and my band today. I don't use the word often—but I feel blessed to be able to go out and perform with these guys every night.